Prepositions and Particles in English

PREPOSITIONS AND PARTICLES IN ENGLISH

A Discourse-functional Account

Elizabeth M. O'Dowd

New York   Oxford
OXFORD UNIVERSITY PRESS
1998

Oxford University Press

Oxford   New York
Athens   Auckland   Bangkok   Bogota   Bombay
Buenos Aires   Calcutta   Cape Town   Dar es Salaam
Delhi   Florence   Hong Kong   Istanbul   Karachi
Kuala Lumpur   Madras   Madrid   Melbourne
Mexico City   Nairobi   Paris   Singapore
Taipei   Tokyo   Toronto   Warsaw

and associated companies in
Berlin   Ibadan

Copyright © 1998 by Elizabeth O'Dowd

Published by Oxford University Press, Inc.
198 Madison Avenue, New York, New York 10016

Oxford is a registered trademark of Oxford University Press

Library of Congress Cataloging-in-Publication Data
O'Dowd, Elizabeth M.
Prepositions and particles in English : a discourse-
functional account / Elizabeth O'Dowd
p.   cm.
Based on the author's thesis (Ph. D.,
University of Colorado, Boulder, 1994)
Includes bibliographical refrerences and index.
ISBN 0-19-511102-8
1. English language—Prepositions.   2. English language—Discourse analysis.
3. English language—Particles.   I. Title.
PE1335.036   1998
425—dc21   98-18309

9 8 7 6 5 4 3 2 1

Printed in the United States of America
on acid-free paper

Acknowledgments

First, I thank Barbara Fox, my dissertation advisor at the University of Colorado, for her example as a teacher and scholar, her laser-like precision in critiquing my work, and her unfailingly cheerful encouragement. She has contributed immeasurably to the production of this book.

I also thank other faculty members of the University of Colorado for their generous contributions: Bill Bright, Susanna Cumming, Zygmunt Frajzyngier, Lise Menn, Jim Martin, and especially Laura Michaelis, whose careful and articulate insights added new dimensions to this book.

I am grateful to several scholars outside Colorado for their assistance: to Sandra Thompson in particular, who gave generously of her time in responding to my work, and to Paul Hopper, Knud Lambrecht, Ron Langacker, and Bernd Heine for helpful conversations about prepositions and particles.

For the recordings and transcripts that make up the database, I thank Emanuel Schegloff for his "Upholstery Shop" data, Charles Goodwin for his "Auto" transcript, Randy Sparks for his "Round the Dinner Table" Conversation, and Bob Jasperson for "Eldora." In addition, Bob helped me greatly with astute comments on conversational transcription. I also thank Tracy and the Red Cross Clinic in Longmont, Colorado, for allowing me to record the "CPR" training conversation.

My friends and colleagues in Colorado, in New Mexico, and at Saint Michael's College have been an invaluable source of help and moral support: Immanuel Barshi, Phyllis Bellver, Linh-Chan Brown, Carolyn Duffy, Alex Eggena, Bob Fox, John Hughes, Kathy Mahnke, Charl Norloff, Mia Thomas-Ruzič, Brian Trouth (who persistenty rescued me from my own computer semiliteracy), and especially Debra Daise. My friend Dean Birkenkamp offered crucial assistance in preparing this manuscript for publication. Lori Heintzelman's excellent indexing was a godsend.

I will always be indebted to GB and Yvonne Oliver of La Luz, New Mexico, who so warmly and graciously provided a home away from home, and nurtured the development of this volume as it if were their own.

Most of all, I thank my parents, to whom this work is dedicated, for their unconditional love and support.

Contents

Abbreviations and Transcription Symbols

Abbreviations

Symbol	Gloss
A	Agent (subject of transitive clause)
S	Subject (of intransitive clause)
O	Object (of transitive clause)
LM	Landmark (of preposition)
NP	Noun phrase
RRG	Role and Reference Grammar
PIE	Proto-Indo-European
IE	Indo-European

Transcription Symbols

	Symbol	Gloss
1.	. . . (0.n)	long (timed) pause
2.	. . .	medium pause
3.	. .	short pause; tempo lag
4.	=	lengthened segment
5.	''[double quote]	primary stress
6.	'[single quote]	secondary stress
7.	. [period]	final pitch contour
8.	, [comma]	continuing pitch contour
9.	?	rising (question) contour
10.	!	exclamatory intonation

Transcription Symbols (continued)

11.	~~	truncated intonation unit
12.	<COMMENT>	researcher's comment (on voice quality, etc.)
13.	%	glottalization
14.	~	truncated word
15.	(.. . .)	intervening (untranscribed or uninterpretable passages)
16.	hh	inhalation
17.	CARRIAGE RETURN	intonation boundary
18.	SPACE	word boundary
19.	CAPITAL	sentence beginning
20.	U:23	transcript reference: e.g., "Upholstery: page 23"

(Adapted, for the purposes of this study, from Du Bois, Cumming, and Schuetze-Coburn, 1988.)

Prepositions and Particles in English

1

The "P" Phenomenon

1.1. Elusive Elements

There is in English a small group of words which, depending on their sentential context, is usually classified as either "preposition" (the (a) examples) or "particle" (the (b) examples):

(1) a. Jack ran <u>up</u> the hill.

      b. Jack ran <u>up</u> the bill.   (Liles, 1987:19)

(2) a. Do you often come <u>along</u> this road?

      b. Do you want to come <u>along</u>?

(3) a. They could send a bullet right <u>through</u> the window.   (R:32)[1]

      b. If you roll an animal onto your hood, I'm sure that it would come roaring <u>through</u>.(R:33)

This group of words, which I will call "P," has defied linguistic description for several hundred years. The descriptive problems have centered traditionally on the issues of how to *categorize* P syntactically and how to account for its many *meanings*.

    If we go by traditional grammatical definitions, examples (1)–(3) are relatively straightforward categorially: we can reason that each underlined (a) example is a *preposition*: that is, "a closed-class, uninflectable morpheme which shows the relationship between its [noun phrase] object and another word in the sentence" (Liles, 1987:229). In these examples, the noun phrase (NP) objects are clearly identifiable as <u>the hill</u>, <u>this road</u>, and <u>the window</u>, respectively.

    Similarly, we can reason from traditional grammatical definitions that each underlined (b) example is a *particle*. Although this term is less clearly defined in the literature, the following characterization, paraphrased from Liles (1987:16) captures its commonly understood meaning: word which may also function as a preposition, but which commonly attaches to verbs in verb-particle combinations. In these (b) examples, there is no prepositional object, and P is attached to the verb to produce a unitary meaning: ran up here roughly means "accumulated"; come along means "accompany (me)"; and roaring through means "penetrating."

In explaining word classes, Liles (1987:16–18) goes on to point out that particles may transform the meaning of the verb (as we see in 1b) or simply add a spatial meaning (as in 3b), and that the particle, unlike the preposition, may be moved after the direct object (e.g., *Jack ran the bill up*).

All these features seem to distinguish prepositions from particles uncontroversially. But even the straightforward examples given here raise some logical questions about the categorial status and function of P.

For example, why should the same lexical form — up, along, or through — have membership in two different lexical categories? And why should through in (3b) have a different categorial status here than in (3a), an utterance which differs only in that the understood object (the window) is left unspecified?

Example (4) raises even more questions. It unveils some of the complexities of a single P-form, up — one of the most useful words in the English language. We will see that pinning down the meaning of up is trickier than it was for the P-forms in examples (1)–(3), and that even categorizing up as a preposition or particle can give us problems. Example (4) presents naturally occurring utterances from my original database.[2]

(4) a. She'll cli-'try to 'climb up your ''leg 'man .   (U:83)

  b. An ''I'm gonna clean up the 'me=ss ?   (U:2)

  c. When we 'clean up the ''table it'll˜˜   (R:34)

  d. . . .and I uh-an I . .an I 'messed you ''up .   (U:30)

  e. There 'used to be a 'place up in ''Toledo   (A:31)

  f. laid 'off a . . .bunch of . .'really high up ''people ,   (R:19)

The first utterance contains a clear token of up as a preposition, according to the traditional definition: up shows a directional relationship between its object, your leg, and the subject of the sentence, she, which moves upward.

For (4b), we have to rely on semantics, rather than word order, to identify up as a particle rather than a preposition. Up is followed by a noun phrase (the mess), but has a very different relationship to it than to your leg in (4a). In (4a), your leg serves as a sort of *landmark* — a stable entity in terms of which the movement of another entity is defined: "your leg" does not move. However, in (4b), the mess is not a landmark but, rather, the entity that moves: we can think of "the mess" as being "up" (in a dustpan, perhaps), as a result of the cleaning. And that movement is not defined in relation to any other landmark element in the sentence. Therefore, we conclude that clean up constitutes a verb-particle construction, with the mess as the object of the construction.

Example (4c) looks very similar to (4b): the table functions as the object of clean up, so we might expect that clean up here means the same as clean up in

(4b). However, in (4b), "the mess" moves "up" as the result of cleaning; but in (4c), "the table" does not move at all. The meaning contributed to the verb by up in (4c) seems to be more abstract than in (4b); a sense of completion — of doing the cleaning thoroughly — rather than one of direction. Therefore, even in these apparently identical verb-particle constructions, up has two different meanings.

Again, in (4d), we can identify a verb-particle construction, for the same reasons as in (4b) and (4c); but here the meaning of up becomes even more obscure, since neither messed nor up makes sense independently of the construction (here, messed up means "inconvenienced"). Rather than adding some independent meaning, the particle seems to be idiomatically collocated with the verb; and the collocation carries no spatiodirectional sense at all.

So far, we have been able to categorize up as either a particle or a preposition. But what about up in (4e)? It does not meet our definition of preposition, nor does it seem to form any construction with the verb phrase used to be. However, it does form a semantic and syntactic unit with the prepositional phrase, in Toledo: if we repositioned the prepositional phrase (as in 5a), or removed it altogether (as in 5b), up would have to go along with it:

(5)   a.   Up in Toledo, there used to be a place.

      b.   *There used to be a place up.

Traditionally, this use of up would be classified as neither a preposition nor a particle, but simply as an "adverb" (traditionally defined as a word modifying some sentence element other than a noun). As for the meaning of up, it does share some of the spatiodirectional reference of up in (4a–4c) — after all, it tells you where "a place" is — but not in the literal sense of vertical movement. The meaning of P here is more like "somewhere north of where I am now."

Finally, in (4f) we have a case of up that does not meet the traditional definitions of preposition, particle, or adverb, but could only be classified as an *adjective*: a word that modifies a noun. Here, up modifies people and means something like "senior" or "important." Again, we detect a directional meaning, but not in any literal sense. It is as if we are placing "people" on some metaphorical ladder of success, where more successful people are positioned "higher" than less successful people.

In summary, the simple questions "How can we classify the word up?" and "What does up mean?" have no simple answers in traditional grammatical or dictionary terms. What we have with up is a word that seems to belong to several lexical categories (or word classes), with a wide variety of meanings sometimes but not always clearly related to the notions of space and direction. Furthermore, there is no direct correspondence between lexical category and meaning: similar meanings may be expressed across different categories (for example, the preposition in 4a and the particle in 4b both express directional movement); or different meanings may be expressed within the same category (the particle in 4b expresses vertical movement, in 4c it expresses some abstract sense of completion, and in 4d it seems to have no meaning independent of the idiomatic construction messed up).

1.2. Preposition or Particle?

1.2.1. *Teaching and Learning Difficulties*

The study reported here was undertaken to solve the "problem of P," which may be formulated as a central theoretical question: How can linguists define and describe these multipurpose P-forms in a way that accounts for their categorial flexibility and semantic versatility, as well as their syntactic constraints?

In answering this question, I will directly address many smaller ones. Several of them are often raised by students of English grammar, and in particular by nonnative speakers of English who, in my experience, find prepositions and particles (and P-forms in particular) among the most difficult, but also the most intriguing, forms that they have to master in learning the English language. In fact, it was in the context of teaching English as a Second/Foreign Language (TES/FL) that my interest in P-forms was aroused.

Nonnative speakers, grappling with long lists of "phrasal verbs" (common verb-particle collocations) in their grammar textbooks, wonder why some, such as think over, are "separable" and others, such as think about, are "inseparable": you can *think over* a problem, and *think about* a problem; and you can *think a problem over* — but you can't *think a problem about*.

Nonnative speakers also despair of memorizing which preposition goes with which verb: care about, or care for? think about, or think on — or in — or of? None of these prepositions seems to have any distinct spatial meaning, so what *do* they mean?

Particles can seem even more arbitrary in their assignment to specific verbs. Why does something that is *burning up* seem to be getting hotter, while something that is *burning out* seems to be getting colder? And would a building on fire be burning *up* or *down*?

Learners of English concerned about writing style may ask why so many verb-particle or verb-preposition combinations — put out, look into, and climb up — have one-word synonyms, such as "extinguish," "investigate," and "ascend," respectively; and which alternative is "better." They have heard somewhere that verb-particle combinations are "informal," but why should this be?

Another very good question to be addressed in this study is: Why isn't every preposition and particle a P-form? Certain prepositions (of, at, from) never function as particles, while certain adverbial particles (for example, away), never function as prepositions. Only a certain subset of forms, including those illustrated in examples (1)–(4), seems to have dual membership in both categories. Why is it that out can sometimes function alone as a simple preposition but other times has to be followed by of — *I threw it out the window* but not *I threw it out the room*?

In my experience, the most common reaction by language learners to P-forms is that of fascination at the richness of P's idiomatic possibilities. They marvel that the simple combination of a verb such as *make* with a particle such as up can yield so many different meanings e.g., "invent," "apply cosmetics," "put together," "compensate for an inadequacy," "make friends after fighting," and "act obsequiously." (Consider the combinations make out, take up, and put out for a similarly wide range of meanings.) In their eagerness to become real communicators of conversational, idiomatic English, second language learners generally share Bolinger's delight in P as the source of "an outpouring of lexical creativeness that surpasses anything else in our language" (1971:xi). Still, learners wonder what the source of all this creativeness may be, and what its limits are.

I propose that grammar textbooks have never satisfactorily addressed such questions because they have always treated prepositions and particles as "fixed" elements within a static model of grammar. They take little account of how P's meanings can vary, depending on its interaction with other elements in the same utterance, or on its use in different communicative contexts.

The goal of this study is to propose a theoretical model of P within which both the larger and the smaller questions can be answered. P is approached here as a dynamic discourse-pragmatic element, highly productive but highly principled in the range of meanings that it generates. Although the study focuses centrally on data from the "P" subgroup, the scope of its conclusions includes the larger group of nonalternating prepositions and particles, other grammatical elements that overlap functionally with prepositions and particles, and, finally, the counterparts of English prepositions and particles in the world's languages.

The model proposed here synthesizes many insights from leading cognitive and discourse-functional linguistic theories. These theories, although well known to scholars, have not generally been brought to bear on the specific issues that interest learners and teachers of English grammar. I hope to offer insights that will be useful pedagogically, not only for understanding prepositions and particles but also for a new way of looking at grammar and language. When we begin to understand how language is rooted in human cognition, experience, and interaction, we can more readily describe its elements in terms that invoke universal, commonsense communicative purposes.

This study is not intended as a grammar textbook, but as a theoretical contribution to the field of linguistics. Nevertheless, its conclusions should be interesting and useful for applied linguists, too, helping to bridge the well-known gap between linguistic theory and language teaching practice. Its conclusions about categoriality may also be of use to lexicographers seeking more practical ways of documenting P's meanings.

1.2.2. *Evolving Descriptions*

English language scholars have not always shared Bolinger's delight in prepositions and particles as a fountainhead of creative language use. In fact, some of them warned their readers not to be seduced into linguistic sloth by the easy fluency of these vernacular forms and not to abandon the purer structures of Latin-based grammar. In 1655, William Walker wrote a treatise on English particles, explaining how their meanings could be rendered in correct Latin. He was spurred on to do so by "the great variety of use that is made . . . of English Particles (the ignorance whereof is the cause of those many gross and ridiculous barbarisms committed daily by young learners, for whose use chiefly this work is designed)" (Walker, 1970: Preface). Although "particles" for Walker included many forms that would be differently categorized today, such as possessive and demonstrative pronouns, they also included most of the P-forms addressed in this study.

In the eighteenth century, Dryden was preoccupied with the phenomenon of sentence-final, "stranded" prepositions (as in, *This is the field we walked through*). He labeled this phenomenon an "idiom" and frowned on it as a rather immodest and potentially cancerous growth within the English language. After careful examination of his linguistic conscience, Dryden found "no other way to clear my doubts but by translating my English into Latin" (in Visser, 1984:402). By the higher authority of that translation, he was forced to condemn the end-preposition as "inadmissible" and to purge it from his own usage.

The flavor of this dogma persisted at least through the first part of this century, and is reflected in Arthur Kennedy's 1920 admonition on verb-particle combinations. While Kennedy values the creativity of many combinations, he warns:

> beyond all these, there lie a great number of colloquial or slang combinations which should not be encouraged, not merely because they are bizarre and render impossible that modest reticence which characterizes good breeding in speech as well as in dress, but largely because they detract from the simple expression of the unqualified idea. (1920:45)

It would seem that such value judgments as Dryden's and Kennedy's directly reflected a contemporaneous linguistic puritanism, which considered that the most "correct" English was that which most closely resembled the grammar of Latin. Elizabeth Close Traugott explains that the genre of prescriptive grammar, which extended from the last half of the eighteenth century to the first part of this one, developed in response to cultural pressures, where "three major issues were at stake: social, literary, and philosophical":

> Perhaps the main social factor in the development of prescriptive grammars was the rise of the middle class. In urban communities the gentry felt threatened and sought ways to keep themselves apart from the middle class. They looked for overt behavioral tokens by which to single themselves out . . . which would create barriers between themselves and the middle class. Language was an obvious vehicle for such an aim. (1972:163)

Today, the evolution of descriptive linguistics has produced a more tolerant attitude, along with an acceptance of workaday language as an object worthy of study. It is in the workaday domain of conversation that P-constructions are most productive, especially in the formation of new meanings through verb-particle combinations.

But instead of helping define and describe P-forms efficiently, descriptivism has simply uncovered the complexities of the task. For every major theoretical approach to linguistics, there have been several attempts to account for the "P" phenomenon. The questions asked in these studies reflect the assumptions of the approaches. Traditional, structural, and generative grammarians focus on the lexical categoriality and syntactic function of P. More semantically oriented linguists tend to focus on P's wide range of meanings and try to explain its semantic productivity. Depending on their conceptual frameworks, these scholars have used a bewildering variety of names to classify P-forms, prepositions, and particles, including the following: preposition, particle, adverb, locative auxiliary, stative predicate, predicator, modifier, preverb, adprep, verbal adjunct, aspect marker, satellite, intransitive preposition, transitive adverb.

Verb-particle and prepositional-phrase constructions have been assigned an even more dazzling variety of names, including: phrasal verb, polyverb, compound verb, two-word verb, group verb, discontinuous verb, prepositional phrase, prepositional verb, conjunct, adjunct, disjunct, adverbial phrase.

When faced with all the versatility and polysemy of P-forms, scholars respond in a variety of ways. Some scholars have simply concentrated on classifying all their meanings without attempting to explain their differences—for example, Hill (1968) lists thousands of sequences but makes "no rigid and fundamental distinction . . . between prepositions, on the one hand, and adverbial particles, on the other" (1968:vii).

In contrast, most syntactically oriented studies have claimed that we can successfully categorize P as either a preposition or a particle in any given sentence, on the basis of "tests," involving invented sentences, which reveal different predictable patterns for prepositions as opposed to particles. Unfortunately, these tests do not produce very satisfying results, and their authors have had to acknowledge a certain amount of overlap and indeterminacy between the two categories. Furthermore, syntactically oriented studies have done little to explain why, although both preposition and particle categories are labeled "closed class," they seem to offer an almost inexhaustible supply of new meanings, especially in combination with other sentence elements. And these studies do not begin to explain why, although different P-forms all seem to share a common property of spatiodirectional meaning, the most frequently used Ps have several meanings that do not refer to the spatiodirectional or physical domain at all.

The semantically oriented literature has been more promising and has explained some of P's variation as an effect of its interaction with other constituents at different syntactic levels. The main concern of this literature has been with P's multiple meanings, or polysemy, rather than with its categoriality. In particular, recent cognitive-semantic frameworks have produced very useful models to account for much of this polysemy in terms of radial categories, semantic webs, and extensions from prototypical "core" meanings. When they have addressed the categoriality question, their answer has been either, as with grammarians, to assign prepositions and particles to discrete lexical categories, or to unify them by positing that particles are some sort of "intransitive preposition."

While the latter interpretation is promising in that it acknowledges the obvious overlap between P-prepositions and P-particles (that they share the same lexical forms, and often refer to the same spatiodirectional notions), it leaves unanswered some intriguing questions about the grammar and distribution of certain Ps, including the one I asked previously: Why are all prepositions and particles not like P in their property of alternation? In other words, why are some prepositions, such as of, for, and at *always* transitive (or prepositional), while the particle away is never transitive?

Furthermore, the data from the present study reveal that, even within the P-group, alternation is very predictably constrained. For example, up and out function as particles 98% of the time and as prepositions only 2% of the time in the present database. To my knowledge, cognitive-semantic approaches to P have not addressed this problem of categorial specialization at all.

What previous syntactic and semantic approaches have in common is that, as with traditional grammar textbooks, they assume a static model of grammar, where lexical categories and grammatical relations have an autonomous status in the structure of the language itself or in our mental models of the language, rather than being shaped by the purposes of particular communicative contexts. Thus, their descriptions and accounts are generally based on made-up sentences rather than on evidence from real conversations. Since such sentences come from the inventor's memory rather than from actual observation and are presented in isolation without any anchoring or explanatory context, they can only provide rather speculative distillations of what we speakers actually do with language. As a result, "mental model" approaches are unlikely to uncover intriguing facts about P's usage (such as the categorial specialization mentioned previously) that could provide significant clues to its pragmatic, semantic, and syntactic functions.

This study was grounded in the following premises: that language can best be understood when observed in its natural setting — conversation; that language forms and meanings are not static, but fluid and constantly susceptible to change over time and space; and that these changes are driven primarily in conversational contexts, where speakers are constantly using language in creative and strategic ways to achieve their interactive purposes. Therefore, my theoretical perspective aligns itself with that of recent grammaticization research, which views language variation in present-day contexts as possible evidence for language change or shift. And, consistent with current discourse-functional linguistic theory, I look for clues to P's functions in the conversational contexts where it is used: clues which show what kind of information is being focused by P, how P interacts with other linguistic elements, how information is constructed between speaker and hearer, and so on.

1.3.   Developing a New Approach

The central thesis to be developed by the following chapters is that P-forms are best understood, not as syntactic or semantic elements, but as pragmatic, *discourse-orienting* elements. It is this orientational function that determines their grammatical function as prepositions, particles, or other lexical categories, and that drives their semantic extensions into a variety of meanings.

In elaborating this hypothesis, I will place English P-forms — prepositions and particles — in the wider context of the world's languages by showing how they exemplify universal principles of language variation and change. The approach takes the form of a cumulative argument, based on the analysis of five American English conversations from a database containing 1,245 P tokens. The argument is driven by findings from the database and supported by cognitive and functional linguistic theories that provide independent evidence for my claims.

Chapters 2 and 3 set the stage for the argument by explaining the shortcomings of purely syntactic or semantic solutions to the problem of P. Chapter 4 argues for a corpus-based approach to the problem that will reveal semantic-pragmatic motivations for the observed variation of P's meanings, and then briefly outlines the methodological features of this approach.

The remaining chapters present the details of this study and elaborate a discourse-functional account that solves the "problem" of P. Chapter 5 defines the semantic-pragmatic function of *Orientation* as that of *situating elements of information in relation to other, contextual elements.* This function is as basic in the construction of discourse as it is in human cognition and experience of the physical world. The prototypical orienting element is the *adprep*, an element originally introduced by Dwight Bolinger (1971).

Orientation involves both *situating* (predicating states or changes of state) and *linking* (introducing contextual information). I argue that *particles* situate and *prepositions* link. The basic difference between a particle and a preposition is the omission of the prepositional object, or contextual information; the choice of one form over the other is determined by issues of pragmatic focus in specific conversational environments. Evidence for these arguments is presented in the prosodic, semantic, and information properties of elements in utterances containing P (chapters 6 and 7). Indirect support comes from current theories of information structure and assertion (Givón, 1984b; Lambrecht, 1994).

Moving from the basic functional distinction between prepositions and particles, chapter 8 examines in detail their constructional capabilities. It sketches a template for preposition and particle constructions which shows how their respective linking and situating functions generate a wide variety of meanings at many levels of constituency. The template makes it possible to account coherently for the previously confusing results of syntactic categoriality tests and to answer several of the specific questions already raised in the present chapter.

Chapter 9 answers the remaining questions from a diachronic perspective, which provides the last major piece of the "P-puzzle." It explains why P-forms seem to specialize as either particles or prepositions but not as both, and why all particles and prepositions are not P-forms. In the process, P is revealed as an element constantly evolving in response to situating and linking requirements and takes its place in the larger picture of universal tendencies for linguistic change and grammaticization.

By chapter 10, there is a comprehensive account of P as a discourse-orienting element and a new theoretical model for prepositions and particles in English. The conclusion for this study revisits the "problem of P," recasting the questions raised in the present chapter as fundamental theoretical ones about linguistic categoriality and variation. It suggests several lines of inquiry for further research and, finally, it addresses the implications of this study for language scholars in general, and for teachers of English to nonnative speakers in particular.

1.3.1. *Defining "P"*

The argument outlined in the preceding section is based on evidence from a corpus of 1,245 utterances containing P-forms recorded and transcribed from a series of five unrelated, naturally occurring conversations in American English, representing about three and a half hours of discourse in total.

In these data, a preliminary working definition was used to identify P. P is a form that alternates between the traditional functions of preposition and particle, and which displays the same kinds of variation seen in examples (1)–(4) for in, along, off, and up. From this corpus, at least twenty alternating P-forms have been identified:

about	around	down	over
above	before	in	through
across	behind	off	to
after	between	on	under
along	by	out	up

This list requires a few words of explanation. First, it is not exhaustive; a larger database would undoubtedly reveal a larger number of words alternating as prepositions and particles. For example, since is listed in W. Nelson Francis and Henry Kučera's (1982) frequency analysis of English words as a conjunction, a preposition, and a particle; however, it is excluded from the working list because it occurred only as a conjunction in my own database. Since my purpose here is to analyze the properties of these words in their different syntactic distributions, I have limited my focus to those words that yield some basis for comparison.

Conversely, about is included even though it never actually appeared in the role of a particle in the database. It revealed variation of a different kind, which turns out to be of particular theoretical interest to this study. The potential occurrence of about as a particle *is* documented, however, by dictionaries and will be discussed more fully in subsequent chapters.

Second, my working definition of P effectively disqualifies certain nonalternating words from P-membership — such exclusively "prepositional" words as from, of, and with, and such exclusively "particle" words as away. However, even these words may yield surprises; for example, in my own idiolect I have experienced the use of with as a particle co-occurring with the verb take (e.g., *You might need your raincoat, so let's take it with*). It will be argued later that these words are not categorially distinct from P-prepositions, and that their more limited syntactic potential simply reflects their greater specialization as linking elements. Therefore, certain "pure" prepositions and particles are coded in the corpus when their occurrence is of particular interest.

Finally, within this group of twenty words, I take the rather nontraditional step of coding certain instances as "particles" even when they do not attach to a verb in verb-particle constructions. For instance, in examples (6e) and (6f) up is coded as a particle:

(6)   e.   There 'used to be a 'place up in ''Toledo.   (A:31)

      f.   laid 'off a . . .bunch of . .'really high up ''people ,   (R:19)

I apply the term "particle" to these instances for want of a better working definition to distinguish them from clearly prepositional forms. It will become clear that this distinction is a crucial one; that nonprepositional uses have certain functional commonalities that justify their consideration as a set. Traditionally, such nonprepositional uses would be labeled "adverbial." In fact, several scholars classify P-forms in verb-particle combinations as "adverbial particles" even though Bruce Liles avoids this classification in the definition paraphrased above (1987:15–18). However, such a label is problematic. The category "adverb" includes many other forms not directly related to P, including adjectivally derived adverbs of manner, so the term is too broad. As well, this category is itself in need of clearer definition; many adverbs have meanings that do not involve modification of or attachment to a verb, so there is little explanatory value in this term. Since a major goal of the present study is to redefine the traditional categories of preposition and particle (chapter 10), the reader is asked to suspend judgment and accept these terms as convenient coding devices only: "prepositions" will be defined ad hoc as P-forms that appear with following landmarks and "particles" as P-forms that appear without them.

1.4.   Conclusion

This brief overview outlines the task and approach taken in this study. In more general terms, the following chapters are intended to follow the lead suggested by Bolinger's (1971) work, *The Phrasal Verb in English*. While drawing extensively on Bolinger's insights, the study presented here goes beyond them by unifying prepositions and particles, by uncovering new phenomena about both categories, and by refocusing his analysis in light of current theoretical research. In the process, it is hoped that this present account of P's versatility may help untangle the processes by which a language may "coin out of its own substance" (Bolinger, 1971:xi) in the continuous creation of new meanings.

2

Syntactic Solutions to
the Problem of P

2.1. Preposition vs. Particle Tests

This chapter presents the "problem of P" from a syntactic standpoint. It will show
why attempts to define P as a lexical category by means of syntactic tests can only
produce indeterminate results. The most useful of these tests draw on semantic and
pragmatic criteria, which indicates that we cannot analyze syntactic patterns without
looking at the *meaning and use* of the elements involved.

Much of the syntactic literature seems to agree on a polarization of P between
the two categories of preposition and particle. The definition of these terms varies
according to theoretical perspective, but it is generally agreed that prepositional Ps
are somehow bound in constituency to a following NP, whereas adverbial particles
are more bound to the verb. Traditionally, the justification for the categorial split
comes from a variety of sentence-level tests designed to disambiguate prepositions
from adverbial particles in terms of their syntactic, semantic, and prosodic properties.

2.1.1. *Some Categoriality Tests*

Some of the more widely accepted tests for prepositions and adverbial particles are
summarized in table 2.1, which have been synthesized and paraphrased for purposes
of simplicity, from a variety of studies.[1]

2.1.2. *Analysis of Tests*

The general principle underlying these tests is that in certain verb-P sequences, P
constructs closely with the verb, performing an adverbial function while in others

Table 2.1:   Preposition/Particle Categoriality Tests

Test	Example
Only Prepositional (not Particle) constructions:	
A1. Conjunction-reduction	We turned off the road and onto the highway.
	*We turned off the light and on the stereo.
A2. Verb-gapping	He sped up the street, and she, up the alleyway.
	*He sped up the process and she, up the distribution.
A3. Adverb-insertion	We turned quickly off the road.
	*We turned quickly off the light.
A4. P-fronting	Up the hill John ran.
	*Up a bill John ran.
A5. NP-ellipsis	We turned off (the road).
	*We turned off (the light).
Only Particle (not Prepositional) constructions:	
B1. Passivization	The light was turned off.
	*The road was turned off.
B2. Verb-substitution	The light was extinguished.
	(= The light was turned off)
B3. NP-insertion	We turned the light off.
	*We turned the road off.
B4. P-stress	The button was sewed ON (particle).
	The dress was SEWED on (preposition).
B5. V-nominalization	His looking up of the information.
	*His looking into of the information.

it constructs with the following NP, performing a prepositional function. This principle explains why what appear to be lexically similar sequences may actually be syntactically different. For example, test A1 (conjunction-reduction) predicts that the following example is ungrammatical (as indicated by an asterisk).

(1) *We turned off the light and on the stereo.

According to test 1A, the underlined P is seen as an element inseparable from the verb turned, a fact which prohibits verb-ellipsis in the conjoined clause. This inseparability indicates that P is a particle. However, the following contrasting sentence does allow verb ellipsis, because the underlined P is interpreted as a preposition: it forms a phrasal unit, not with the verb, but with the following NP:

(2) We turned off the road and onto the highway,

Thus, off the road and onto the highway are interpreted as two prepositional phrases conjoined in a parallel syntactic relation to the same verb. The same principle of verb-particle unity explains the constraints in tests A2–A4. It also accounts for the semantic possibilities of the verb-substitution test in B2: if combinations such as turned off and put in are considered verbal units, then it makes sense that they can be paraphrased with simplex verbs such as "extinguished" and "install."

Conversely, the passivization, NP-insertion, and nominalization tests (B1, B3,

B5) work on the principle of preposition-NP unity: that a preposition must precede its object and may not be separated from or inverted with it.

(3)   *The road was turned <u>off</u>, (passivization test)

   *We turned the road <u>off</u>, (NP-insertion test)

   *His looking <u>into</u> of the information, (nominalization test)

Tests such as those in table 2.1 demonstrate that all Ps do not pattern the same way. However, the results, on examination, are not consistent enough to justify any absolute categorial distinction between adverbial particles and prepositions. The following discussion will show that several of the tests listed in table 2.1 allow plenty of overlap and indeterminacy between the two P-categories (see also Lindner 1981:18–25 for a critical review of the gapping, adverb-insertion and nominalization tests).

   Two of the most popular tests for adverbial particles versus prepositions are the NP-insertion or particle movement test (B3), and the passivization test (B1). Unfortunately, these two tests do not produce the same results. The NP-insertion test has been used as the main criterion (for example, by Martin, 1990:5–7) to distinguish phrasal verbs (another name for verb-particle constructions) such as <u>take out</u> from verb-plus-preposition sequences such as <u>talk about</u>. The test predicts that prepositions will fail the NP-insertion test since they do not allow the intervention of a NP between verb and P: the following (invented) examples are not acceptable:

(4)   *We're talking you <u>about</u>.

(5)   *We turned the road <u>off</u>.

Unfortunately, however, when the passivization test is applied to these examples, P easily passes the test in (4) (*You were being talked about*) but has much more difficulty with (5). Verb-preposition sequences are supposed to be intransitive and therefore not passivizable, but in (4), P behaves just like a transitive particle. Similarly, given the sequence in example (6), we find that P behaves like a preposition in failing the NP-insertion test (7), but more like a particle in passing the passivization test (8):

(6)   George Washington slept <u>in</u> this bed,

(7)   *George Washington slept this bed <u>in</u>,

(8)   This bed was slept <u>in</u> by George Washington.

This result, furthermore, contradicts the expectations of Anna Live (1965:435) and R.M.W. Dixon (1982:12), who suggest that literal meanings for P (in the sense of spatiodirectional reference) imply nonpassivizability. The meaning of <u>in</u> is clearly spatial in (3) and yet this P-form participates in passivization.

   How can we account for such ambivalence? The best answer may well come from the perspective of Cognitive Grammar, which makes the point that we cannot meaningfully analyze the patterning of a sentence unless we consider its *semantic-pragmatic context*. Only transitive verb phrases can be passivized, but Sally Rice (1987) claims that the "transitive" potential of a verb-preposition construction is determined by contextual considerations, or, as she puts it, by the overall "scene construal properties" of the proposition.

In example (8), <u>this bed</u> is seen as somehow affected by association with a significant event (the encounter with George Washington). For the purposes of this particular utterance, we might interpret <u>slept in</u> as a two-word verb, representing the "affecting" event, with <u>this bed</u> as its notional object. Therefore, in this context at least, we cannot explain P's categoriality without considering the semantic and pragmatic import of the whole sentence. In this way, transitivity is determined according to the semantic property of affectedness, and this property itself is assigned strategically by the speaker for pragmatic effect — that is, to mark his/her attitude to the overall situation.

The NP-insertion test is problematic in other ways, too. First, even when applied in isolation (rather than matched with the passivization test), it fails to disambiguate prepositions from particles consistently. For example, Live's (1965) study, dealing with discontinuous verbs (by which she means verb-particle constructions), divides P-forms into three different groups mainly on the basis of the NP-insertion test. Group 1 particles (e.g., <u>up</u>, <u>down</u>, <u>out</u>, and <u>off</u>) are distinguished from Group 3 particles (e.g., <u>in</u>, <u>on</u>, and <u>after</u>) on the grounds that the object of the discontinuous verb, if it is a pronoun, is usually placed before a group 1 particle (e.g., *look <u>it</u> up*), whereas the pronoun objects of group 3 particles always follow the particle (e.g., *look after <u>it</u>*).

However, Live concedes that these two word order patterns do overlap for a "special category" of particles (group 2), consisting of <u>over</u>, <u>through</u>, <u>across</u>, <u>along</u>, <u>about</u>, <u>around</u>, and <u>by</u>. The group 2 category "occasions both constructions": for example, we can say *talked <u>it</u> over* as well as *went over <u>it</u>* (1965:432–443). Furthermore, Live notes that <u>in</u> and <u>on</u> — group 3 particles — may sometimes pattern like those of group 1, since we do find sequences like *swear him <u>in</u>* or *lay it <u>on</u>*.

Both the distinctions and the overlaps between these P-groups are instructive. Live acknowledges that "most of the common prepositions double as adverbs, the bases of distinction between the two being closeness of association with the verb or with a following noun or pronoun, and relative stress" (1965:432). However, her grouping system implies that particular Ps seem intrinsically more likely to pattern as either adverbs or prepositions, but not as both. This tendency for a given P to specialize in one syntactic role or another has not been explored in the literature, and will be discussed more fully in chapter 9.

Live's group 2 seems to be the most flexible group categorially. But the exceptions noted for <u>in</u> and <u>on</u> suggest that, even within group 3, P's categoriality is not entirely predictable: we need to look at the particular verbal collocation in which it participates. In other words, we need to look at semantics again. Live does not address these implications, which will be explored in later chapters under the claim that prepositions and particles are not inherently separate categories — that although most Ps tend to specialize as either particle or preposition, they do have the potential to perform as both.

Another interesting problem with the NP-insertion test is that it only works for certain kinds of object NPs, as illustrated in the following invented examples (the NP object is underlined). Some NPs must be inserted (9a), others may (9b–c), and still others may not (9d).

(9) a. We turned <u>it</u> off.

b.   We turned off <u>the light</u>.

c.   We turned <u>the light</u> off.

d.   *We turned <u>those lights that had been blinking on and off like crazy for the last two days</u> off.

It is well known that pronouns can and must be inserted between verb and particle (9a); but it is more difficult to predict exactly which *lexical* NPs are possible in that position. For instance, (9c) seems quite acceptable, but (9d) does not. Therefore, once again, we must qualify the generalization in table 2.1 that particles allow NP-insertion.

Bruce Fraser (1976) claims that such qualifications can be accounted for in terms of underlying syntax, without resorting to semantic criteria. However, his explanations seem to involve a fair amount of subjectivity. For example, he invokes a sort of "heavy NP shift" rule which states that "whenever the direct object noun phrase is long and complicated, the particle must remain next to the verb" (1976:19). But, as Anthony Kroch's (1979) review points out, "long" and "complicated" are semantic value judgments rather than syntactically definitive criteria.

A more detailed syntactic account of NP-insertion comes from the field of generative syntax — from government-binding theory (GB). Bas Aarts (1989) suggests that the basic underlying structure of a sentence such as (9) is that of (9a) and (9c): verb-NP-particle. The word order in (9b) comes about by rightward movement of the object. As an explanation for the rule that pronoun objects must be inserted, Aarts posits the "lightness" of the pronoun, which consists only of a nominal head with no modifying elements. For "heavier" NPs, as in (9b) and (9d), there exists the option of rightward movement (1989:286–287).

However, this rule of optional movement begs the question as to why the speaker's option seems to become more constrained as objects get progressively more heavy. In other words, why is movement in (9d) not only possible but almost obligatory?

To answer this question, we must once again consider semantic-pragmatic motivations, as we did for the passivization test. A more satisfying account of NP-insertion and heavy NP-shift has been offered from a semantic-pragmatic perspective by both Dwight Bolinger (1971) and Ping Chen (1986). As Bolinger puts it, "the longer an element is, the more likely it is to contain critical information and hence to take the normal position for semantic focus, at the end" (1971:66). Similarly, in a detailed study of particle movement (or NP-insertion), Chen argues from a discourse perspective that word order is largely determined by the information status of the direct object (1986:93). He presents evidence to show that the medial position (between verb and object) tends to be the place conventionally reserved for familiar and predictable elements of information (e.g., pronouns, whose referent is already known to the hearer). New and unpredictable information tends to be staged later in the utterance — i.e., in clause-final position. Example (9d) would be unacceptable by Chen's analysis, not because the object NP is so long, but because it contains so much new and unpredictable information. Further discussions on this point, as well as the pragmatics of P's word order, can be found in chapter 7.

In summary, the passivization and NP-insertion tests are most instructive precisely where they fail to produce consistent results. Although they show strong constraints on P's patterning, they also show that adverbial particles cannot be clearly disambiguated from prepositions in all cases. In several instances, the overlap between these categories is best accounted for, not by syntactic rules, but in terms of semantic and pragmatic motivations.

The NP-ellipsis test (A5) is instructive in the same way. By this test, a preposition may sometimes occur with or without its object NP (10a). However, a lexically identical verb-P collocation does not allow the same alternation (10b):

(10)   a.   We turned <u>off</u> (the road).

     b.   *We turned <u>off</u> (the light).

From such examples, the test is intended to distinguish prepositions (as in 10a) from particles (as in 10b). However, the results are less than satisfactory since it is possible to find alternations such as the following, recorded in the present database:

(11)   a.   And I'm goan clean <u>up</u> the mess?

     b.   I'm cleanin <u>up</u> , right?   (U:2)

     c.   And I'm goan clean <u>it</u> up.

The NP-insertion test shows that <u>up</u> in (11a) must be a particle and not a preposition, since this sentence would presumably allow NP-insertion (11c). Nevertheless, this particle evidently passes the NP-ellipsis test in (11b). It would seem then, that NP-ellipsis is not the prerogative of prepositions, but also applies to verb-particle constructions. In other words, we could interpret both (10a) and (11b) as cases of null complementation (Fillmore, 1986). In (10a), it is the complement of the preposition which is not expressed and in (11b) it is the complement of the verb-particle collocation, <u>cleaning up</u>, which is omitted.

But now we are left with the question: why is null complementation not permissible for the verb-particle collocation in (10b)? Why can't we say *We turned off* and mean *We turned off the light*? In order to answer this question, the semantic difference between the two verb-particle sequences must be considered:

(12)   a.   We <u>turned off</u> the light.

     b.   I'm goan <u>clean up</u> the mess.

In interpreting this difference, Sue Lindner's (1981) Trajector-Landmark schema becomes useful. In her lexico-semantic analysis of <u>up</u> and <u>out</u> particle constructions, she examines their semantic relations from a Cognitive Grammar perspective, where P-forms express a relationship between their *trajector* (generally speaking, the entity that moves) and their *landmark* (the stable entity in relation to which movement is defined). This two-term relationship loosely corresponds to Leonard Talmy's (1985) Figure-Ground schema. Within this schema, the effect of P is predicated on the trajector: for example, in (13), <u>John</u> represents the trajector of <u>up</u>, which predicates the effect of the running — that is, a change of state for John — in relation to the landmark (*the hill*).

(13)   John ran <u>up</u> the hill.

By the same logic, <u>the light</u> in (12a) represents the trajector of <u>off</u>, even though the relationship with its landmark does not refer to the physical spatiodirectional domain. Lindner has an analogous example (repeated here as 14):

(14)   The lights went out; did you turn them out?

According to Lindner's explanation, the trajector is the lights, which change their state, or become imperceptible. The landmark is unexpressed, but implicitly understood as that state where the trajector would be perceptible: once the trajector "leaves the landmark, it becomes inaccessible to the viewer" (1981:88). Using Lindner's schema, we can see why NP-ellipsis is not possible in (12a). As the trajector affected by the predication of off, the light may not undergo ellipsis. If it could, the hearer might mistakenly construe a different NP — we — as the trajector of off, a construal which in fact holds for (15):

(15)   We turned off (the road).

In contrast, no such misinterpretation could apply to (16a) and (16b), because they have a different semantic composition from that of (12a):

(16)   a. I'm goan clean up the mess.

   b. I'm cleanin up, right?

In these two sentences, there is no risk that the hearer will attribute the up predication to the wrong NP (which is what happens with the unacceptable sequence We turned off in 10b). I is clearly not the trajector of up in either sentence, since the I referent does not change its state as a result of the cleaning. Furthermore, Lindner suggests that ellipsis is facilitated in sentences such as these, by the interpretation of clean up as a verbal unit, with a meaning which is not the sum of its parts:

> Clean and clean up code different sets of activities. Clean refers to removing dirt, making sanitary. .... Cleaning up the room need not involve cleaning it, but rather implies putting clothes away, shoving things into the closet, stacking things neatly — changing the overall appearance of the room. (Lindner, 1981:157)

Under this interpretation of clean up, the mess is construed, not as the trajector of up, but as the (ellided) complement of the whole verb-particle combination.

In conclusion, the NP-ellipsis test reveals more about the semantic construal of verb-P collocations and about how speakers choose to package information for their hearers than about the preposition/particle distinction.

Turning from considerations of transitivity and word order, we may briefly consider another test: verb-substitution (B2 in table 2.1). This test shows that verb-particle constructions such as turn off (the light) may be replaced by simplex verbs (usually derived from Latin) such as exit. Bolinger objects that this test is too vague to be very informative: for example, he points out that take off is not really a synonym for "depart," because it is more specific semantically (1971:6). Furthermore, Mario Pelli notes that this test yields "only fragmentary results" (1976:28): Latinate paraphrases are simply not available for many verb-particle sequences. Even if they were, it is unlikely that we would be any closer to an unequivocal test for particles, because we can also find Latinate paraphrases for verb-plus-preposition sequences — for example, turn off (the road) = "leave", look into (the problem) = "investigate," and so on. Once again, the results of this test suggest overlap, rather than clear distinction, between prepositions and particles in that both may form unitary concepts or lexicalizations with the verb.

Finally, in this discussion of categoriality we must consider the stress test (B4 in table 2.1). Stress (or accent placement) is one of the properties most often claimed to disambiguate prepositions from particles. In the majority of cases, it works predictably: particles receive stress, and prepositions do not. However, there are enough exceptions to the rule to raise questions about categorial distinctness; and once again, semantic-pragmatic considerations are required to answer these questions.

It is well established in the literature that there are different *levels* of stress placement in any given utterance (Halliday, 1967; Chafe, 1987, 1993; Du Bois et al., 1988). The stress test should perhaps then be reformulated, to predict that particles rather than prepositions receive primary stress, which represents the prosodic peak of an intonation contour. But even this prediction may fail. In the present database, for example, we can find a particular pattern where prepositions receive primary stress (marked here by double quote marks, following Du Bois et al., 1988):

(17)   Just kinda ''tiptoe because you have to go right ''by them.   (C:14)

(18)   They can't call out , from Germany ,) ''on AT&T lines   (R:7)

(19)   (You know where they introduce competition ,) ''to AT&T   (R:8)

(20)   (Where they actually bring ''in , an ''MCI line or a US ''SPRINT line) ''into
       your office ,   (R:10)

Examples (17)–(20) have prepositions (underlined) that introduce a NP object which is already familiar and topical in the conversational context. In (17), for example, them refers to a class which is going on upstairs from the speaker's group, and this antecedent has just been mentioned in the previous utterance. This pattern of stress placement is very common among native speakers of English and seems to have nothing to do with emphasis or contrastive marking. Yet it clearly violates the prediction of the stress test — namely, that only particles, and not prepositions, should be stressed.

An explanatory account of this pattern is offered by Knud Lambrecht whose theory of pragmatic focus predicts that primary stress falls on "the last accentable constituent" in a sentence (1994:251). This would normally be the object of the preposition; but in cases where this object is familiar or presupposed, the stress is placed elsewhere by a strategy of default accentuation, or destressing, which marks a normally focal constituent as nonfocal (1994:248–251). Further discussion of Lambrecht's account of pragmatic relations can be found in chapter 8; for the moment, it is enough to say that his account explains an apparently arbitrary set of exceptions to the Stress rule, by appealing to semantic-pragmatic considerations.

Finally, one particular P-pattern that remains unresolved by categorial tests is the one in which P functions sometimes like a preposition (the (a) sentences) and sometimes like a postposition (the (b) sentences):

(21)   a. John walked over the field (to get to the other side).

b. John walked the field <u>over</u> (looking for a wallet).

(22)   a. The director ran <u>over</u> the idea (with the scriptwriters).

b. The director ran the idea <u>over</u> (in his head — to examine it very closely).

(Dixon, 1982:27)

In Live's (1965) analysis, <u>over</u> is contained within the group 2 set of Ps, which may pattern as both prepositions (in the (a) sentences) and particles (in the (b) sentences). Admittedly, the P-form in the (b) sentences may, at first glance, look like a particle. However, Bolinger, Dixon, and Talmy (1975, 1985) all claim that such Ps are more like postpositions than particles, arguing from the premise that the (a) and (b) versions in examples (21) and (22) seem to have identical meanings. For Bolinger, this pattern is evidence that word order differentiation between prepositions and particles "is not absolute" (1971:37). In other words, if we interpret a postposition as a rightward-moved preposition (as Bolinger does), then we can say that prepositions and particles sometimes follow exactly the same syntactic pattern. Looked at this way, examples (21b) and (22b) seem to display a flagrant violation of the NP-insertion rule, with prepositional objects being inserted between the verb and the preposition.

Talmy's (1985) semantically based theory of motion accounts for this pattern by invoking a variable "valence precedence," where certain Ps may place either Figure or Ground (i.e., the trajector or the landmark, respectively) in direct object position. For example, in (23a), the Figure NP (<u>it</u> — the entity that moves) occurs in the direct object slot, while in (23b) the Ground NP (<u>him</u> — the stable entity) occurs in this slot. In this example, <u>it</u> refers to "my sword":

(23)   a. I ran it <u>through</u> him.

b. I ran him <u>through</u> with it.   (Talmy, 1985:119)

What remains puzzling, however, is why postpositional examples are so marginal in the English language. Bolinger, Dixon and Talmy all acknowledge that postpositional constructions are limited to a small set of Ps (such as <u>over</u>, <u>through</u>, and <u>by</u>) and to an even smaller set of verb-P collocations. In fact, Dixon reports that he cannot find any examples of <u>by</u> as a postposition, except in collocation with the verb <u>pass</u>.

(24)   a. Mary passed <u>by</u> John.[2]

b. Mary passed John <u>by</u>.   (Dixon, 1982:28)

To understand the marginality of such P-constructions, we must once again look beyond purely syntactic descriptions. What postpositional Ps illustrate is apparently a diachronic layer of usage from an earlier stage of English word order. Bolinger interprets these Ps as "fossils" which "retain in Modern English their old freedom with transitive verbs to go either before the object or after it in what appear to be identical functions" (1971:37–38). But why should this old freedom be retained? Apparently, for pragmatic purposes: for the expression of speaker attitude. Dixon mentions that these postposed Ps "imply a more *thorough* treatment of the referent of the prepositional object" (1982:27; italics mine). Thus, example (25) might, according to Dixon, "be paraphrased *John walked all over the field*," and example (26) "could be *The director ran over every facet of the idea*" (1982:27).

(25)   John walked the field <u>over</u>

(26)   The director ran the idea <u>over</u>

It would seem that the postposition survives in a restricted group of idiomatic collocations because of the effectiveness of these idioms in producing a particular subjective connotation. In conclusion, we can see once again that P's patterning is not predictable from syntactic rules alone: we must also take into account its semantic and pragmatic functions in construction with other elements and within particular contexts, and we must acknowledge that syntactic irregularities, or violations of the rules, may be occasioned by the dynamics of language change.

2.2.   The "Adprep" Category

Having considered the difficulty of distinguishing prepositions from particles, I will now introduce Bolinger's notion of the "adprep" as a further indication that binary categoriality tests may be heading in the wrong direction.

The adprep has been identified as a third, intermediate category for P. Constructionally, adpreps seem to "belong" to the verb as much as to the following NP (Bolinger, 1971; Sroka, 1972). Example (27), paraphrased from Bolinger (1971:26–27), illustrates the three-way distinction for particle, preposition, and adprep Ps, respectively.

(27)   a. She swept <u>off</u> the stage (cleaned it).

       b. She swept <u>off</u> the stage (did her sweeping elsewhere).

       c. She swept <u>off</u> the stage (departed majestically).

In (27a), <u>swept off</u> may be taken as a verb-particle construction, where <u>off</u> adds a completive adverbial meaning to the verb: she completed the job of sweeping the stage. In (27b), <u>off the stage</u> is interpreted as a prepositional phrase, modifying the preceding clause by expressing the location where the event took place (offstage, as opposed to onstage). In (27c), Bolinger sees an adprep, or "a case of dual constituency" (1971:27), where <u>off</u> contributes meaning both to the verb and to the following NP object: we can construe <u>swept off</u> as a directional verbal unit but we can also construe <u>off the stage</u> as a directional prepositional phrase.

Accordingly, as we might expect, categorial tests such as those outlined in table 2.1 reveal the adprep in (27c) as patterning in some ways like a preposition and in some ways like an adverbial particle. For example, like a preposition, <u>off</u> fails the NP-insertion test in (28) but passes the Adverb-insertion test in (29).

(28)   a. She swept <u>off</u> it majestically.

       b. *She swept it <u>off</u> majestically.

(29)   She swept majestically <u>off</u> the stage.

However, the adprep also passes the stress test, which we should expect only for particles; Bolinger points out that "the in-between status of the adprep shows up in the possibility of accenting either way" (1971:42). Thus, we could presumably place stress either on <u>off</u> (30a), or on <u>swept</u> (30b).

(30)   a. Show me the stage she swept "<u>off</u>.

      b. Show me the stage she "swept <u>off</u>.

So what does the adprep tell us about the categoriality of P? Bolinger's explanation for the adprep phenomenon is that "Adpreps are portmanteau words, *fusions* of elements that are syntactically distinct but semantically identical" (1971:31; italics mine). In other words, according to Bolinger, we should interpret (27c) as meaning "She (swept <u>off</u>), (<u>off</u> the stage)."

The same kind of intuition seems to be expressed by Talmy's decompositional semantic analysis of motion events, where he notes that <u>past</u> in a sentence such as (31) "has properties of both a satellite (i.e., particle) and a preposition" (1985:105–106).

(31)   I went <u>past</u> him.

Talmy argues that this P constitutes a coalescence, where the satellite "is coupled with a zero preposition." In other words, (31) can be interpreted to mean "I (went past), (past him)," where the second prepositional <u>past</u> is omitted, and its meaning is carried by the first satellite <u>past</u>.

Both Bolinger's and Talmy's interpretations seem to hold to the principle that, at some underlying level of syntax, the preposition and the particle are categorially distinct, even though they may be semantically identical. This principle is supported by Talmy's evidence that prepositions are formally distinct from particles in other Indo-European languages (in Latin, for example), where "the satellite is bound prefixally to the verb while the preposition accompanies the noun ... and governs its case" (1985:105). Furthermore, Talmy points out that particles and prepositions do not have identical lexical memberships:

> There are forms with only one function or the other. For example, <u>together</u>, <u>apart</u> and <u>forth</u> are satellites that never act as prepositions, while <u>from</u>, <u>at</u> and <u>toward</u> are prepositions that never act as satellites. Furthermore, forms serving in both functions often have different senses in each. Thus, <u>to</u> as a preposition (*I went to the store*) is different from <u>to</u> as a satellite (*I came to*). (1985:105)

Bolinger makes a similar point about underlying distinctness when he claims that the fused elements of the adprep separate "when an object noun is inserted, though the second element undergoes a stylistic change" (1971:31):

(32)   a. He drove the chickens <u>off</u> the lawn.

      b. *He drove <u>off</u> the chickens <u>off</u> the lawn.

      c. He drove <u>off</u> the chickens <u>from</u> the lawn.   (1971:31)

However, I am not sure that Talmy's and Bolinger's arguments must lead to the conclusion that there is any inherent categorial distinction between prepositions and particles. It is clear that syntactic, semantic, and lexical differences show up in particular constructions and collocations. But this is also true of other elements, particularly those which have undergone grammatical shift. For example, the historical development of the verb <u>do</u> into a main verb and an auxiliary has resulted in different patterning constraints in modern English. In the negative-interrogative construction, we can invert an auxiliary <u>do</u> in (33), but not a main-verb <u>do</u> (in 34):

(33)   a.   I <u>don</u>'t like linguistics.

     b.   <u>Don</u>'t you like linguistics?

(34)   a.   I <u>do</u> linguistics.

     b.   *<u>Do</u> you linguistics?

We would say, therefore, that <u>do</u> performs differentiated semantic and syntactic functions. We can also say that it has differentiated morphosyntactic properties, since only the auxiliary form allows the negative contraction <u>don</u>'t. However, we know that historically both uses of <u>do</u> derive from the same verb. Subsequent chapters of the present study will argue an analogous pattern of divergence for prepositions and particles from a common adprep source. Evidence for this argument comes from

1. the literature reviewed in this chapter, which shows so much categorial overlap between prepositions and particles that even some formalists posit a unitary category — for example, Joseph Emonds (1972), who defines adverbs as "intransitive prepositions"
2. the present database, which also contains many examples of preposition-particle overlap
3. the diachronic and typological literature discussed in chapter 9, which shows that prepositions and particles have always displayed overlap in an intermediate adprep-like function — even, contrary to Talmy's claim, in Latin and other Indo-European languages
4. the conclusions of several discourse-pragmatic studies, which suggest that categoriality for other parts of speech (such as nouns and verbs) is similarly ambivalent.

2.3.   The Inadequacy of Syntactic Tests

In conclusion to this chapter on categoriality, I suggest that syntactic tests do not clearly establish a dichotomy between prepositions and particles, although they do reveal a tendency for P-forms to participate in constructions and collocations which constrain their syntactic role. The most satisfactory explanations for the test results all seem to suggest that categoriality is flexible, influenced by semantic and pragmatic considerations. Furthermore, the existence of an intermediate adprep category suggests a possible diachronic source for the divergence of prepositions and particles.

Another limitation of syntactic approaches to P is that they do not explain why P-forms have so many meanings. Having established that many of P's meanings are generated only in certain types of constructions and collocations, several scholars have examined the semantics of these constructions for clues to the problem of P. The next chapter summarizes the most significant insights of the semantics literature for the purposes of this study and indicates some issues still unresolved.

3

Semantic Solutions to
the Problem of P

Following the analysis in chapter 2 of P's categoriality and the inadequacy of purely syntactic explanations, this chapter examines what semantically oriented explanations can tell us. Specifically, we want to know what it is about P's function that can produce such different interpretations for one word, so that, for example, *run up the hill* has a different meaning for up than *run up the flag*; and *believe in* has a different meaning for in than *in the library*. We also want to know, following chapter 2 (section 2.1.2), why different syntactic constraints seem to apply not only to prepositions and particles but also to different kinds of prepositional sequences, so that, for example, these sequences may be passivized in some sequences but not in others.

In this chapter we will see that early semantic accounts of prepositions and particles do little to explain such phenomena satisfactorily; however, three more recent theoretical models hold more promise. Although these models are not centrally concerned with explaining the preposition-particle distinction, they do suggest that at least part of the answer lies in the level of constituency at which P attaches to other elements. The first model (Lindner, 1981) deals with the functions of verb-particle combinations, while the remaining two (Vestergaard, 1977; Foley and Van Valin, 1984) examine the functions of prepositional phrases. Although these models provide important insights for discussions in later chapters, I argue here that their semantic-syntactic accounts still fall short of solving the problem of P — particularly, of explaining what *motivates* P's many meanings, and what constrains certain Ps to specialize as either prepositions or particles.

3.1. Particle Constructions

As explained in chapter 1, "particle," for the immediate purposes of this study, refers to all constructions where P takes no prepositional object. Particles usually follow the verb in an utterance and their meaning is construed with the verb. We know from section 1.1 that not all particles function postverbally — or even adverbially, if we define adverbial functions as modifying something other than nouns, and we will consider these non-postverbal cases in due course (particularly, in chapter 8).

Most P-studies, however, have overlooked these more unusual cases and have focused on the much larger group of adverbial particles in verb-particle constructions. The meanings of these constructions range from clearly literal combinations, where P adds spatiodirectional force to the situation expressed by the verb (e.g., look up, meaning "glance upward," and take off, meaning "remove from a surface") to combinations where P's sense is more abstract (e.g., adding a completive sense in *look up the information*), and finally, to completely idiomatic fusions of verb and particle, as in take off, meaning "impersonate."

Early accounts of verb-particle constructions — also commonly called separable phrasal verbs, verb-adverb constructions, polyverbs, or compound verbs — display some vagueness in the way they either ignore important syntactic distinctions or assume them inappropriately.

In one of the most important early accounts, Arthur G. Kennedy (1920) is primarily interested in P-forms that have non-literal meanings and have entered into some sort of welded association with the verb. Acknowledging the difficulty of clearly distinguishing prepositions from particles, Kennedy finally identifies sixteen prepositional adverbs as his focus which, in combination with different verbs, produce a corpus of over 900 constructions with several thousand meanings.

Kennedy's is one of the first attempts to explain the polysemy of P in a principled way. He takes literal, spatially referring verb-plus-P combinations as a sort of semantic prototype from which more abstract or figurative meanings can be inferred metaphorically. His account in many ways is a precursor to later semantic models which also look for cognitive principles to explain how P-meanings can extend into so many domains of reference (Lindner, 1981, 1982; Brugman, 1981; Hawkins, 1984; Lakoff, 1987). For example, Kennedy offers some very helpful speculations as to why a P such as *on* could come to be interpreted as a continuative aspect marker, as in *He just talked on and on*. According to Kennedy, when something is *on* a surface it can be seen, and as long as a process is continuing, it can be perceived. Therefore, the relationship expressed by on may also refer to a nonspatial domain of reference, such as the activity of talking, where a similar relationship of continuous perceptibility holds.

However, since he does not take on the problem of categoriality, Kennedy's verb + adverb set includes combinations that are clearly not parallel in their syntactic status. For example, he includes come by (= "find") and set about (= "begin") in his corpus, together with let out (= "release") and spruce up (= "decorate") (1920:16–17). He does not attempt to explain why the first two combinations, but not the last two, would fail the NP-insertion test (*I came it by) or the stress test (*How was that money come by?). This syntactic difference, however, would be crucial to any analysis that attempted a comprehensive account of P's functions since it would prohibit the inclusion of both pairs in a single set.

A different kind of definitional vagueness occurs when semantic and syntactic criteria are inadvertently mixed up. In a later survey of the research on phrasal verbs, K.A. Sroka (1972) searches for some semantic unity that may characterize this group. Discussing L.P. Smith's (1948) account, he finds it most satisfying to the extent that it captures several correspondences between English phrasal verbs and other Indo-European prefixed compounds:

> Thus "fall out" has the meaning of the Latin excidere, the German ausfallen. . . . As a matter of fact, we have in English both compound and phrasal verbs, often composed of the same elements — "upgather" and "gather up," "uproot" and "root up," "under- lie" and "lie under." In these instances the meaning is the same in each, but in other cases the meaning is changed by the grouping of the different elements: "undergo" and "go under," "overtake" and "take over," have not the same signification; and "upset" and "set up" are almost opposite in meaning. (Sroka, 1972:181)

This account is vague because the parallelism attested here between phrasal verbs and Indo-European compounds cannot be substantiated; it is only the *forms*, not the meanings, which are parallel. Smith's study defines the phrasal verb a priori as an idiomatic construction; however, fall out as a phrasal verb (meaning, perhaps, "hap- pen" or "have an argument") is not semantically parallel to ausfallen and excidere, which have literal spatiodirectional meanings. By the same logic, Smith is inaccurate in labeling gather up and root up as phrasal verbs, since their meaning is also literal rather than idiomatic; in this paragraph he seems to be inconsistent with his own definitions in classifying these combinations on the basis of their phrasal *form* rather than their meaning.

W.P. Jowett, also cited in Sroka, assumes a similarly semantic definition of "phrasal verb" when he posits a "lexical indivisibility" between verb and particle to differentiate phrasal verbs as in (2) from literal, composite constructions as in (1). As with Kennedy's "verb-adverb" set, Jowett's "phrasal verb" set does not seem to exclude combinations which, according to any categoriality test, would be classified as prepositions.

(1)   Flowers grow on plants.

(2)   This coffee will grow on you.   (in Sroka, 1972:182–184)

However, this semantic definition once again breaks down when Jowett includes the following combinations as phrasal verbs:

(3)   He came into [entered] the room, picked up [seized] a book, looked at [regarded] it casually, put it down [discarded it] and went out [exited].   (in Sroka, 1972:183; paraphrases added)

Jowett identifies these verbal combinations as phrasal verbs because they each allow simplex verb paraphrases — in other words, they all pass the verb-substitution test of table 2.1.

However, this raises the question of what lexical indivisibility means. The "indi- visibility" that Jowett points to in the paraphrases is formal: morphosyntactic rather than semantic. It is difficult to see the semantic justification for classifying grow on in (1) as more "divisible" than came into and looked at, since all of these combi- nations have literal, composite meanings. In contrast, grow on in (2) has a figura- tive meaning — for which Jowett offers no simplex verb paraphrase. Therefore, his rationale for classifying (2) and (3) together as phrasal verbs but excluding (1) is far from clear.

Recently, more promising and systematic approaches to particles have been developed within cognitively oriented models of grammar (Langacker, 1986, 1991; Lakoff, 1987) which explain syntactic constructions in terms of underlying semantic relationships. In the previous chapter's discussion on categoriality, we saw that these models can offer some useful explanations for certain syntactic irregularities of prepositions and particles. These models are especially valuable for their mental "maps," which explain how certain grammatical phenomena are conceptually organized. The maps invoke psychological principles from prototype theory and cognitive operations such as metaphorical inference or image-schematic organization, to explain how the semantic features of a core reference can be extended via "radial categories," "fuzzy boundaries," or other conceptual paths to produce an ever-widening network of meanings from a single word.

Several studies, using this cognitive perspective, have approached the problem of P-forms and mapped out many of their meanings (Lindner, 1981, 1982; Brugman, 1981; Hawkins, 1984; Lakoff, 1987). Perhaps the most thorough analysis, which also faces the issue of P's categoriality and accounts for several syntactic constraints, comes from Sue Lindner's research into verb-particle constructions containing up and out.

Lindner defines prepositions and particles in general as "extended locative relations," which predicate relations between the trajector and landmark of the P-form. The only difference between a preposition and a particle for Lindner is that a preposition specifies a landmark, whereas a particle "sublexicalizes," or leaves it unspecified. Lindner proposes that this difference

> is not best explained in terms of distinct word classes like preposition and adverb, which entails that we posit a preposition out and an adverb out as distinct, homophonous lexical items. Instead, we may attribute to OUT [in both particle and preposition constructions] the same intrinsic semantic structure and show that the real differences lie at the level of construction, that is, in the way the substructures present in the predicates involved are "hooked up" to each other. (1981:195)

In Lindner's account, the core semantic structure of up and out is decomposed into various semantic features so that the extensions from this core can be explained in detail. For example, she explains how a difference in one feature — the relation with the landmark — can produce two different meaning schemata for up: thus, The cat climbed up the tree posits the tree-landmark itself as the upward path of motion, whereas He rushed up and said hello posits the nonspecified landmark (me, perhaps) as the goal of the motion (1981:112–139).

This decompositional approach has perhaps been more enlightening than any other in accounting for the impressive polysemy of P-forms. A similar approach is applied to the semantic extensions of over by Claudia Brugman (1981), and to the meanings of English prepositions by Bruce Hawkins (1984). This study will draw extensively on Lindner's and Hawkins's insights to describe some of P's extensions.

Lindner's research is especially helpful in accounting for certain alternative interpretations of verb-particle constructions which have not been approached elsewhere in the semantic literature. She points out that the same word may be construed at different levels of constituency, as in the following set of examples.

(4)   He ran <u>up</u>.

(5)   He ran <u>up</u> the hill.

(6)   He ran <u>up</u> the flag.

(7)   He ran the flag <u>up</u>.

In both (4) and the prepositional example (5), the subject of the sentence (<u>he</u>) is the trajector of <u>up</u>, and the only difference is that the landmark NP (<u>the hill</u>) is sublexicalized in (4) but expressed in (5). However, in (6) and (7), the trajector of <u>up</u> is now the object of the sentence (<u>the flag</u>), with the landmark (<u>the pole</u>) sublexicalized.

The word order difference between (6) and (7) is explained in terms of alternative constituencies: <u>run up</u> is construed as a "composite scene" (or verbal unit) in (6), with <u>flag</u> as its direct object. But in (7), <u>ran the flag</u> is construed as a composite scene (or verb-object predication), modified (or "elaborated") by <u>up</u> (Lindner, 1981:188–189).

These interpretations provide some valuable principles to explain some of the syntactic constraints discussed previously, in section 2.1.2. As explained there, the Trajector- Landmark schema can be used to clarify the results of the NP-ellipsis test: we can say *We turned off*, meaning *We turned off the road*, but we cannot say *We turned off*, meaning *We turned off the lights*, because <u>the road</u>, as a landmark, may be sublexicalized, whereas <u>the lights</u>, as a trajector, may not.

The trajector-landmark schema also ties in with Ping Chen's (1986) and Dwight Bolinger's (1971) pragmatic interpretation of NP-insertion. For them, pronouns are inserted between verb and particle because they express familiar information whereas lexical NPs are more likely to be placed after the particle, according to how much new information they express (see 2.1.2). Lindner's schema suggests a useful iconic frame for this pragmatic interpretation, in the following way. Example (8) groups verb and particle together syntactically as a composite event, isolating <u>the lights</u> as the new information; however, example (9) groups verb and object together, isolating the P-form <u>off</u> as new information, which represents a change of state.

(8)   We <u>turned off</u> the lights.

(9)   We (<u>turned the lights</u>) off.

Thus Lindner's account allows us to interpret syntactic patterns in a way that mirrors the pragmatic purposes of the speaker.

Furthermore, this schema helps clarify Bolinger's (1971) and R.M.W. Dixon's (1982) postpositional constructions, as in "He walked the field over." If we construe <u>walked the field</u> as a verb-object unit analogous to <u>ran the flag</u>, with <u>over</u> as the "new" information, then we can translate Dixon's intuition of a "more thorough treatment" as meaning *focal* treatment: after all, that which is new is likely to be focused. More will be said about the relationship between particles and focused information in chapter 7.

Following Lindner's lead, we can also now schematize the semantic and syntactic differences in Bolinger's riddle (1971:26–27):

(10) a. She (swept <u>off)</u> the stage. (particle)

    b. (She swept) (<u>off</u> the stage). (preposition)

    c. She (swept[<u>off)</u> the stage]. (adprep)

In (10a), <u>the stage</u> is construed as the complement of the verbal unit <u>swept off</u> (mean-ing "cleaned"). In (10b), <u>she swept</u> is a whole event, construed as the trajector of <u>off</u>, with <u>the stage</u> as the landmark: the relationship could be paraphrased as "Her sweeping was off the stage." In (10c), <u>she</u> is construed as the trajector of <u>off</u>, meaning that "she" changed her position as a result of the sweeping, with <u>the stage</u> as the land-mark. Example (10c) is an adprep sentence; that is, the adverbial particle <u>off</u> adds a resultative meaning to the verb <u>swept</u> and also serves as a preposition. It represents a prototypical motion event in Leonard Talmy's (1985) terms, where the figure (<u>she</u>) follows a path (<u>off</u>) in relation to a ground NP (<u>the stage</u>).

And finally, with Lindner's insights we can return to my introductory examples of the problem of P (section 1.1.1) to explain the difference between "I'm goan clean up the mess" and "I'm cleaning up the table." In that discussion I posed the question as to why two apparently identical verb-particle phrases predicated two different states: if "the mess" moves in the former example, why doesn't "the table" move in the latter?

Now we can answer that question by positing two possible construals for "clean up the mess." In one construal, <u>the mess</u> is the trajector of <u>up</u>: it moves upward as a result of cleaning (analogous to "pick up the pieces"). In the other construal, <u>the mess</u> is the complement of a verbal unit, <u>clean up</u>. For "clean up the table," however, only the latter construal is possible: <u>up</u> does not add directional force, but, rather, completive force to the verb, and the whole situation is interpreted not as a motion event but as an event being performed to completion.

Thus, Lindner's semantic analysis of <u>up</u> and <u>out</u> is very helpful in our approach to the problem of P. We have now uncovered and explained several syntactic idiosyn-cracies, and caught a glimpse of several paths along which P's meanings can extend, depending on how speakers choose to construe P-forms with verbs, landmarks, and other elements.

However, several issues remain unresolved. For example, Lindner's analysis, like Brugman's and Hawkins's, interprets all prepositions as being extended locative relations. Presumably, then, they should all have the same property of optional land-mark sublexicalization as <u>up</u>, <u>out</u>, and <u>over</u>. In other words, they should be optionally usable as particles.

But we know that this is not true. Certain prepositions (e.g., <u>from</u>, <u>of</u>, <u>at</u>) never sublexicalize their landmarks no matter what the context. They always appear as prepositions and never as particles. Conversely, other words that express extended locative relations (<u>away</u>, <u>toward</u>, <u>forth</u>) never lexicalize their landmarks. They always appear as particles and never as prepositions.

The semantic accounts of P have not addressed this issue. Lindner does propose a principle of "salience" to motivate sublexicalization — that landmarks which are nonsalient do not get lexicalized; but she never clearly defines this notion of salience. Nor does she explain why preposition-particle alternation is possible only for P-forms and not for all prepositions and particles. This problem will be defined in more detail in chapter 7.

Table 3.1: Frequencies and Particle/Preposition Distribution of
P-Lexemes in the Corpus

P-Lexeme	% Particles	% Prepositions	Other	Total
in	18%	81%	1%	204
on	15%	83%	2%	175
up	98%	2%	0%	132
out	98%	1%	1%	114
over	73%	24%	3%	71
about	0%	97%	3%	66
down	94%	4%	2%	52
by	4%	89%	7%	35
around	66%	34%	0%	35
off	79%	21%	0%	34
through	31%	65%	4%	23
number of P-uses:				941

Furthermore, even within the P-group, sublexicalization does not seem to be as optional for some Ps as it is for others. The conversational database used in the current study uncovers an intriguing pattern of skewed distribution for its P-tokens and shows that certain Ps, such as up and out, almost always occur as particles, while others, such as on and by, rarely do. Table 3.1 summarizes the distribution of the eleven most frequently occurring P-forms in this database. Percentages refer to the number of times a certain P-form is used as either a preposition or a particle, relative to the total number of uses of that P-form. The "Other" column refers to repeats, repaired utterances and uninterpretable uses. These P-forms are listed in order of decreasing frequency.

The skewed distributions in the sample are clearly mirrored by those of W. Nelson Francis and Henry Kučera's (1982) word frequency analysis for American English (see chapter 9 for a more detailed comparison between their study and this one). In fact, the Francis and Kučera study shows strongly skewed distributions for all twenty P-forms included in the study presented here, whereas table 3.1 only shows the eleven most frequently occurring Ps in my own database. That is, it would appear that the patterns illustrated by the tests in table 2.1 are strongly representative of P-use in American English generally.

As we can see, none of the forms listed in table 3.1 occurs with equal frequency as both preposition and adverbial particle. Over, around, and through are relatively flexible while others display very little flexibility. In particular, up and out come close to resembling such pure adverbial particles as away and together, while about and by are almost as purely prepositional as to, with, and from.

These results suggest that the usage of P-forms in actual conversation is constrained by certain principles that have not been uncovered by semantic models such as Lindner's. Chapter 9 will address the phenomenon of P-skewing in more detail, as a logical result of discourse-pragmatic requirements in conversation.

Lindner's alternative constituency approach to particles is mirrored to some extent by two semantic-syntactic approaches to prepositional sequences. The next

section shows that these approaches are similarly helpful in explaining some interpretations and constraints, while leaving some key issues unresolved.

3.2.   Preposition Constructions

3.2.1.   *The Functions of Prepositional Phrases*

Prepositional phrases occur in a wide variety of syntactic contexts: for example,
after the verb (*I live in Boulder*), clause-initially (*On the other hand* . . .), or clause-
finally (*I've lived there for three years; you should be tired by now*; and so on). Such
prepositional phrases are traditionally classified as adverbial since they modify verbs
or whole clauses.

    However, prepositional phrases may also modify nouns, thus functioning like ad-
jectives: *angels from heaven* could be paraphrased as "heavenly angels"; and *medicine
in a bottle* is generally synonymous with "bottled medicine". We cannot, therefore,
assume adverbial status for all prepositional phrases any more than we can assume a
priori categoriality for prepositions and particles.

    Like particles, prepositions construct with other elements to produce a wide
variety of meanings, ranging from transparently spatiodirectional to abstract, as in
the examples of the previous paragraph. For example, in English, prepositions have
almost totally replaced inflections as case-marking morphemes at the clause level: *to*
marks dative case by specifying that its landmark is the recipient in events of giving,
showing, and telling (*I gave the letter to my mother*). The P-form *in* is often interpreted
as a locative case marker specifying its landmark as a location (*I live in Boulder*),
and it may also refer nonspatially, in prepositional phrases beyond the clause level
(e.g., *I'll be with you in a minute*; *in fact* . . . ; *in particular*, . . . ; and so on).

    With clause-external constructions such as these, we have no trouble identifying
the P-form as a preposition rather than a particle. Categorial indeterminacy between
preposition and particle is an issue only in syntactic contexts where the two functions
overlap: that is, postverbally in clause-level constructions such as we saw in the
categoriality tests of chapter 2 (table 2.1). However, here I will examine prepositional
constructions at all levels of constituency (see chapter 8) in an attempt to unify
them functionally. By examining the syntax and semantics of prepositions both in
postverbal contexts and beyond, we hope to find some clues as to how prepositions
are similar to particles, and how they are different. We also hope to discover why it
is that even prepositional phrases do not all pattern alike; for this we turn to Torben
Vestergaard's model.

3.2.2.   *Vestergaard's Semantic–Syntactic Continuum*

Vestergaard's (1977) monograph examines the semantic–syntactic role of the prepositional object in relation to the clause. He plots five different roles along a five-point
semantic continuum, ranging from non-role-playing prepositional objects, with relative syntactic freedom from the clause, to central participants in a tightly bound
case-marking function:

(11)   a. *Non-Role-Playing*:
       <u>On the other hand</u>, it is true that ...

       b. *Abstract Circumstantial*:
       George appeared <u>on the appointed day</u>.

       c. *Concrete Circumstantial*:
       The lizards ran <u>on these steps</u>.

       d. *Marginal Participant*:
       He was sitting <u>on a beer crate</u>.

       e. *Central Participant*:
       I shouldn't be imposing <u>on you</u>.   (compiled from Vestergaard, 1977)

Of these functions, (11a) would traditionally be classified as a sentential adverb, or conjunct, (11b) and (11c) as free adjuncts, and (11d) and (11e) as prepositional complements (Quirk et al., 1972).

Vestergaard's analysis successfully captures the semantic continuity among these constructions, which have traditionally been seen as discrete. It also helps clarify their syntactic constraints in a way that mirrors their progressive centrality to the clause predication. The least central sentence, (11a), is the most free syntactically: we know from experience that sentential adverbs can be moved to the end of the sentence or inserted into a sentence-medial position (e.g., *It is, on the other hand, true that ...*). Furthermore, this sentential adverb is not entailed in any sense by the other elements in the sentence. In contrast, the most central prepositional phrase, in (11e), is so tightly construed with the verb that it cannot be placed elsewhere in the sentence, while the verb <u>imposing</u> entails, or sets up, the expectation that it will be followed by the preposition <u>on</u>.

In fact, this kind of verb-preposition combination has been described as having a transitivizing effect on the verb, and bringing the prepositional object into the construction as the direct object of a two-word verb, <u>imposed on.</u> English contains many verb-preposition constructions like (11e). Some of them use P-forms that alternate as particles in other constructions (e.g., *depend <u>on</u>, talk <u>about</u>, believe in*), but many others use "pure prepositions" (e.g., *care <u>for</u>, see <u>to</u>, believe in*). The tight construction between verb and preposition has also earned such combinations the label of "inseparable phrasal verb" in some grammar-teaching textbooks (e.g., Azar, 1989). However, this term is misleading since it suggests some syntactic or semantic parallel with separable phrasal verbs (or verb-particle constructions), when in fact they perform very different functions and pattern quite differently (to be discussed in chapter 8).

Vestergaard's scale allows us to explain the syntactic constraints in the following invented examples whereby (12), but not (13), passes the passivization test. Passivization is a process in which the object of the verb becomes the subject of the passive construction. Therefore, it can only take place with transitive verbs.

(12)   a.   They're imposing <u>on</u> you,

       b.   You're being imposed <u>on</u>,

(13)   a.   They came <u>on</u> the same day,

       b.   *The same day was come <u>on</u>.

In (12), the prepositional object <u>you</u> is a central participant in the clause. <u>Imposing on</u> therefore has a transitivizing effect, and we can interpret <u>you</u> as its direct object. Thus, passivization is possible. However, in (13) the prepositional object <u>the same day</u> has an abstract circumstantial relation to the clause so the prepositional phrase cannot be interpreted as the object of the verb.

Vestergaard's model, by revealing the parallelism between semantic central-ity and syntactic constraints, might be considered a precursor to later studies that acknowledge the iconicity with which form mirrors function (Haiman, 1985; By-bee, 1985). More specifically, his insights about the different types of prepositional meaning that emerge at different levels of constituency parallel those of Lindner for verb-particle combinations. These insights will be helpful for mapping out P's polysemy in chapter 8.

However, Vestergaard does not integrate particles into his scale. He concedes that the same words may function as both prepositions and particles, but he categorizes the latter with multiword verbs and excludes them from his corpus (1977:3–5). Even though, as mentioned above, verb-preposition constructions are also sometimes interpreted as multiword (or phrasal) verbs, this area of overlap is not addressed. Furthermore, although Bolinger's adpreps are included on the scale, they are only treated as prepositions; their dual function and their potential for particle alternation are not explored by Vestergaard (1977:95–96).

3.2.3. *Role and Reference Grammar: Insights and Problems*

More recently, Vestergaard's constituency approach to prepositional meanings has been developed from a functionally oriented perspective in Role and Reference Grammar (RRG: see Foley and Van Valin, 1984; Van Valin, 1993; Jolly, 1993). The RRG framework is helpful here for two reasons. First, like Vestergaard's, it shows how different constituencies can produce different meanings; second, it goes beyond Vestergaard in offering a systematic cross-linguistic model of "layered clause structure" within which we can account for prepositions as "predicators."

In the RRG framework, the primary constituent units of the clause are

> the *nucleus*, which contains the predicate (usually a verb), the *core*, which contains
> the nucleus and the arguments of the predicate, and the *periphery*, which is an adjunct
> to the core and subsumes non-arguments of the predicate, e.g. setting locative and
> temporal phrases. (Van Valin, 1993:5)

Prepositional phrases may be slotted into this structure at different levels, as repre-sented diagrammatically in (14) below.[1]

(14)   John   showed   the book   to Mary   in the library
        ARG   PRED   ARG   ARG   PRED ARG
               (_ NUCLEUS _)
        (_____ CORE _____)   (__ PERIPHERY __)

With reference to Robert D. Van Valin (1993:7–20), we can explain the structure of (14) as follows. The prepositional object <u>Mary</u> is part of the clause *core*, as a NP-argument of the verb <u>show</u>. The preposition <u>to</u> functions as a case marker, marking <u>Mary</u>'s relation to the verb. This kind of case-marking relationship is labeled nonpredicative in RRG since such prepositions do not add any substantive semantic content to the clause and they do not license the following argument. Their objects would be classed as "participants" in Vestergaard's continuum (14).

In contrast, the prepositional phrase <u>in the library</u> is clause-peripheral: it does not construe with the verb and is not part of the clause structure. Rather, it has its own internal structure, with the preposition <u>in</u> functioning as a predicator, the nucleus of its own phrase, licensing its own NP-argument <u>library</u>. Prepositions in this context "contribute substantive semantic information" to the utterance, "both in terms of their own meaning and the meaning of the argument that they license" (Van Valin, 1993:19). The information contributed seems to be of the abstract circumstantial type, in Vestergaard's semantic scale.

These notions of clause-layering and prepositional predication account for some of the variation in prepositional meanings. For example, <u>in</u> has a different kind of meaning for the verb-preposition sequence <u>believe in</u> than it does for the phrase <u>in the library</u>. In fact, in the former case, it has very little independent meaning at all; its only reason for being there is apparently its entailment by the verb.

This semantic difference follows from the scope assigned to <u>in</u>, in the layered structure of the clause. I would suggest (although this suggestion has not been made by RRG) that the preposition <u>in</u> refers under nuclear, rather than core scope, in the verb-preposition sequence <u>believe in</u>. It refers only to the verb, relating this rather than any other core argument to the following NP. In other words, the sequence *She believes in you* does not predicate a state of containment on <u>she</u> in the same way that *She sits in the garden* does. Rather, the preposition simply defines the scope of operation (or Range; see Halliday, 1985:136) of <u>believes</u>, adding a transitivity feature, as I explained in the preceding section. Its meaning is therefore grammatical rather than spatiodirectional: it marks a case relation between the nucleus and the following argument.

In contrast, for the sequence <u>in the library,</u> <u>in</u> is under peripheral scope to the whole preceding clause and predicates a spatiodirectional relationship between the situation expressed by the clause and <u>the library</u>. This accounts for its greater semantic substance and its status as a predicator rather than a case-marker.

The notion of prepositions as predicators echoes M.A.K. Halliday's claim that prepositions work as "mini-verbs" (1985:142). However, the RRG framework does not define particles as predicators. Like Vestergaard's model, it makes a categorial distinction between prepositions and particles. Postverbal particles are classified as directional "operators," which modify different layers of the clause. Under core scope, they "specify the direction of motion and orientation of core arguments" (Foley and Van Valin, 1984:393). This function is presumably illustrated in (15), an example from the present database, which refers to a broken window.

(15)   Put it back <u>up</u>. (= core)   (U:1)

Here, <u>up</u> specifies the direction of motion for a core participant, <u>it</u>, thus qualifying itself as a core-scope operator in RRG.

In contrast, under nuclear scope, operators "express a directional orientation of the nucleus" (Foley and Van Valin, 1984:212), which refers to the verb itself rather than to core participants of the clause. Again, this function can be illustrated from the present database.

(16)   I'm cleanin <u>up</u>, right? (= nuclear)   (U:1)

In this case, <u>up</u> does not specify motion for a core participant. Instead, it refers only to the verb, completing its meaning (as Lindner 1981 explains for <u>clean up</u>; see section 2.2).

The core–nuclear distinction will prove to be very useful subsequently in explaining the functions of different P-constructions (in chapter 8). However, RRG's categorial distinction between preposition and particle is problematic. First, according to the findings of my own data, the distinction collapses in many environments, most notably in adprep environments where P performs both functions. Consider example (17):

(17)   I'll ''throw it <u>in</u> the 'furnace an ''I'm not gonna be sorry , when I 'throw him ''<u>in</u> (U:95)

In this sequence (referring to an unfortunate cat that needs to be disposed of) it is clear, from our analysis up to this point, that the only difference between the two underlined uses of <u>in</u> is that the former expresses a prepositional object/landmark (<u>the furnace</u>), and the latter merely infers it from the context—or sublexicalizes it, in Lindner's (1981) terms. In this case, the only difference between prepositional "predicator" and particle "operator" is in the lexicalization of the landmark. Semantically, both functions of <u>in</u> are identical: both uses are predicative, and both modify the orientation of the participant (= the cat). Therefore, the notions of predicator and modifier offer no meaningful basis for the distinction between preposition and particle.

Second, if we do not accept the distinction between postverbal particles as operators and prepositions as predicators, how are we to classify the same P-forms when they show up in different contexts which are neither postverbal nor prepositional, as in (18) and (19)?

(18)   He was <u>up</u> on the back of his pickup truck.   (A:12)

(19)   . .laid off a bunch of really high <u>up</u> people.   (R:19)

These P-uses obviously overlap functionally with those of both predicator and operator in the RRG framework. In (18), <u>up</u> predicates a position on a clause participant (a "predicate adjective," in traditional grammar). It also expresses the orientation of one participant (<u>he</u>) in terms of another (<u>his pickup truck</u>), which is the RRG definition of an operator. However, in this context, <u>up</u> differs from a prototypical postverbal operator because it does more than modify the orientation of action or event. Since the only verb in the clause is a linking verb (or copula) <u>was</u>, which predicates no independent action, we would have to say that <u>up</u> carries the whole predicative meaning of the clause rather than modifying the verb directionally (as it would in a sequence such as He <u>jumped up</u> on the back of his pickup truck). Therefore, in this context at least, <u>up</u> looks even more like a predicator than many prepositions do.

Similarly, in (19), <u>up</u> functions as a predicator. In traditional grammar, <u>up</u> would be labeled an adjective here, and adjectives predicate, as Thompson (1986) has argued. In fact, we could paraphrase the meaning of (19) in a "predicate adjective" construction: "laid off a bunch of people *who were really high up*." In other words, the verb predicates the event of laying off and the P-form predicates the relatively senior status of the people.

However, up in (19) also functions as an operator, in RRG terms, since it specifies the orientation of a core participant, people. In this utterance, up has the effect of positioning people as "higher" than other people on some metaphorical scale. In short, up in this example functions as both a predicator *and* an operator, even though syntactically it could not be labeled as either a preposition or a postverbal particle.

Thus, RRG's functional framework does not explain the difference between particles and prepositions with any greater meaning than the traditional syntactic tests of table 2.1. Rather, it reinforces the conclusion reached in chapter 2 that a priori categorial distinctions between preposition and particle do not hold up under scrutiny. This conclusion applies whether the distinctions are defined syntactically or semantically. There is simply too much overlap between the functions of these two categories and with the functions of other categories, such as verb or adjective. Any valid attempt to define P-forms must look beyond such categorial distinctions, which only obscure important commonalities. I would suggest that it is necessary to discover how adpreps, prepositions, and particles are similar before one can understand what motivates them to pattern differently.

Nevertheless, the RRG framework offers promising clues to P's polysemy, by revealing how a preposition's meanings can be influenced by its constituency or scope of operation in the clause. Within this framework, we can understand the semantic–syntactic difference between prepositions used as predicators and P-prepositions used as case markers. Moreover, if the predicator–operator distinction is dissolved and prepositions are grouped together functionally with particles, the framework becomes even more promising. Its potential for tracing the polysemy of P-constructions will be explored in detail in chapter 8.

Another useful RRG insight is provided by Julia Jolly's (1993) detailed analysis of preposition assignment. She argues that the predicative–nonpredicative distinction for prepositions is not quite binary and proposes a semipredicative function for some prepositions. Her three-point scale is illustrated in (20).

(20)   a. John showed a book to Mary. (nonpredicative)

      b. John baked a cake for Mary. (semipredicative)

      c. John prayed before noon. (predicative)

Jolly explains the distinction in terms of involvement with the clausal verb. Her explanation may be summarized as follows. In (20a), the verb showed requires a following "recipient" argument and to simply marks the case relation of this argument, Mary, to the verb. The preposition predicates no information by itself. In (20b), bake does not require any argument other than its direct object, a cake, so for actually predicates something, by specifying a benefactive relationship between the verb phrase and Mary. In (20c), before predicates quite independently from the verb: it specifies the entire preceding clause (John prayed) as one argument in a two-term relationship, with noon as the other.

Jolly's analysis is intriguing because, by placing the predicative property on a continuum, it may allow us to view prepositional meanings on a sort of grammati-cization scale, where nonpredicative case markers are most grammaticized and fully predicative prepositions are least grammaticized. In fact, such a scale would reflect the principles of current grammaticization theory, which show a universal historical tendency for prepositions to evolve toward greater grammaticization. Although Jolly herself does not propose this line of inquiry, it will be followed in chapter 9.

However, Jolly's predicative continuum is problematic in that she seems to see case-marking as the only kind of nonpredicative function for P. Taking the fully predicative function as basic, on the grounds that case-marking functions can be predicted from it (1993:276), she explains that predicative prepositions occur in peripheral-scope sequences (e.g., *in the library, before noon*) and core-scope se-quences (e.g., *for Mary*). Limiting her examples of nonpredicative prepositions to case markers within the clause, she does not mention that nonpredicative functions may also occur under peripheral scope.

But "predicative" in RRG implies "semantically substantive" (Van Valin, 1993: 9); and, if we look at the P-prepositions from my own database, we find that many of them are no more substantive under peripheral scope than they are as case markers under core scope. For example, in and on have no more independent meaning in sentence adverbials such as in contrast or on the other hand than they do in verb-preposition constructions such as believe in or depend on, where they mark case on the verb. They are grammatically fixed, or required, by the construction in which they participate and predicate no independent meaning.

To my knowledge, the RRG model has not made a distinction between substantial peripheral prepositions (e.g., *in the library*) and nonsubstantial ones (e.g., *in contrast*). The difference, however, is captured by Vestergaard's syntactic–semantic scale. The substantial type would be classified as Circumstantial and positioned more centrally on his scale, whereas the nonsubstantial type would be classified as Non-Role-Playing and positioned more marginally. But Vestergaard does not attempt to explain why semantically nonsubstantial prepositions should also be syntactically marginal to the clause.

I believe that the occurrence of nonsubstantial prepositions under peripheral scope is significant because it shows that nonpredicative (i.e., nonsubstantial) mean-ings are not limited to the case-marking function alone. The reduction of substantial, spatially referring properties may characterize prepositions both within and beyond the clause. In chapters 8 and 9, I will account for the difference between predicative and nonpredicative meanings under all scopes as a pragmatically driven one, as an effect of the specialized situating or linking functions under all scopes.

3.3.   Inadequacy of Syntactic–Semantic Explanations

We are now in a position to summarize what both a syntactic and a semantic analysis have contributed to solving the problem of P.

First, to consider categoriality. We saw in chapter 2 that syntactic tests, performed on isolated sentences and based on the notion of a priori categorial status, do not consistently distinguish between prepositions and particles. They do reveal interesting idiosyncratic constraints on P's patterning in different constructions, but they do not explain them.

We also saw that several of these constraints can be better explained by appealing to semantic or pragmatic considerations: for example, constraints on passivization (Rice, 1987), particle movement or NP-insertion (Bolinger, 1971; Chen, 1986), NP-ellipsis (Lindner, 1981, 1982; Fillmore, 1986), stress placement (Lambrecht, 1994) and postposed word order (Dixon, 1982; Lindner, 1981). Furthermore, the adprep function performed by many P-forms (Bolinger, 1971) invites the hypothesis that prepositions and particles may diverge conceptually from a single source.

In this chapter, Lindner's trajector-landmark schema has further invited this unifying hypothesis of divergence from the adprep, in her very plausible interpretation of particles as prepositions without landmarks. In contrast, the RRG framework categorially distinguishes prepositions from particles; however, as argued in section 3.2.3, the distinction is not justifiable in functional terms.

In short, the categoriality of a given P as particle, preposition, or even postposition is apparently not an inherent property, but a contextual one: syntactic patterning is determined at least partly by the specific construction and semantic-pragmatic function in which it is being used.

Second, we can consider P's polysemy. The preceding discussion has shown that semantically and cognitively oriented models of grammar offer significant insights for explaining P's wide range of meanings. One such insight is in the semantic structure of P-forms, which allows different spatiodirectional features to be extended in a variety of directions via such cognitive operations as metaphorical transfer and prototype extension or as different interpretations of the trajector-landmark schema. The other insight is in the level of constituency at which P interacts with other elements, both in verb- particle constructions (Lindner, 1981) and in prepositional constructions (Vestergaard, 1977; Jolly, 1993; Foley and van Valin, 1984; Van Valin, 1993).

However, we have not yet solved the problem of P. Neither Lindner's account of verb-particle sequences nor Vestergaard's and RRG's account of prepositional sequences has actually explained why we have particles and prepositions at all — why the same lexical form should take two very clear syntactic directions and construct either with the verb as a particle, or with the landmark as a preposition. Lindner's model identifies the semantic commonality between P-prepositions and P-particles but not the reasons for their different syntactic behavior. The RRG framework has identified the predicative function of some prepositions but has not explained why this function is shared by particles.

And finally, we still do not know why only P-forms may alternate as both prepositions and particles whereas other words such as from, for, away, and forth are "fixed" as one or the other. Nor do we know why, even within the P-group, certain words (e.g., up) nearly always appear as particles, whereas other words (e.g., by or in) nearly always appear as prepositions. In fact, this last phenomenon of specialized distribution has not even surfaced in the models described in this chapter, a point that leads me to argue in the next chapter for a data-driven approach to the problem of P, which is more likely to uncover such empirical phenomena.

4

The Problem Revisited:
A Data-driven Approach

The conclusions of the last two chapters leave the categorial status of prepositions and particles still unclear: What functions do they have in common and how are they different? Those conclusions lead me to argue in this chapter for a reconceptualization of the problem of P—one that looks beyond syntax and semantics to explain P's versatility and idiosyncracies. Following the lead of discourse-functional research, as developed by Paul Hopper and Sandra Thompson (1980, 1984, 1985, 1993; Hopper, 1995) and others, I point out that pragmatic motivations are crucial in determining the syntactic or semantic use a speaker will make of a particular linguistic element. To uncover these motivations we must look carefully at the discourse contexts in which they occur.

This requires an approach and methodology radically different from those seen in previous studies of P; they must collect data from linguistic events that are authentic rather than artificial, and they must follow from those data rather than from a priori theoretical models. The remainder of the chapter describes the methodology for this study in general terms: how the database was put together from the conversational corpus, the types of questions asked of the data, and why these questions were considered significant. A more detailed description of the sample and explanation of the features coded can be found in the appendix.

4.1.   The Need for Naturalistic Texts

As mentioned previously, most studies of P have based their conclusions on intro-spective reasoning from invented sentences rather than on the evidence of naturally occurring utterances. Explanations based on theory rather than data may fail to un-earth important facts about the actual use of P. For example, the patterns of specialized distribution in particle and prepositional uses for certain P-forms (table 3.1) would not have been anticipated by logical reasoning or native-speaker intuition alone; rather, they have emerged from a systematic coding of P's properties in the present database. These patterns turn out to have great significance for understanding P-forms as elements in the process of grammaticization (chapter 9).

Intuitions and theoretical expectations run the risk of obscuring the facts. For example, by is discussed quite extensively in the literature as an adverbial particle in such collocations as pass by (Live, 1965; Talmy, 1975, 1985; Dixon, 1982). This might lead one to think that such collocations are frequent in English, and yet the present data reveal only one example of by as a particle, out of thirty-five tokens. This finding is supported by Francis and Kučera's (1982) analysis of word frequencies; in fact, their analysis marginalizes the particle even more, tagging by as prepositional 99% of the time. In short, the conspicuousness of a function is not a reliable indicator of its frequency in everyday speech. It may be very easy to think of an example of a particular usage (e.g., *pass me by*) precisely because it is unusual and sticks in our memory. But if theoretical discussions then treat this example as being representative, they are likely to produce generalizations that distort the realities of language use.

In addition, explanations based on artificially generated sentences produce the persistent problem of forcing us to make grammaticality judgments for these sentences. Most studies of P use such judgments liberally — I have already used a few myself in this study — but they are messy indeed. There is no question that judgments by native speakers of English do help us carve out a rough-hewn core of prototypically grammatical sentences, but these rules are not very reliable as a premise for theoretical arguments. Native speakers often surprise themselves by what they actually do say. It is precisely at the borders of acceptability that new meanings are often created in speech: for example, the current database includes what looks like a new verb-preposition collocation: "to attitude on (someone)." Formed by the combination of a noun and a preposition, this apparently ungrammatical innovation is a surprise, an unexpected example of what is "possible" in English. But having been observed, it represents an example of categorial flexibility and speaker creativity in manipulating language to "coin out of its own substance" (Bolinger, 1971:xi).

Furthermore, even for more conventional collocations, grammaticality judgments are not very satisfactory since they are often inconsistent across different judges (see Kroch's critique of Fraser's judgments, 1979:220–221). As a result, most studies of verb-particle constructions are notable for the overabundance of asterisks or noncommittal question marks prefacing their sentence examples. It seems fair to conclude that the grammaticality of many sentences cannot be judged unless the context in which they are produced it is understood.

For these reasons, a database of naturally occurring conversation is crucial for the goals of the present study. This is the approach taken by a large body of discourse-functional studies that have been concerned with issues of categoriality and idiosyncratic patterning similar to those issues raised here regarding prepositions and particles.

4.2. The Discourse-Functional Approach

Discourse-functional research takes naturally occurring texts and conversation as its starting point and draws conclusions from the phenomena observed. Over the last twenty years or so, this research has led "inescapably to the conclusion that grammars are shaped by patterns in the way people talk" (Hopper and Thompson, 1993:358) and has motivated an emphasis on spoken conversation as a primary source of evidence. Analyses of various grammatical phenomena in English and other languages have interpreted them convincingly as regularities

> that have become temporarily stabilized in the language ... because of certain strategies people habitually use in negotiating what they have to say with their hearers, in terms of what the hearer is likely to know or be able to identify, what needs to be highlighted or presented as newsworthy, what makes a good story, and so forth. (Hopper and Thompson, 1993:358)

Hopper and Thompson have argued convincingly that the categoriality of such word classes as nouns, verbs, and adjectives is not inherent but rather, is imposed by the function of these words in particular discourse contexts (Hopper and Thompson, 1984, 1985; Thompson, 1986; see also section 10.2.1).

Syntactic constructions such as past participle sequences, relative clauses, and adverbial clauses have been interpreted as interactive strategies for packaging information or for directing the flow of information in a way that will be accessible to the hearer (Fox, 1983; Matthiessen and Thomson, 1988; Fox and Thompson, 1990; Ford, 1993). Similar approaches have been taken to word order variations such as dative shift and passivization (Givón, 1984a; Shibatani, 1985). As well, properties traditionally considered purely syntactic or semantic, such as transitivity, ergativity, subjecthood, noun incorporation, switch reference, and animacy, have all been interpreted as responses to particular discourse requirements such as foregrounding and backgrounding, topic identification and continuity, distinguishing old from new information, and keeping track of participants through discourse (Hopper and Thompson, 1980, 1984, 1993; Du Bois, 1987; Schachter, 1976).

One principle that emerges clearly through all this research is that grammar cannot be explained without reference to semantics, while semantics itself cannot be explained without reference to discourse pragmatics. The more recent, cognitively oriented semantic models of grammar, such as those described in chapter 3, share much common ground with the discourse-functional approach: as functional analyses, they all question the notion of grammar as an innate system, universally hard-wired in the human brain, whose rules exist independently of human behavior. The cognitive-semantic approaches stress the autonomy of meaning over grammar: words represent concepts and have an inherent semantic structure that can be manipulated and constructed with other words into progressively more complex meaning relationships. Grammar from such a perspective amounts to "frozen semantics" (Dixon, in Hopper and Thompson, 1993), deriving from the constant coding of semantic properties in predictable ways.

From this perspective, semantic studies have approached many of the same grammatical phenomena as those listed in the discourse-pragmatic research and have offered their own interpretations. However, in an article that reviews these studies and examines the issue of competition between semantic and discourse-pragmatic accounts, Hopper and Thompson (1993) point out for each study that the semantic accounts alone do not satisfactorily account for the data. In fact, since the semantic accounts are not grounded in actual examples of language use, they may sometimes overlook striking facts about the data, as Hopper and Thompson point out in their discussion of the predicative function of adjectives (1993:369). This is precisely the point I made earlier about the skewing of certain P-forms toward particle or preposition functions.

Hopper and Thompson's review concludes by recommending a research orientation that integrates cognitive, semantic, and pragmatic insights, and that takes pragmatic discourse motivations as the driving force for grammaticization (defined as "the process of the emergence of structure" 1993:358):

> The primary source of explanations for grammatical observations is the set of discourse (i.e. "global") motivations for the grammaticization of forms rather than the conceptually later semantic motivations that are derivative of them. One consequence of this is that while memory and intuition can provide the linguist with a limited number of contexts for forms, it is ultimately not a reliable source of data. Only actual texts can tell us indisputably what has been said and inform us about the real contexts for speech forms in a way that can give us clues to the motivations for these forms. (1993:372)

4.3.   P as a Discourse-Functional Element

The conclusion just noted is clearly echoed here in chapters 2 and 3, where it was shown that the most satisfactory answers for P's syntactic constraints have come not from rule-based grammatical accounts but from insights that integrate semantics with pragmatics. And, if we consider these insights once more, we can see that in each case it is the discourse-pragmatic motivation that seems to drive the semantic.

For example, Rice's (1987) account of passivization (see section 2.1.2), which allows passivization only for "affected" prepositional objects, explains why we might say *This bed was slept in by George Washington*. But the unusual strategy of *designating* a prepositional object (this bed) as affected is not prompted by the inherent meaning of the referent itself. Rather, it is prompted by the speaker's subjective attitude about the significance bestowed on that referent by the whole event.

Another example from the same section is the semantic intuition that verb-particle constructions prohibit NP-insertion when NPs are too long or "heavy." This is more clearly defined by Ping Chen's and Dwight Bolinger's pragmatic explanations, pointing out that NP-insertion involves moving the particle to clause-final position, which marks it as new or focal information. This explanation also motivates Sue Lindner's alternative consituency account (section 3.1) of the same phenomenon. Lindner shows that *He ran up the flag* involves P at a level of constituency different from *He ran the flag up*, but she does not say why speakers might be inclined to use either construction. The pragmatic explanation offers a clue by showing that the two constructions assign focus to two different elements by placing them in clause-final position.

As yet another example, Lambrecht's (1994) theory of pragmatic focus offers a helpful explanation for the irregularities, as well as the regularities, of stress assignment for prepositions and particles by showing that stress can be used to mark prepositions as antitopical (section 2.1.2).

And, as a final example from the same section: the idiosyncratic postposed word order of certain P-forms is accounted for plausibly by Leonard Talmy's figure-ground schemata, but this syntactic-semantic model leaves us wondering what motivates such an antiquated usage. The answer seems to lie, once again, in pragmatic motivations. R.M.W. Dixon (1982) suggests that *John walked the field over* expresses a more "thorough treatment" of *the field*. But this "thorough treatment" is predicated by <u>over</u>, which expresses a sense of covering the whole area, thus adding a sense of totality and completion to the verb. By postposing, or focusing this P-form clause-finally, the speaker conveys the subjective meaning captured by Dixon's intuition.

In summary, for all these examples, it seems that discourse-pragmatic considerations drive the meanings conveyed by the different syntactic patterning of P-forms.

Further clues to P's discourse-functional role come from the distributions observed in table 3.1, which reveal a clear tendency for certain Ps to specialize as either prepositions or particles. Although cognitive-semantic models provide us with the conceptual framework to map out P's meanings, these maps are introspectively constructed. Thus, they offer no explanation for the empirically observed fixing of certain words in preposition or particle functions. Furthermore, as static constructions based on memory rather than on naturally occurring data, these maps represent patterns of usage that are known to be "there," without revealing how or why they came to be there or how they may still be evolving.

Similarly, the Role and Reference Grammar map of layered clause structure (section 3.2.3) shows us where prepositions "fit" under different scopes to produce different meanings. But it doesn't explain why some meanings are predicative and some are not. Furthermore, since the RRG model does not accommodate the fluid dynamics of language use, it doesn't capture the functional overlap between prepositions and particles and offers no account for the fact that the same P-form may function as a preposition, a particle, or a predicate adjective.

With regard to this categorial fluidity, it seems clear from our examination so far that P-forms follow Hopper and Thompson's (1984, 1985) principle for nouns, verbs, and other lexical categories: that categoriality is largely determined by context.

The next logical step, then, is to explore the contexts in which P-forms occur, to discover the pragmatic motivations that drive their categoriality and meanings. Having established that theoretical "mental models" can only take us so far, we are encouraged to take a fresh look at the problem of P from the perspective of how it is actually used in everyday conversation. This requires observing and coding certain facts of occurrence which may open a window onto P's discourse function. We need to observe, for example, what kinds of contexts require particles or prepositions, how pragmatic focus is distributed in these contexts, what kind of information is contributed by prepositional objects, which contexts allow sublexicalization of these objects, which P-forms enter into construction with which elements under which scope, and what kinds of meanings result from these constructions.

4.4.   A Discourse-Based Methodology

This section will briefly explain how the above questions are answered by the methodology of the present study, and how the discourse-functional approach to P is operationalized. What is given here is a retrospective distillation rather than a step-by-step account of the methodology. As explained previously, the goal was to discover functions of P in the discourse, rather than to posit them a priori. In practice, this turned out to be a rather circuitous process.

First, to a certain extent, research problems are always defined in terms that bring their own set of premises to the methodology. In this case, the starting point was the problem of P: to identify a motivation for its categorial flexibility and constraints, and to explain its polysemy. The theoretical premise is that this problem requires a naturalistic text-based approach. The premise is based partly on an analysis of the previous introspective literature, which does not satisfactorily solve the problem of P (chapters 2 and 3), and partly on the precedent of other discourse-functional studies which have satisfactorily solved problems similar to those presented here (section 3.2).

However, this premise was actually tested as a hypothesis throughout the research process itself, confirming itself as the data revealed unexpected findings — such as P's skewed distribution — which were obviously important and which would not have been revealed by a more traditional, introspective, sentence-based approach.

Second, one difficulty with a discovery- rather than a theory-driven approach is knowing what questions to ask of the data, in searching for clues to the problem of P. The data should speak for themselves; but the questions asked will naturally limit the kinds of answers that appear. If those answers do not unearth any relevant clues, we need to reformulate the questions. Consequently, the process becomes one of trial and error, constantly refining itself as new answers provoke new lines of inquiry. In the course of the present study, many features and properties were coded, in the hope that they might be significant: for example, semantic properties associated with verb transitivity, or the topicality of P's arguments. However, many of them turned out not to be centrally important to solving the problem of P and they are not included here.

In summary, the following methodological description spares the reader the details of the circuitous research process. Instead, it presents an abstract of those features which offered essential clues and which will be discussed subsequently as evidence for the arguments in chapters 6 through 10. Some of these features invoke theoretical frameworks already discussed: "scope of assertion" is partly defined by Knud Lambrecht's (1994) theory of pragmatic focus, and "scope of operation" by RRG's theory of layered clause structure (Foley and Van Valin, 1984; Van Valin, 1993). These theories are not invoked as predictive models but, rather, as a source of valuable concepts and insights. Their nomenclature provides the tools to unearth and analyze significant semantic, syntactic, prosodic, and pragmatic properties of P.

4.4.1.   *The Corpus*

The corpus of 1,245 utterances comes from a series of five conversations in American English, recorded in the 1970s, 1980s, and 1990s. Two of them (U and A) were recorded during the 1970s, and the three others (coded R, C, and E) were recorded after 1987.

The "Upholstery Shop" (U) conversation takes place in an upholstery shop and primarily involves five men and one woman, of mixed ethnicity. One interlocutor (V) is the superintendent of an apartment complex, and a persistent topic of conversation involves a recent incident where a tenant from a neighboring complex broke a glass door and then entered into an altercation with V about whose responsibility it was to clean up. Another topic involves the negotiation of what to do with some unwanted kittens. The transcribed conversation lasts about half an hour and produces 225 utterances for the database.

The "Auto Discussion" transcript ("A") also contains about thirty minutes of social conversation, mostly about racing cars. The conversation emerges during a picnic and involves three men, two women, and a child. It represents 223 utterances.

The "Round the Table" conversation (R) comes from an informal dinner party involving two married couples and one child. It covers a variety of topics, including long-distance telephone systems, linguistics classes, child-bearing, and the construction of the loop highway around Denver, Colorado. The conversation lasts for about one hour and represents 496 coded utterances in the database.

The "CPR" conversation (C) consists of a training session in CPR (cardiopulmonary resuscitation), delivered by two Red Cross officers. About ten participants are involved, including myself. The conversation is roughly divided into three sequences. The first is an instructional monologue by the female officer introducing the training session and CPR manual, with interjections and questions from the participants. The second sequence involves a hands-on practice session, where a small group of trainees practices CPR on a dummy (called "Annie" by the officers). The third sequence is a whole-group discussion, involving more contributions from the trainees and responses from both officers (one female, one male). The entire conversation lasts about one and a half hours and represents 275 utterances in the database.

The "Eldora" transcript ("E") contains only about five minutes of conversation (26 utterances), extracted from a longer recording. It comes from a social conversation between friends and primarily involves two men and one woman. The topic of conversation here is teacher-student relations. One participant (B), a university instructor, is describing his experience with a disrespectful student and getting reactions to the situation from his interlocutors.

In sum, the extracts represent about three and a half hours of conversation, transcribed and accompanied by videotaped (for A and E) or audiotaped (for R, C, and U) recordings.

4.4.2. Database Encoding

From these conversations, every clear utterance involving a P-form was entered into the relational database system *Paradox*, where various properties of the utterance were coded and logged into in two tables. The larger P-unit table coded properties of P-forms themselves and of the elements around them. The smaller NP table coded a subsample of utterances containing prepositional Ps and focused on the semantic and information properties of their prepositional objects. Prepositional objects are coded as "Landmarks," a term borrowed from Lindner (1981) since it captures the semantic function of prepositional objects. Accordingly, in the remainder of this study, I will also use the term "landmark" to refer to prepositional objects, even when they do not refer to concrete entities in the spatiodirectional domain.

The remainder of this section briefly defines the features that have yielded important findings for this study and explains why they were selected. For a more detailed explication of coding methodology, decisions, and rationale, see the appendix.

4.4.3. *P-Units*

A P-unit is an intonation unit containing at least one use of a P-form. Intonation units were chosen as the basic unit of analysis (see next paragraph). Thus, every entry in this table consists of one P-unit. As indicated in section 4.4.1, the five conversations provided a total of 1,245 utterances containing P-units: 225 in U, 223 in A, 496 in R, 275 in C, and only 26 in E.

INTONATION UNITS   (IUs) are defined prosodically by Wallace Chafe as single-speaker utterances, consisting of

> a single coherent intonation contour characterized by one or more intonation peaks and a cadence that is recognizable as either clause-final or sentence-final (and usually) separated by pauses that last anywhere from a fraction of a second to several seconds. (1988:1)

Both Chafe (1986, 1987, 1988) and M.A.K. Halliday (1967) argue that IUs offer a better window to the processes of information flow than do clauses. This claim is supported by the data presented here, which show, for example, that certain constituents — notably, prepositional phrases — tend to be separated by means of intonation from other elements in the clause, depending on the kind of information that they contain.

Halliday claims that the "information unit" (roughly corresponding to Chafe's IU) "is what speakers choose to encode as a unit of discourse" (1967:202):

> much of discourse structure involves patterns of reference, ellipsis and the like which lie outside the more restricted conceptions of linguistic structure and whose range extends across the boundaries of recognized structural units. (1967:243)

For Halliday, the clause is the intersection point for "options ... associated with experiential meaning, speech function and discourse organization" (1967:243). Thus, many information units do correspond with clause units, but not exclusively so.

Chafe identifies the clause as the basic unit of written discourse while the IU is the basic unit of spoken discourse. IUs package information in a way that is "optimally accessible" to the hearer. Example (1) consists of only two clauses (1a, 1b, and 1c–1h), but eight IUs. The units are separated by commas to indicate nonfinal intonation breaks, and dotted lines represent pauses.

(1)   a. . . . But . . . the first time I was in Japan ,

     b. . . . in nineteen fifty . . . nine ,

     c. . . . I was out on the street ,

d.   . .late at night ,

e.   . .in downtown Kyoto ,

f.   . . . wi-th

g.   . .uh in the bar district ,

h.   . . . with an American man,   (Chafe, 1986:15)

Chafe argues convincingly that spoken conversation is the most natural domain for language (1986:12). And since the present study is centrally concerned with phenomena considered to be informal and conversational (e.g., verb-particle collocations), IUs are a natural choice as the basic coding unit. However, within these IUs, *clause-level* information is also coded, as we will see in the discussion of "Unit Form."

The corpus includes 1,000 different IUs, each containing at least one use of a P-form. Since each use of a P-form is entered and analyzed separately, this produces a total of 1,245 entries in all. An example of a double entry is given in (2), where about and out, from the same IU, are coded as two different entries.

(2)   'He's about the only 'good regular ''out there .   (A:8)

UNIT FORM   refers to the syntactic form of the IU — as a clause, prepositional phrase, subject NP, or any other recognizable constituent. The interaction between prosody (stress, intonation patterns, pauses, etc.) and syntactic form has received a great deal of attention in the literature, and is considered significant for interpreting information flow and meaning (see also Crystal, 1969; Allerton and Cruttenden, 1974; Bing, 1984; Cruttenden, 1997; Fox, 1984; Bolinger, 1986; Tench, 1990).

This unit form feature will help in highlighting interesting properties of landmarks in chapter 6, where it is noted that prepositional phrases, after clauses, are the most frequent unit form in these data.

The coding of unit form is not always a simple matter. In naturally occurring texts, with all their false starts, repairs, and truncations, it is sometimes difficult to know what to include as a well-formed unit. Theoretical controversy over what can be called a clause — whether, for example, gerunds, infinitives, and nominalizations count as clausal verbs (Givón, 1980; Hopper and Thompson, 1984, 1985) — complicates matters further. Appendix A.2 explains how this issue is resolved for the present study.

P-FORM   Every token of a P-form was typed into the database to allow for frequency counts of different words. These counts are particularly relevant to the analysis of P-specialization in chapter 9 in either preposition or particle functions.

P-words were identified by the criteria outlined in chapter 1: if any word in the transcripts appeared as both a preposition and a particle in different contexts, then it was included in the database as a P-word. The number of P-words identified in this way totaled eighteen for the present corpus. Although a larger sample would undoubtedly produce a greater number of alternating P-forms, the smallness of this sample is itself instructive as a frequency measure, indicating which words are most likely to be used as both preposition and particle.

However, to this P-set I have added two more forms — about and after — even though these words never actually appear as particles in my data. I did this because their unexpected distribution offers interesting insights regarding the specialization of P-forms, as I will explain in chapter 9.

The final "P-set," then, includes the twenty forms listed in (3).

(3)

about	around	down	over
above	before	in	through
across	behind	off	to
after	between	on	under
along	by	out	up

Together with these P-tokens, I occasionally coded such non-P-forms as the "pure" prepositions of and with when their distributions were instructive — for example, when they formed a complex with P-forms (out of, in to). Their significance will be explained in chapter 8.

To avoid making categorial judgments at the coding stage, all P-manifestations were coded even when they occurred as prefixes and suffixes (turnoff, upcoming), and even, in certain cases, the conflated forms here and there, when these were clearly interpreted as meaning "in this/that place" (see Appendix A.3 for justification). Although such occurrences are only occasional in the database, they are important for the purposes of a study such as the current one, which seeks to offer a comprehensive account of P's functions.

PARTICLE/PREPOSITION   P-words were coded as either prepositions or particles, depending on whether or not they occurred with a landmark NP. This criterion, as explained in section 1.2.4, is an ad hoc response to the problem of distinguishing one form from the other as it appears in the data, and implies no assumptions about inherent categoriality.

Thus, even P-forms that function syntactically like adjectives were coded as "particles" since they appeared independently of a landmark. The same criterion was applied to affixes such as those mentioned earlier. Some prefixes denote a landmark relation for the following NP; for example, if I underline a word, then I write a line under the word, and the word may be viewed as a landmark. On the other hand, if I underuse or overuse a word, nothing is under or over the word. Rather, the word is the direct object of the verb use, and under or over serve an Aktionsart-marking function on the verb (to be explained in the following chapter). As a result, these prefixes were coded as particles rather than as prepositions.

To distinguish landmarks from direct objects, I invoked Lindner's semantic trajector-landmark schema (1981, 1982), which offers a more coherent basis for distinction than the syntactic tests previously used in the literature. For example, the road in (4a) is the landmark for the relationship expressed by off. I is the trajector, which changes its state and becomes separated from the landmark. Off is a preposition here.

(4)   a. I turned off the road.

b. I took off my hat.

However, my hat in (4b) is not a landmark: it is the trajector, the entity that changes its state. The landmark from which <u>my hat</u> is separated is sublexicalized, and can only be inferred as "my head." Thus, <u>off</u> is a particle in (4b).

The distinction becomes more tricky when nonspatial relationships are involved, or when the P-form has uses that do not clearly involve either preposition or particle. For instance, <u>about</u> performs a variety of functions, one of which seems to be that of an all-purpose *Qualifier*, meaning "approximately":

(5)   'Usually it 'takes <u>about</u> a ''teaspoon , that's <u>about</u> all the 'water they can ''get in their
      'lungs .   (C:6)

Coding problems also arise with such sequences as <u>over there</u> or <u>on here</u>. In all such cases, the coding rationale was consistent: if the P-form was followed by a NP, which could, through logical inference, be considered a landmark, it was coded as a preposition. If not, it was coded as a particle, whether or not it occurred postverbally. Appendix A.3 explains the coding rationale for instances like <u>over there</u> above, and more detailed discussion will be devoted to <u>about</u> in chapter 9.

STRESS PLACEMENT   offers important clues for pragmatic focus, topic continuity and speaker attitude (Halliday, 1967; Bolinger, 1971, 1978; Ladd, 1986, 1990; Boyce and Menn, 1979; Lindsey, 1981; Cutler, 1984; Chafe, 1987, 1993). In particular, Lambrecht's theory of focus (1994) claims that stress placement is the primary focus-marking device in English. Pragmatic focus is a significant principle in the analysis developed in chapter 7 of particle-preposition alternation, so Lambrecht's theory will be discussed in more detail there.

Lambrecht's theory of focus is only concerned with primary stress placement. However, IUs generally display different levels of stress, and secondary stress placement carries its own pragmatic significance (Chafe, 1993; Bolinger, 1971:45). Therefore, secondary stress was coded in these data (for details, see Appendix A.4).

ASSERTION   According to Lambrecht, pragmatic focus is attributed to that portion of an utterance which is asserted — "that portion of the proposition which cannot be taken for granted at the time of speech" (1994:207). Lambrecht's model predicts that asserted elements are marked by stress placement. However, Givón (1984) proposes an independent definition of assertion in terms of the epistemic contract between speaker and hearer (i.e., what the speaker assumes the hearer knows and accepts), and this can be coded. Therefore, by coding P-forms as "asserted" or "presupposed" (in Givón's terms) and then checking the correlation between their assertion status and their stress placement, we can not only doublecheck Lambrecht's predictions but also bring independent evidence to bear on the focal status of different P-constructions. This issue is also developed in chapter 7.

The procedures used here for coding P-forms and landmarks as being asserted or not differ from Lambrecht's in that he takes phrasal categories rather than individual words as the basic unit for a focal domain. Thus, within his theory, a preposition would not be tagged as asserted, but rather the whole prepositional phrase would be taken as the focal domain. For theoretical reasons that will be explained in chapter 7, I coded assertion more locally: if a P-form or a landmark displayed the information properties that Givón would associate with asserted information, then I coded that word as asserted. For details on coding operations and decisions, see Appendix A.5.

SCOPE OF OPERATION   refers to the level of constituency at which P operates in the layered structure of the clause, and uses the nomenclature of Role and Reference Grammar (RRG). As already mentioned in section 3.2.3, P's construction with different elements under different scopes offers some clues toward the generation of P's various meanings.

In general, coding decisions draw on RRG's schemata (Foley and Van Valin, 1984; Van Valin, 1993). However, I have modified these schemata to capture more accurately the different structural relationships actually observed in the database. For example, I make no categorial distinction between prepositions and particles ("operators" in RRG terminology). As explained in section 3.2.3, this distinction cannot be maintained satisfactorily on either semantic or syntactic grounds.

Other modifications involve extending the logic of the RRG schemata to finer distinctions: for example, distinguishing between core and nuclear scope for prepositions and identifying a new scope, namely, P-scope, which accounts for particle-preposition complexes such as *out of (work)*. Such modifications are explained and justified in chapter 8; also, coding details for this feature are explained in more detail in Appendix A.6.

4.4.4. Landmarks

Landmarks, as already explained, are prepositional objects. These were coded in a noun phrase (NP) table separate from the P-unit table. Since the basic defining difference between prepositions and particles is that the former occur with landmarks and the latter do not, a close examination of these landmarks and their functions suggested a useful line of inquiry for understanding the functions of prepositions and particles.

The main purpose of the NP table is to discover how P's landmarks differ in their properties from other NPs in the clause. These properties determine the function of prepositional phrases and will be discussed in chapter 6. My coding of semantic and pragmatic information properties such as "identifiability" and "tracking" followed Thompson's lead (1997) in her study of oblique arguments, except that it focused more narrowly on P-landmarks than on prepositional landmarks in general, and added a couple of properties to Thompson's list: morphological form (whether the landmark is a lexical noun or a pronoun) and semantic class (whether it refers to people, places, and so on). Both these properties are important in functionally distinguishing landmarks from other NP-roles in the clause (e.g., subject or object), as we will see in chapter 6..

The NP table contains 565 NP entries taken from the first sections of each conversation and representing all syntactic roles. The following properties were coded for the NPs in this table.

SYNTACTIC ROLES   of NPs include intransitive subject (S), transitive subject (A), object (O) — all three following Dixon's (1989) three-way distinction — and landmark (LM). An explanation of these roles, and a discussion of their distribution in this sample, is given in Appendix A.7.

MORPHOLOGICAL FORM   Each landmark NP is coded according to its morphological form, as either lexical or pronominal. I include generic forms such as <u>someone</u> and <u>everything</u> as pronouns, and even <u>you guys</u>, on the principle that this last form functions conventionally like a second-person plural pronoun in some dialects of American English. For lexical forms, I distinguish between proper nouns (names, titles, acronyms, and so on) and common nouns.

SEMANTIC CLASS   This field groups NP arguments into general semantic domains, such as person, place, thing, or quality. The endeavor is intuitive to some extent, but enlightening, since it reveals some striking links between syntactic roles and particular semantic domains (see Appendix A.8 for coding procedures).

INFORMATION STATUS   indicates how new or familiar the NP information is to the hearer. The importance of information status for explaining NP-functions is well documented (Du Bois, 1980, 1987; Prince, 1981; Givón, 1983; Fox and Thompson, 1990) and is again relevant for distinguishing landmarks from other syntactic roles. The present study adopts and slightly modifies Ellen Prince's (1981) six-point scale of Assumed Familiarity (see Appendix A.9).

DEFINITENESS AND REFERENTIALITY   are also important in distinguishing the functions of landmarks (Chafe, 1976; Du Bois, 1980; Hopper and Thompson, 1980, 1984, 1985). In the literature, they are often conflated under the larger property of identifiability: definite and referential NPs are more identifiable than indefinite and nonreferential NPs. In English, definite NPs are usually marked with the article <u>the</u>, indicating that the speaker assumes their identifiability. Referential NPs are used to speak about objects with independent, "continuous identity over time" in the "real" world (Du Bois, 1980:208). For example, <u>work</u> in the phrase *out of work* is not referential because it only exists in the discourse context to define a state: it could be paraphrased as "not working." In contrast, if we indicate, about a specific job, that "this work is hard," we attribute referentiality to the NP.

In the present study, definiteness and referentiality are coded separately, following Du Bois (1980; see Appendix A.10 for more definitional information). The results show that these properties interact intriguingly with morphological form to distinguish landmarks from other NPs.

4.5.   Conclusion

From an analysis of what we know and do not know about the syntax and semantics of P, as revealed by the previous chapters, I have argued that a data-driven, discourse-based approach is necessary, breaking a long tradition of introspective, theory-driven accounts of P that depend on artificially generated sentences for their examples.

We know that P's categoriality is flexible and contextually determined, but we do not know what the determining principles are. We know that cognitive-semantic models offer insightful mental maps of P's meanings and explain some of these meanings in terms of alternative constituency, but we do not know why the meanings are systematically structured in patterns of particle versus preposition. We know that pragmatic motivations help account for several of P's idiosyncracies, and that previous discourse-pragmatic studies have successfully explained many equally idiosyncratic grammatical phenomena in English and other languages.

All of this warrants a new, data-driven approach to the problem of P. Section 4.4 of this chapter has outlined the general methodology for this approach, introducing the corpus and the features to be coded, which will throw light on the discourse function of P in the course of this book.

The remaining chapters are presented as an argument, based on the findings from the text data and supported by existing theoretical insights. The argument is constructed step-by-step, building from its central thesis about the discourse function of P-forms (chapters 5 through 7) to explain how this function is taken up differently by particle constructions than by prepositional constructions at all syntactic levels (chapter 8), and how P's variation reflects semantic extension and grammar change in progress (chapter 9).

As I explained, this argument is presented as a posthoc construction rather than as a description of the inductive research process. Its major claims are therefore presented as conclusions, not hypotheses; as insights that were suggested, modified, and confirmed by the data themselves. I hope that this reconstruction of the study will result in a more coherent and readable document.

5

P in Discourse:
Orienting, Situating, and Linking

Previous chapters have set the stage for a discourse-pragmatic approach to the problem of P. The first task is to tackle the issue of categoriality. This chapter does so by defending a new, functional definition of P, which forms the central thesis of this study:

(1)   *P is a discourse-orienting element.*

The first part of this chapter defines orientation and argues that this function is as basic in our cognitive makeup as is our perception of people, objects and events — in fact, it helps to define our perception of these entities. The adprep is represented as the prototypical orientating element. I will then argue from the data that orientation involves two subfunctions: situating and linking. I will illustrate how these subfunctions are taken up by particles and prepositions, respectively. Finally, I will consider some possible counterarguments and will conclude that the notion of orientation is meaningful as a theoretical principle, for both unifying and distinguishing prepositions and particles.

5.1.   Orientation and Cognition

According to the *Oxford English Dictionary* (1969), orientation means "to bring into clearly specified relations" or "to turn in a specified direction." Orientation has been defined in various ways according to different theoretical perspectives in the psychological, sociological, and phenomenological literature; but all approaches invoke the notions of space, of reference points, and of a subject's relation to these points.

Orientation is basic to our perception of the world and to our thinking. We see the world in terms of forms whose size, shape, function, and significance are defined in relation to ourselves or to one other. Similarly, we experience events as changes of state, made visible in changed relationships between the forms around us;

even motion itself can be defined as "the perception of recurrent changes of spatial relations" (Svorou, 1994:24).

Without orientation, we cannot move purposefully or act upon the world. This point is made from a clinical psychological perspective by Emerson Foulke (1983), whose laboratory-based research on perceptual systems and impairments leads him to claim that "mobility must be purposeful and goal-oriented":

> One can imagine a blind pedestrian who ... could avoid every obstacle while moving through space but whose course of travel was random. Without this last criterion [of goal-orientation], a blind pedestrian might be able to satisfy every other criterion while meandering aimlessly, but such ability would be of little value to blind pedestrians. (1983:127)

Navigation is effected by constantly checking our location in relation to relevant objects surrounding us. As George Psathas points out in his phenomenological analysis of movement and navigation, "Orientation requires skills and knowledge about what are relevant objects and places in one's social world, how these may be identified, and what the spatial relationships of various types of objects and places are" (1989:150). "Relevant objects and places" are those that help us know where we are and where we are going:

> Blind pedestrians who know where they want to go are oriented in space. In order to know how to get there, they must know where they are, and where their goals are in relation to their present positions. To achieve this orientation, they must be able to gather relevant information about the spaces in which they are operating; that is, they must have spatial ability. (Foulke, 1983:127)

5.2.   Orientation and Discourse

Human language systems, like our knowledge of the world, are embedded in human experience. When we use language to refer to objects, events, and situations, we represent our own subjective understanding about how things are related to one other. But language is more than reference and representation. Essentially, language is communication — interaction with other people — and in order for it to work, our representations have to make sense to others.

To this extent, meaning in language is constructed intersubjectively. Words, phrases, and grammatical structures have meanings only to the extent that interlocutors agree on those meanings. Therefore, as these language forms are manipulated and combined to construct progressively more complex meanings, it is essential that each interlocutor be involved in the construction process. In this way, conversational discourse becomes an exercise in the cooperative construction, or negotiation, of meaning. This involves, on the part of speakers, a great deal of sensitivity and accommodation to their hearers: an awareness of what they can be assumed to know already, of where their attention is at the moment, of how to signal a shift of topic or a return to an old one, and so on.

The negotiation of meaning in discourse, like navigation in the real world, requires orientation if it is to be purposefully directed. No matter what my discourse purpose—to report or elicit information, to express an attitude, to get you to do something, or just to be friendly—a significant part of my conversational effort will be directed to aligning your discourse perspective with mine. The proliferation of conventional metaphors referring to interpersonal communication in spatiodirectional terms testifies to the conceptual significance of orientation. To mention just a few:

Are you with me?

We're not tracking

Try to see it from my point of view.

Let me talk you through it.

Let's put it this way.

If I may back up for a second.

I don't follow.

Do you catch my drift?

You're way ahead of me.

I was just coming to that.

Going back to what you were saying.

Let's look at it this way.

On the other hand, . . .

That's a garden path argument.

You're rambling.

In the present study, I define discourse orientation as follows:

(2)   *Orientation is the function of situating elements of information in relation to contextual information.*

Like Foulke's blind pedestrian, we could wander aimlessly, going through the motions of exchanging random utterances with one other, but we would not be constructing a meaningful conversation and our linguistic ability would be of no more value than the undirected motor ability of the pedestrian. Talking, like walking, needs orientation.

Some explanation of the terms in (2) will be useful here. First, "to situate elements of information" means to represent the things we talk about as being in a certain relative state: a state that can only be defined in terms of its relation to something else. That something else is contextual information. Contextual information may be familiar or new, but to assist orientation it must be relevant to the construction of the discourse perspective, just as surrounding objects and places must be relevant in the physical world of orientation.

What is relevant varies according to present position and immediate goal. Emanuel Schegloff (1972:76) explains that conversation is sequentially organized, in the sense that utterances are warranted, or made relevant, by the occurrence of preceding utterances. To take a very simple example: if I remark that the room is cold, my remark gives relevance to your announcement that I may close a window if I like. In Schegloff's terms, this means that your announcement is "conditionally relevant" on my remark. It is conditional relevance that makes the utterances in an exchange meaningful and produces "sequence" (the discourse corollary of navigation) rather than mere "subsequent occurrence."

Conditional relevance is important not only in turn-taking exchanges between speakers but also in the general construction of meaning. Participants and events need to be introduced in a way that warrants their presence in the discourse. Thus, if I say *There's a fly on your nose*, the introduction of *a fly* is warranted by the "here and now" of *your nose*; presumably, the physical context is what makes the fly relevant to you.

New contexts may provide relevance in a slightly different way by opening up new frames of reference in which subsequent utterances may be situated: they may take us from the "here and now" to the "there and then." For instance, in "There was an old woman who lived in a shoe," the first line of the nursery rhyme introduces a setting that helps us visualize and evaluate the old woman's circumstances in a rather unusual way.

In the process of discourse orientation, we are in a sense more impoverished than Foulke's blind pedestrian since we don't even have tangible objects much of the time for reference points. Whatever we refer to in discourse has to be "put there," or constructed, by speakers. As Wolfgang Klein (1983) convincingly argues, reference itself is dependent on establishing links with already established concepts in discourse. To illustrate his point, he asks us to close our eyes and imagine two little red squares:

> The two squares exist only in your imagination. No one but you knows their exact size or their exact colour. But I can refer to them. . . . I can also refer to each of them individually, although they are identical in all their attributes: they are both little, red, rectangular, and have sides of equal length. So, I can't use their properties. I can't use their position, as I could do if they were drawn on a blackboard or printed in a textbook. They have no material substance which would "individualize" them . . .

> The only way to keep them separate and to refer to them individually is through deixis. I can say, for example, "Erase the first square" or, "Put a triangle on that square, which, in your view, is on the left." . . . [These] expressions . . . relate the square in question to factors of the speech act. (1983:286)

Deixis is defined by Klein as the process of linking concepts to the speech situation, of constructing them in relation to the speaker's subjective experience of what exists "here and now." This comes very close to my own definition of orientation. However, orientation is a broader term. It includes links not only to the here and now, and to previously established, familiar concepts, but also to new concepts. It may involve casting familiar information in unfamiliar settings, projecting new horizons, and creating new reference points, so that the discourse can move from frame to frame in a purposeful and goal-directed way.

In this process of discourse orientation, it is logical that words that refer to space should have a central role. In the physical world, it is spatial relations that orient us — relations of containment, separation, anteriority, and posteriority, and so on. Several linguists have postulated that language is conceptually structured by our perception of spatial relationships, that references to the concrete world of space become transferred to progressively more abstract domains in the world of ideas. A slightly different way of looking at it is that language is structured by the need to communicate, and that the same kinds of relations obtain between linguistic elements as between elements in the physical world, so the same words emerge to refer to relationships in both domains. We could say then that the relationships are conceptually basic, whether they refer to discourse or to the physical world.

The conceptual basis of language is a phenomenological issue beyond the scope of the present study, but what seems certain is that words are the building blocks of language and their arrangement is driven by our pragmatic purposes in conversation: we make them mean what we want them to mean.

Prepositions and particles are the primary building blocks for expressing both spatial orientation and discourse orientation in English. The remainder of this chapter is devoted to explaining how prepositions and particles are used for discourse-orientational purposes. It should be borne in mind, however, that orientation may be performed by a wide variety of linguistic expressions and constructions. It may be lexicalized, or built into the meanings of many nouns, verbs, adjectives, and adverbs. Furthermore, certain grammatical constructions seem to have orientational functions, some of which will be exemplified in section 5.6.2, and their relation to P-forms will be considered in the conclusion to this book (chapter 10). In this chapter, however, my main concern is to show that P-forms constitute a special group whose purpose is specifically to provide orientation, and whose productivity and scope in this function therefore far exceed those of other linguistic elements.

In this endeavor, this book complements previous discourse-oriented analyses of other lexical classes. Just as the class of nouns has been shown to specialize in conferring "participant" status on their referents and the class of verbs to represent "events" (Hopper and Thompson, 1984, 1985), I will show that prepositions and particles also have a specialized discourse function: to provide orientation for participants, events, episodes, and larger rhetorical units.

P-forms constitute a particular subset of orienting words that may occur as either prepositions or particles. As outlined previously, in section 2.2, P-forms are commonly used postverbally as adpreps, and here I argue that adpreps perform the prototypical function of orientation and offer essential clues about the difference between prepositions and particles.

5.3. Situating and Linking Adpreps

Adpreps were introduced as "a case of dual constituency," where a preposition could quite acceptably be used as a particle: *She swept off the stage majestically* can also be rendered *She swept off majestically*. I have suggested that adpreps may provide a clue to P's apparently indeterminate categoriality since they reveal a functional context where particles and prepositions coincide semantically and syntactically as the same element, and differ only in the presence or absence of a landmark. Lindner's semantic account of particles as prepositions with sublexicalized landmarks (section 3) reinforces this interpretation.

We can examine the discourse function of the adprep in the conversational data from the present study. Consider the following examples.

(3)   Whyncha 'just' throw em <u>out</u> the ''window .   (U:78)

(4)   What's 'bad is they could send a 'bullet right <u>through</u> the ''window .   (R:6)

Adpreps, in general, refer to the spatiodirectional domain, so their orientational function is semantically quite transparent. In (3), the speaker is suggesting what to do with some unwanted kittens. The P-form <u>out</u> situates or predicates a change of state for the kittens. This change of state is defined specifically in terms of their path of exit, <u>the window</u>, which serves as a contextual reference point. In (4), the speaker is talking about some hunters shooting irresponsibly in a field. The adprep <u>through</u> situates <u>the bullet</u> in relation to <u>the window</u>, once again, which defines the path of motion.

So, in the most concrete sense of physical motion, these adpreps situate discourse participants in relation to contextual information — they perform the prototypical function of orientation. But there is a duality in this function, to match the "dual constituency" noticed by Bolinger. Adpreps situate and but they also link.

In the present volume, situating is defined as predicating states. "Predicating" is used here in a broader sense than that of clause-level predication by verbs: it is used in the dictionary sense of "expressing something about a subject." This interpretation is consistent with much of the semantic and syntactic literature where prepositions are seen as predicators or predicates (Halliday, 1985:142; Van Valin, 1993:19; Lambrecht, 1994; Jacobs, 1993:25–26). Also, the word "state" is used here in a broad sense, to encompass evolving states (i.e., directions), end-states, changes of state, and temporary states. Thus, in (3), <u>out</u> predicates a change of state — from containment to separation — for the kittens, and in (4) <u>through</u> predicates an evolving direction for the bullet.

In syntactic terms, predication is traditionally considered the central function of the verb. The verbs <u>throw</u> and <u>send</u> in (3) and (4) predicate particular types of activities on their clause subjects. Since the adpreps modify the verbs by contributing spatiodirectional meaning to the activities predicated by the verb, they carry what would traditionally be termed an adverbial function.

However, these adpreps also link: that is, they introduce contextual information to the discourse context. They do this by establishing a relation between the element being situated and the information being introduced. Thus, in the preceding examples, <u>the window</u> has no status in the utterance — no reason for being there — other than its relation to <u>the kittens</u> and <u>the bullet</u>, respectively. It helps to define their situation but only when licensed by a preposition that expresses the configurational nature of the relationship. Therefore, in addition to their adverbial function, these adpreps also carry a prepositional function, in traditional grammar terms. In semantic terms, we would say that they establish a relation between a landmark (<u>the window</u>) and a trajector (<u>the kittens</u>, or <u>the bullet</u>).

The same functional duality that we have seen for (3) and (4) can be observed next for the adpreps <u>off</u>, <u>up</u>, and <u>in</u>. All of the following utterances come from the same conversational "cats" episode in example (3).

(5) a. I 'knocked it <u>off</u> the ''bed, 'right ?   (U:24)

   b. She'll cl-'try to ''climb <u>up</u> your ''leg man .   (U:83)

   c. 'Throw him <u>in</u> the 'goddamn ''furnace ,   (U:94)

In each of these utterances, the particle situates, or predicates a change of state, for a participant (<u>I</u>, <u>she</u>, or <u>him</u>). It also links or introduces the context defining that state (<u>the bed</u>, <u>your leg</u>, <u>the goddam furnace</u>).

By definition, adpreps can alternate as particles. This alternation is illustrated in the paired conversational sequences in (7), which nicely juxtapose the functions of adprep and particle.

(6) a. M: And you know 6:30 in the morning . . . guns you know.

        Cause there's farms over there .

        R: What's 'bad is they could send a 'bullet right <u>through</u> the ''window .   (R:32)

   b. Hondas have these-have a real big windshield and so — and so , if you roll an animal onto your hood I'm sure that it would . .come 'roaring ''<u>through</u> .   (R:33)

The meaning of <u>through</u> is very similar in these two sequences, which occurred contiguously in the conversation. The only difference, in syntactic and semantic terms, is that in (6b) <u>through</u> does not occur with a landmark. The landmark is sublexicalized — but it is clearly and implicitly recoverable as <u>the windshield</u> from the first clause. The pragmatic effect of this sublexicalization is that in (6a), <u>through</u> both situates and links while it only situates in (68b). The first utterance introduces a new context: the hearer's attention is directed, via <u>the window</u>, to the interior of the farmhouse. But in the second utterance, the hearer's attention is directed only to the evolving state of <u>the bullet</u>.

To take another example of the interplay between adpreps and particles (parentheses suggest intervals between utterances, or interruptions by other sequences):

(7) a. M: Wyncha 'just 'throw em <u>out</u> the ''window .

        (. . . . . .)

   b. C: 'I'm gonna put eh ''<u>out</u> in the 'yard .

        (. . . . .)

   c. J: 'Throw the 'goddam things '<u>out</u> in the ''street !

        (. . . . .)

   d. M: Put ''food <u>out</u> every 'day .

   e. J: [damn? cats] , just 'throw em ''<u>out</u> !   (U:78–94)

In this sequence, speaker M first uses <u>out</u> as an adprep in (7a). In other words, <u>out</u> serves the dual purpose of situating the kittens by predicating their direction of motion and of defining that direction contextually, by introducing the path of their trajectory (<u>the window</u>) as a landmark. This path is not defined in the remaining utterances, where <u>out</u>, as a particle, merely situates the kittens. It predicates their change of state, but does not define that state in terms of any landmark or contextual reference point — although we can infer the path of exit as <u>the window</u>, perhaps, or <u>the door</u>.

Unlike the other utterances, (7b) and (7c) actually involve <u>two</u> P-predications: a particle predication with <u>out</u>,and a prepositional predication with <u>in</u>. The <u>out</u> predications express directional movement, whereas the <u>in</u> predications define a new location for the kittens following their ejection.

5.4.   Situating Particles

In the preceding examples, we have seen that a P-particle differs from an adprep in that it expresses only the situating part of orientation as opposed to the linking part. The juxtaposition of adpreps with particles in chronologically or semantically close sequences allows us to infer the sublexicalized landmark fairly easily in (7). Often, however, particles are not juxtaposed with adpreps in the course of conversation, and the precise nature of the implied landmark is a little harder to recover, as in (8):

(8)   a. You 'wanna 'hand stuff ''<u>over</u> ?   (R:27)

      b. It sure is 'fun, to be ''moved '<u>in</u> ,   (R:33)

The function of these particles is clearly to situate, in a spatiodirectional sense. In (8a), the speaker is at the dinner table offering to take some plates from the server. The particle <u>over</u> predicates a direction on the plates (the <u>stuff</u>). No contextual information is offered to define this direction. However, given the spatiodirectional and deictic context, the hearer (and reader) can infer a path-landmark fairly easily: <u>the table</u>, perhaps. Similarly, in (8b), since the speakers have been talking about their new home, their use of <u>in</u> clearly predicates a state of containment, defined in terms of an implicit context such as "our new home."

The particles in (8) do not link — they introduce no contextual information. However, as with the adpreps in (3)–(7), they appear as adverbial elements and refer to the spatio-directional domain. Therefore, we can infer, from our knowledge of spatial orientation what kinds of contextual links might be associated with them. We can also make such inferences with nonspatially referring particles.

(9)   a. . . .and by then it was so far <u>along</u> ,   (R:24)

      b. . . . You'd be <u>out</u> , after that   (R:28)

      c. . .laid off a bunch of really high <u>up</u> people .   (R:19)

Once again, these P-particles situate, but now in a nonphysical domain. Furthermore, they do not perform the adverbial modification associated with adpreps. Both (7a) and (9b) refer to the same conversational topic: a doctor's misdiagnosis of a cancerous breast tumor. In (9a), the speaker uses <u>along</u> to predicate a state of advancement on <u>it</u>, the tumor. There is no defining context to specify the path of advancement, but we could reasonably infer that "cancer" itself is viewed metaphorically as a progressive path. In (9b), the interlocutor responds by indicating that, in the United States, the doctor (who was German) would have been expelled from the medical profession for his misdiagnosis. Therefore, in this utterance, <u>out</u> predicates a change of state. Even though it does not link to any context, we could again perhaps infer "the door of the medical profession" as the reference point defining this new state of separation.

Example (9c) occurs earlier in the same conversation, where the speakers are referring to corporate layoffs. Once again, the P-form, which functions syntactically as an adjective rather than an adverb, situates in the nonspatial domain. It predicates a state of seniority on people. Although the landmark is not mentioned, we can infer from our knowledge of social relationships that this state is defined in relation to some kind of social ladder on which people can be positioned higher or lower.

In all these nonspatial examples, P-particles predicate states which, if defined, would invoke links to contextual landmarks. However, to attempt such a definition is something of an academic exercise which would distort the pragmatic meaning of the utterance,because a particle rather than a preposition is used in all these utterances precisely not to express links — but to situate.

The third set of particle examples is semantically more obscure. It contains particles whose sublexicalized landmark is hard to recover, even in a metaphorical sense, from the spatiodirectional domain.

(10) a. . .I 'checked the ashtray out ''first but ,   (U:85)

      b. Ah it's gonna 'clean up ''nice .   (U:3)

      c. . .there isn't that . . . I 'guess that 'joking ''around ,   (R:21)

      d. . .and it 'keeps ''on .   (U:12)

These examples represent a particular kind of verb-particle construction, often referred to as a "phrasal verb," where certain particles are construed with certain verbs to add an *aspectual* meaning (or, more properly, a meaning of Aktionsart, which Brinton 1988 defines as lexical rather than grammatical aspect).

Aspect and Aktionsart meanings express a variety of interpretations for the activity expressed by the verb: "whether it is static or dynamic, punctual or durative, bounded or unbounded, continuous or iterative" (Brinton, 1988:3). These interpretations are assigned subjectively by the speaker in a given context: for example, Bernard Comrie explains imperfective aspect in terms of a "situation viewed from the inside" (in Bybee, 1995:174). In other words, aspectual meanings represent the verb's meaning from the speaker's point of view, just as *Webster's Collegiate Dictionary* definition of "aspect" suggests:

> 1 . . . b: a position facing in a particular direction   2. a.(1): appearance to the eye or
> mind. b: a particular status or phase in which something appears or may be regarded
> 3. (archaic): an act of looking.

What out and up contribute to the verb in (10a) and (10b) is the notion of "goal-orientation," which is analogous to purposeful direction in the world of physical orientation. Brinton defines this notion as "telic aspect" (1988:169); in addition to *clean up*, Brinton offers such examples as *heal up, flatten out, wrap up, cool off/down*). The goal itself does not need to be specified. In fact, there is no goal that could be referred to semantically as a landmark. The landmark exists only as an abstraction, a progressive path that defines the state of goal orientation. That is, it situates the verb in relation to "some arbitrary endpoint which the speaker considers sufficient or adequate" (Brinton 1988:169–170). Thus, in (10a), checked out suggests that the checking was done to the speaker's satisfaction; similarly, in (10b), <u>clean up</u> suggests a process of cleaning until the job is adequately done or complete.

The particles <u>around</u> in (10c) and <u>on</u> in (10d) have an opposite aspectual effect: <u>around</u> contributes a sense of undirected activity or aimlessness rather than of purposeful direction to the activity of <u>joking</u>; <u>on</u> reinforces the sense of continuation already expressed by the verb <u>keeps</u> rather than predicating completion. For Sandra Chung and Alan Timberlake, "aspect characterizes the relationship of a predicate to the time interval over which it occurs" (1985:213). By this interpretation, <u>keeps on</u> refers to an undesirable situation which, from the speaker's point of view, has extended beyond the limits of a reasonable time frame.

In all these aspectual uses, therefore, we see that the adverbial particles predicate states — of goal-orientation, continuation, or nondirectedness — on the events that they represent. In other words, they situate their verbs.

5.5. Linking Prepositions

As consistently as particles situate, so prepositions link. We have already observed this linking function for adpreps, which perform adverbial and prepositional functions at the same time. In the following examples, the underlined prepositions, like adpreps, both situate and link in the spatiodirectional semantic domain.

(11) a. . . 'He was ''up <u>on</u> the . . . 'trailer hhh , or 'up on the back of his ''pickup truck .(A:12)

b. . . .I had my ''weight , my 'head and 'shoulders ''<u>over</u> my 'hands ,   (C:22)

However, these underlined prepositions are not adpreps. At the risk of making ill-advised grammaticality judgments, I suggest that <u>on</u> and <u>over</u> could not alternate as particles in these utterances; that is, the utterances would not make sense if the landmarks were sublexicalized. This syntactic requirement reflects a pragmatic and semantic reality about these prepositions, that regardless of any situating function they may have, their linking function is crucial. If we examine their landmarks, we see that they are necessary for defining the situations predicated by P.

In (11a), <u>on</u> predicates a state on <u>he</u> and also functions to introduce a new location (<u>the trailer</u>) for one of the participants. The location is in fact an important element in the scenario being constructed here because <u>he</u> is using it as a defensive position, "trying to keep himself from getting his ass beat" by some companions he has angered. Linking, then, is the crucial function of <u>on</u> here rather than situating. In fact, the situating function is primarily performed by the particle <u>up</u> while the prepositional phrase <u>on the trailer</u> independently defines a new setting.

In (11b), linking is also crucial. The speaker (a CPR instructor) is demonstrating CPR procedures and instructing the trainees how to position themselves in relation to the "victim" (a dummy). If the landmark <u>my hands</u> were not specified here as a reference point, the situation would not be precisely defined: hearers could interpret "<u>over</u> the dummy," for example. And precise definition of reference points is all-important in this CPR scenario.

Moving to a more abstract domain, the next set of examples shows P-prepositions which do not refer to physical space.

(12)   a. If 'you believe <u>in</u> ''that , (U:31)

    b. <u>In</u> ''particular , this ''one kid I remember was ... (0.7) he was in a ... ''road 'accident ,   (C:20)

    c. . .it 'depends <u>on</u> if it's a 'partial or a ''full .   (C:21)

    d. . .for people who're spending <u>under</u> ''three hundred 'dollars a 'month ,   (R:10)

These prepositions all link certain elements in the utterance to an interpretive context. <u>That</u> in (12a) contextualizes <u>believe</u>: it provides a frame of reference (namely, a previous proposition that "we may all be Jesus reincarnated") within which the belief operates. In other words, it defines the range of the belief.

    <u>In particular</u> in (12b) provides metalinguistic orientation. This phrase has a text-transitional function, signaling the upcoming statement as a specific case of a previous generalization (about the problems of performing CPR on children). It directs the hearer's attention to the new, specific frame of reference and indicates where the speaker is "going" in the construction of text.

    <u>Depends on</u> in (12c), like <u>believe in</u> in (12a), defines the scope of the verb's operation — the conditions within which the "depending" operates. The speaker in (12c) is talking about a full as opposed to a partial "stoma" (a tube inserted in the air passage of the CPR recipient). The P-form <u>on</u> links to the following proposition (<u>if it's a partial or a full</u>), and this landmark actually opens up a whole new frame of reference, as we can see in the continuation of the sequence in (13).

(13)   Okay . .it 'depends <u>on</u> if it's a 'partial or a ''full . Um . .if it's a full, then there's no connection between the two (. ...) If it's a partial you might have to close the mouth .   (C:21)

    Similarly, the preposition <u>under</u> in (14) introduces a landmark that defines limits (a sort of "ceiling") to the range of activity expressed by the verb <u>spending</u>. This limit is relevant as a landmark because it helps to define, in the larger utterance, the newly introduced topic of conversation, <u>MTS service</u>:

(14)   It's called MTS service. It's just your basic service for people who're spending <u>under</u> three hundred dollars a month in long distance.   (R:10)

    Finally, one more interesting example of the linking function is given in (15):

(15)   .<u>about</u> 'four or five ''weeks ago .   (A:22)

The preposition <u>about</u> functions as a sort of qualifier: it has the effect of hedging, or reducing the precision, of the measurement term following it. In fact, <u>about</u> in this function is listed as a qualifying adverb by several dictionaries and by W. Nelson Francis and Henry Kučera's (1982) word frequency list. However, if we adhere to the defining principle that prepositions take landmarks, <u>about</u> behaves more preposi-tionally in these data than adverbially. This argument will be developed in chapters 8 and 9; for now, we need only note that <u>about</u> serves a clear linking function in (15). The landmark <u>four or five weeks ago</u> provides a temporal reference point for an event just reported ("We went over to Norwalk"). <u>About</u> expresses a relationship of approximation between the event and the reference point.

In summary, all the prepositional examples in this section have displayed a linking function for P. In some examples, (11a and 11b), where the preposition predicates a spatiodirectional state, it serves a situating function, too. However, in other examples, such as <u>believe in</u> or <u>depend on</u> in (12), P has very little meaning independently of the verb-preposition construction. Its only function, in other words, is to link.

5.6.   Possible Counterarguments

The preceding discussion accounts for adpreps as "dual constituency" uses of P-forms that carry both situating and linking functions equally, thus suggesting the adprep as the prototypical orienting element. In effect, the adprep is a unifying category for prepositions and particles. This claim will be supported in subsequent chapters as we examine pragmatic, syntactic, and semantic extensions from the central adprep function.

But now we need a reality check. To support the claim that discourse orientation is really a meaningful pragmatic motivation rather than a theoretical abstraction, we need to consider what would disprove this characterization for P, and to suggest what kinds of functions are not orientational. For this purpose, I will consider three counterarguments to my own thesis:

1. The meanings of P-forms are so wide-ranging, in many cases so idiomatic, that it is unrealistic to posit any unifying function for them, other than as an academic exercise.

2. Orientation is provided by several elements other than P- forms, so this function does not constitute a distinguishing characteristic for P.

3. P-meanings can be paraphrased by other, nonorientational words and phrases, again suggesting that P-forms make no singular functional contribution as a lexical group.

These counterarguments are addressed next.

5.6.1.   *Idiomatic and Lexicalized Uses of P*

Argument (1) is most persuasive when we consider idiomatic verb-particle collocationss such as <u>run in</u> (= "send to jail"), <u>run out</u> (= "exhaust supplies"), <u>hang out</u> (= "relax"), and <u>screw up</u> (= "perform badly"). In such collocations, neither the verb nor the particle has any independent meaning. How the meaning of both forms came to be fused, or lexicalized, in such cases is beyond the scope of this study, but the phenomenon of lexicalization presents few problems for the thesis defended here.

First, lexicalization is not confined to P-forms. On the contrary, all lexical categories seem susceptible to loss of syntactic and semantic independence in certain collocations. For example, all the following represent lexical idioms whose meanings do not equal the sum of their parts: *the long and the short of it*; *day in, day out*; *not at all*; *the be all and end all*; and so on. Nevertheless, the existence of these idioms does not suggest that such words as <u>long</u>, <u>day</u>, <u>come</u>, and <u>all</u> are too unpredictable in their meanings to permit analysis. In other sequences, these words behave in very orderly ways, and it turns out that P-forms generally do, too, despite their well-known participation in idiomatic collocations.

In the present data, from a total of 490 particle uses and 627 prepositional uses, there were very few cases in which the meanings of P-forms were coded "uninterpretable." Spatiodirectional meanings were common to all the P-forms (with the exception of <u>about</u>, to be discussed in chapter 9) in at least one of their uses, and were generally the most frequent kind of meaning for most of them. The colorful, idiomatic verb-particle meanings that attract so much attention in the literature do so precisely because they are idiomatic, but they prove the exception rather than the rule.

This conclusion from my own data is backed up statistically by Mario Pelli's (1976) analysis of verb-particle constructions. Given a corpus of 14,021 constructions involving 2,199 different sequences, Pelli classifies these sequences into four groups according to "the semantic relation between the verb and its particle" (1976:65–67). Group 1 particles add a purely directional or locational meaning to the verb (for example, *climb <u>up</u>/<u>down</u>*, *fall <u>off</u>*). Group 2 particles add a spatial meaning "and additional semantic characteristics" such as "extension" or "intensity" (*pay <u>out</u>*, *load <u>down</u>*). Group 3 particles have no spatial reference but contribute aspectual meanings to verbs that retain their own basic meanings (*clean <u>up</u>*, *check <u>out</u>*). Only Group 4 particles form idiomatic, "noncompositional" meanings with verbs (*bump <u>off</u>* = "kill," *run <u>out</u>* = "expire").

When totaled, only 6% (153) of Pelli's verb-particle sequences are classed as being in the idiomatic Group 4. The majority are overwhelmingly Group 1, with 1,500, or 68%, of the combinations expressing spatial reference. The next largest is Group 3, with aspectual particles: the 367 sequences represent 17% of the corpus, suggesting this aspect-marking function is productive enough to be considered at least partially grammaticized.

Thus, it is fair to say that idiomatic P-constructions are not prevalent enough to invalidate the present account of P-forms as orderly elements with systematic meanings.

5.6.2. *Orientation by Other Elements*

The counterargument in (2), that orientation can be provided by other elements, is in fact quite compatible with the current orientational account of P. There are certainly other ways of providing discourse orientation in English, as I acknowledge in section 5.2.

One of these ways is through the lexical meaning of certain nouns, verbs, adjectives, and adverbs. There is no limit to the number of words whose meaning may refer to orientation. For example, the verb <u>arrive</u> situates the subject of its verb in a new location, <u>leave</u> predicates separation from an old location, and <u>finish</u> predicates a temporal endpoint to an activity. Some verbs directly express deictic features (e.g., *come, go*) or other features that situate their subjects in terms of an implicit reference point (sit, lie, vanish). Nouns such as conclusion or introduction refer directly to reference points in texts (generally, of course, as landmarks in prepositional constructions). Adjectives such as alternative, first, or final situate NPs by predicating comparisons. And of course, a large corpus of temporal, spatial, and comparative adverbs perform situating functions.

There are also grammatical constructions that orient beyond the clause level; in particular, adverbial clause constructions have been shown to provide discourse organization, providing temporal, backgrounding, or motivating contexts for main-clause meanings (Matthiessen and Thompson, 1988; Ford, 1993). The following examples are taken from Christian Matthiessen and Sandra Thompson (1988:277).

(16)   Before leaving Krishnapur, ... , the Collector took a strange decision. (= Temporal relation)

(17)   As your floppy drive writes or reads, a Syncom diskette is working four ways ... (= Circumstatial relation)

Ther is no question that orientation can be performed by linguistic devices other than P, and this should come as no surprise. There is no theoretical premise in the field of functional grammar that predicts a one-to-one relationship between pragmatic and syntactic functions. For example, Robert Van Valin explains that focus can be ex-pressed in several ways in English including stress (*a STORM was coming*), syntactic inversion (*there came a storm*), or even *it*-cleft constructions (*it was a storm that was coming*) (1993:26–28). Similarly, some overlap is found between the functions of adjectives and relative clauses since both may be used to identify new referents for subsequent use in the discourse (Thompson 1986; Fox and Thompson, 1990):

(18)   We used to do some awful things though   (Thompson, 1986:11)

(19)   they had one that was a real cheapo thing   (Fox and Thompson, 1990:305–306)

Therefore, I am not claiming that *only* prepositions and particles may perform orientation. But I *am* claiming that the word classes of preposition and particle constitute a special-purpose group that is grammaticized (i.e., structurally assigned) for this function. Prepositions systematically provide discourse links to contextual information, and particles (i.e., P-forms without landmarks) systematically situate discourse elements. The orienting function consistently distinguishes P-forms and P-constructions from other categories (such as adjectives) and constructions (such as resultatives) with which they may sometimes overlap (see chapters 8 and 10 for further discussion of P's functional overlap with other forms and constructions).

Similar claims have been made for the discourse functions of other word classes. For example, Paul Hopper and Sandra Thompson (1984, 1985) claim that nouns are grammaticized for the purpose of conferring discourse-participant status, and verbs for the purpose of conferring eventhood. This grammatical arrangement overrides the semantics of the words involved. For example, an activity like *say* may be mor-phosyntactically marked as a noun in *the sayings of Confucius* not because it denotes a "thing" but because it is assigned a participant role as topic in a particular discourse context. Similarly, sections 5.4 and 5.5 have demonstrated that prepositions link and particles situate, whether or not they refer to spatiodirectional meanings.

Other lexical categories and grammatical constructions may provide orientation, but not as a systematic, structurally assigned set. In chapter 8, it will be shown that particles situate and prepositions link, at every level of constituency, and no matter what elements P-forms construct with.

5.6.3. *Nonorienting Synonyms for P*

We are left with counterargument (3): that, if nonorienting words and phrases can be found which paraphrase P-meanings, then there is nothing clear-cut about the orientational function of P. In other words, how would we know what is not orientational?

The answer is that, if we consider some synonyms for P-meanings, we will see that, in fact, the effective ones do provide orientation and those that do not may be disqualified as synonyms.

To begin, several linguists have drawn attention to the fact that verb-particle collocations often seem to be synonymous with simplex verbs. This has been taken as evidence that particles are components of compound verbs (see section 2.1, and Jowett (in Sroka, 1972) in section 3.1). For example, "enter," "ascend," and "exit" could be substituted for come in, go up, and go out, respectively, and "examined" could be substituted for checked out in the following example from the data.

(20)   I 'checked the ashtray out ''first but ,   (U:85)

Notice, however, that the simplex synonyms are themselves often derived from Latin words that involve the same kind of morphological composition as verb-particle combinations. Enter, ascend, exit, and examine all carry phonologically altered forms of the directional prepositions in, ab, and ex, respectively. In short, these paraphrases are actually borrowings of P-type constructions from Latin that presumably performed orientational functions themselves. It is often quite difficult to think of simplex paraphrases for verb-particle combinations that do not involve originally directional P-prefixes. I can only think of "investigate" or "peruse" as synonyms for check out in (20) and "upset" as a synonym for knock over in (22).

(21)   When I'm straight I knock things over man .   (U:91)

Admittedly, some simplex alternatives do not seem to involve P-attachment, such as "leave" for go out or perhaps "topple" for knock over (a rather ineffective synonym for knock over in 21). As mentioned, the verb leave carries a deictic feature in its meaning, which situates its subject.

However, an important syntactic difference between simplex verbs and verb particle constructions gives a clue to the more explicitly orientational function of P construction: namely, particles can be separated from their verbs and positioned at the end of the utterance. As Dwight Bolinger says, "What needs to be asked is what it is that end position confers" (1971:41). End position, according to Bolinger and to Ping Chen (1986), is the syntactic slot reserved for the important semantic and pragmatic information—the focus—of the sentence predication.

Much has been said about pragmatic focus in the literature (and more will be presented in chapter 7) in relation to the issue of particle-preposition alternation. But for now, suffice it to say that such constructions as go out and knock over allow the speaker to isolate one semantic feature — the state being predicated — from the verb and place it in this focal position. Thus, the endstate of separation rather than the act of leaving itself, can be focused in <u>go out</u> while the state of inversion can be focused in <u>over</u>.

In short, the fragmented structure of verb-particle sequences endows the speaker with a power that Hopper has noted for complex verb phrases in general — namely, to piece meaning together "in the author's image" or to impose a particular, speaker-determined perspective on an event:

> ... not to report an "event" in a simple way, but to combine an account of what is being reported with a set of epistemic attitudes and perspectives, in other words to construct an account of "what happened" with a view to coopting the listener/reader into the narrator's perspective. (Hopper, 1995:146)

The verb-particle construction, unlike the simplex verb, allows the speaker to focus states — in other words, to focus its situating function in the utterance.

Beyond simplex verbs, we could posit another paraphrase for <u>check out</u> in (20), using a manner adverb to carry the aspectual meaning of <u>out</u> — perhaps, "check thoroughly" or "check completely." But here again the meanings are not quite the same. What is lost by the paraphrases is orientation. As explained in section 5.4, <u>out</u> situates the "checking" activity on a goal-oriented path toward a subjectively determined endstate of completion. In contrast, "completely" expresses the manner or quality of the "checking" without this explicit sense of directed activity.

It has already been noted that P-forms sometimes function like adjectives.

(22) a. . .and by then it was so far <u>along</u> ,   (R:24)

      b. . .laid off a bunch of really high <u>up</u> people .   (R:19)

It might seem natural, then, to suggest that such P-forms could be replaced by adjectives. But the only adjectives that would work as effective synonyms would need to carry semantic features of orientation. For example, "advanced" in (22a) or "senior" in (22b) would both imply states that can only be defined in terms that situate them comparatively with other states as reference points. We might suggest a noncomparative adjective such as "important" for (22b), but this adjective would sacrifice the pragmatic force of the utterance, for the following reason. This conversational episode centers on the topic of corporate restructuring and the changes that have happened in the speaker's workplace. In this context, the <u>people</u> being laid off are introduced only as examples of the changes; they have no topical status of their own. Thus, <u>really high up</u> functions not so much to identify the <u>people</u> or to predicate some interesting characteristic about them (the two primary functions of adjectives, according to Thompson, 1986) but to situate them in relation to the company, which *is* topical in the conversation. Thus, the speaker's choice of adjectives here is strategic for maintaining topic relevance.

Therefore, with regard to counterargument (3), I would suggest that synonyms for P-meanings are often not really synonyms at all, and that if they are, their contribution must be orientational.

In summary, this discussion maintains that P-forms systematically express orientation perspectives in a way that distinguishes them from other lexical categories.

Of course, speakers may not know when they access a particular P-construction that they are providing discourse orientation for the hearer, any more than they know when they convert verbs into nouns that they are representing events as discourse participants (Hopper and Thompson, 1984). But such a systematic usage of P does seem to reinforce the discourse-functional claim that conversational requirements drive grammatical regularities.

5.7. Conclusion

This chapter has identified orientation as a basic discourse function. Orientation involves both situating and linking, which are most fully performed by the adprep. Beyond adpreps, particles specialize in the situating subfunction and prepositions in the linking subfunction. These discourse functions distinguish P-forms generally from other lexical classes and constructions in English.

6

Landmarks as Contextual Props

The last chapter claimed that prepositions perform the orientation subfunction of linking discourse elements to contextual information. If this claim is true, then we would expect prepositional objects in general to display properties that identify them as "contexts" for discourse purposes.

This chapter provides empirical evidence for the orientation function of prepositional phrases by showing that prepositional objects (or landmarks) differ semantically and informationally from NP referents in other syntactic positions. Their properties suggest that speakers use them for different purposes, namely, as contextual "props."

Several discourse-functional studies have already identified some significant properties that mark the functions of NP referents in other syntactic slots: the slots of transitive subject or agent (A); intransitive subject (S), and object (O). For example, it is well established that A is the slot reserved for topical participants — most notably, for human referents, the most frequent topical choice in human conversation. Thus, A-slots usually display topic-marking properties: they tend to be definite, referential, and given — that is, representing information that is familiar to the interlocutors from either the physical or the discourse context. (See Appendix A.9 for explanations of these and other information properties.)

The S-slot shares the function of topic continuity with A but may also introduce *new* referents that are likely to become topical (Du Bois, 1987) — for example, human referents who will become protagonists in the development of a narrative. Therefore, NPs in this slot also tend to be referential but may or may not be definite.

The O-slot is normally associated with nontopical referents like inanimate objects and manipulable entities, as well as certain predicating terms (e.g., *eating chocolate*) which define activities (Du Bois, 1980). Therefore, we expect this role to contain more new arguments than A or S and to show a lower incidence of definiteness and referentiality.

Relatively little attention has been given to the difference between "core" (A, S, O) and "oblique" (landmark) NPs. From her preliminary analysis of the core-oblique distinction, Sandra Thompson (1997) concludes that obliques differ from other NPs in their informational properties: they are less likely to be discourse-active (which loosely means given), identifiable (which loosely means definite), or tracking (which loosely means referential). In her study, Thompson introduces the term "orienting" as an example of a nontracking function for obliques (1997: 9). However, she does not develop the idea and attaches no special theoretical importance to the term, as I do here.

The following analysis of landmark properties takes up Thompson's lead, with some modifications, and extends it to consider some different NP-properties, which turn out to be instructive in explaining orientation. Because this study is centrally concerned with P-forms, the analysis focuses on the landmarks of P-forms rather than those of such pure prepositions as of, from, or with (a preliminary survey, however, suggested that both types of landmarks are very similar in their properties). A total of 565 NPs were coded from the first sections of four conversations in the database. These included referents in all syntactic slots: A, S, O, and LM (= landmark). The goal was to compare the properties of the different types of referents to determine what was distinct about the properties of landmarks in particular. The syntactic distributions of these NPs were as follow (see Appendix A.7 for an explanation of the relatively smaller number of A-tokens): A, 66 tokens; O, 88 tokens; S, 180 tokens; LM, 231 tokens; for a total of 565 NPs. The pragmatic, semantic, and prosodic properties of these NPs were then coded and analyzed. The results of the analysis are elaborated in the following sections.

6.1. Information Properties of P-Landmarks

Information status is a good indicator of the pragmatic function of NP referents. Table 6.1 shows the information properties coded for different NP roles in the present database. For the coding, I adopted Ellen Prince's (1981) hierarchy of assumed familiarity rather than the simpler active/inactive distinctions proposed by Wallace Chafe (1987). Prince's scale distinguishes between evoked referents (meaning discourse-active), inferrable referents (which are logically recoverable), and unused referents (which are familiar to the interlocutors, but new in the discourse). These categories are useful since they distinguish LMs from other types of NPs: LMs are more than twice as likely to represent inferrable or unused information. This point will be taken up subsequently

Table 6.1 shows that the NPs in this corpus generally fulfill the predictions of the literature.[1] A-referents are overwhelmingly evoked, definite and referential. S-referents show the same tendencies, but less strongly than As. O-referents are variable in terms of definiteness and referentiality, and less likely to be evoked than A- or S-tokens. LMs are less often evoked than NPs in all other roles, and are less often referential.

This table shows that LMs have more in common with Os than with NPs in any other roles. LMs and Os are more likely to be new, indefinite, and nonreferential than

Table 6.1: Information Properties of Landmarks versus Other NPs in the Database

Role	Evoked	Inferrable	Unused	New	Definite	Referential
A	97%	0%	1%	3%	97%	89%
S	83%	3%	3%	11%	92%	75%
O	59%	6%	3%	32%	60%	55%
LM	36%	14%	8%	42%	65%	43%

To complement the discussion below, Appendix A.9 provides more detailed explanations of Prince's evoked, inferrable, unused, and new categories; Appendix A.10 elaborates on Du Bois's (1980) definitions of definiteness and referentiality.

are A- or S-referents. This is not surprising since both LMs and Os tend to appear in the clause-predicative slot. This slot is associated with the introduction of new referents and predicating terms.

However, LMs are clearly distinct from Os and, in fact, from all other NPs, in their takeup of inferrable and unused referents, and in terms of two other significant properties: semantic class and morphological form. The findings for all these different types of properties support the claim that LMs function as contextual *props*, as I will explain next.

6.2. Semantic Class of Landmarks

Semantic class refers to the domain of meaning in which NPs refer (for details, see Appendix A.8). To some extent, the interaction between semantic class and syntactic role has already been considered in the literature, primarily in studies of animacy. These claim that A- or S-slots are generally occupied by animate referents because such referents are more "topicworthy" than the nonanimate ones generally associated with O-roles (Hopper and Thompson, 1980, 1993).

The results in table 6.2 clearly mark a contrast between the semantic classes represented by landmarks and those represented by other NPs.

The semantic classes listed in table 6.2 account for the majority of NPs in each syntactic role. "Other" classes, such as system, social organization, and abstract concept (see Appendix A.8), are fairly evenly distributed across S-, O-, and LM-roles. They are lumped together in this table since they make little difference to the general picture. We can see that A- and S-roles, as expected, are strongly associated with animate referents (person/animal) whereas the O-role is primarily associated with things (but also, to a slightly lesser extent, with animate referents and with situations).

However, the LM-role is clearly distinct as the slot for place/time referents. Place/time is the most preferred category for LMs, and the least preferred for A-, S-, and O-referents.

It may at first seem self-evident that place/time referents should be preferred in the LM-slot, since LMs follow prepositions and often refer to space and time (e.g., *in Atlanta, at ten o'clock*). However, there is no logical reason for this to be so. Landmarks may quite easily encode things, persons, and situations, and do so quite often in this conversational corpus; for example, *through the window, (depend) on*

Table 6.2: Semantic Classes Represented by LMs and
Other NPs in the Database

Class	A	S	O	LM
Person/Animal	94%	65%	25%	10%
Place/Time	0	3%	2%	34%
Thing	2%	8%	34%	13%
Situation	2%	9%	24%	20%
Totals:	98%	85%	85%	77%
Other	2%	15%	15%	13%

me, in an accident. Any spatiodirectional meaning in these examples is derived from the preposition rather than from the semantic class of the landmarks themselves. Conversely, O- and S-roles may and do encode place, as we see in the following examples:

(1) a. We'll 'make a little ''Erie, just 'over around the ''corner over here ?   (R:12)

    b. I kind of thought this would be a ''nice 'place,
        to 'buy a ''piece of land ,   (R:34)

To avoid the circularity of automatically coding LMs as space/time referents, care was taken to consider the referent *only* as a semantic element, and not to interpret it as a location simply because it was constructed with a spatially referring preposition. For example, in (2), the chair and the highway are coded as things, not places. The semantic class of place is reserved for inherently locational referents, like those in (3).

(2) a. He 'doesn't want to 'sit in the chair .   (R:16)

    b. You're 'driving along on the highway and you 'see an accident ,   (C:3)

(3) a. so . . . 'just like living in ''Longmont.   (R:12)

    b. They didn't 'put Erie in the Denver . .calling zone .   (R:12)

It is therefore reasonable to claim without circularity that place/time referents are strongly associated with LM-roles, and strongly dispreferred in any other role. Now we can ask why there should be a slot that seems to be specially designated for such referents rather than for animate or inanimate entities.

Time and place are clear exemplars of external conditions, or circumstances. The *Oxford English Dictionary* definition of a circumstance is an "external condition that . . . might affect the agent"; the *Random House* definition shows "a condition . . . that accompanies or determines a fact or event." These definitions suggest that circumstances have a relative independence, an external relation to the "agent" or other participants in any situation. Circumstances, in other words, provide contextual information: reference points or "props," in terms of which participants, events, facts, or other discourse elements may be situated and defined.

Semantic class as a property thus distinguishes LMs from other NPs. LM-referents do not manipulate situations, as A-referents do, and they are not manipulated, as O-referents are. Rather, they represent independent contexts.

Table 6.3: Percentage of Landmarks
and Other NPs Pronominalized in the
Database

Role	Pronoun Form (%)	Lexical Form (%)
A	90	10
S	79	21
O	41	59
LM	14	86

The morphological form of LMs also distinguishes them pragmatically from other NPS.

6.3.   Landmarks as Discourse Props

John Du Bois distinguishes between discourse "props" and discourse "participants." A prop is an object "whose continuity of identity is ignored, as opposed to a partici- pant — a human, animal, or object whose continuity of identity is salient enough to be maintained" (1980:269). Du Bois identifies props as being located most often in the O-slot, using this distinction primarily to distinguish object-predicate conflations (e.g., "pear-picking") from referential objects ("the pears").

I suggest that LMs are also props but of a special kind whose function is orien- tational. Support for this suggestion comes from the finding that, more than all otehr NPs, LMs are likely to be lexical rather than pronominal in their morphological form (table 6.3) even if they have definite and referential status (table 6.4).

The function of pronominalization is to assist *tracking* in discourse. Tracking means to establish "an identification with some known referent" (Du Bois, 1980:226). In table 6.3 LMs are the least likely of all NPs to be pronominalized, which strongly suggests that they are not tracking NPs.

In studies of other syntactic roles, pronominalization is generally associated with referentiality and definiteness. Referentiality is also a tracking device, which denotes "continuous identity over time" (Du Bois, 1980:208). An example of a nonreferential NP would be one that is mentioned only to define a situation, as in *I was picking pears*, or *I was in bed*. Unless the speaker goes on to talk about the pears themselves, or the bed, these NPs have no continuous identity; they do not really "refer" (272).

Definiteness also assists tracking. In English it most often applies to proper nouns or to common nouns marked with the definite article the. According to Du Bois, definiteness, when applied to a referential NP, establishes identifiability (*I picked the pears yesterday, Mother's bed*).

Logically, then, if the NP is not identifiable, we would not expect it to be pronominalized since pronominalization serves to track identifiable referents. Con- versely, NPs which *are* identifiable (i.e., both definite and referential) would seem to be ideal candidates for pronominalization. Table 6.3 shows that this prediction is true for NPs in all syntactic roles — except LMs. Not only are landmarks generally less likely to be pronominalized than other NPs (only 14% of the time), but they are also

Table 6.4: Percentage of Definite and Referential
NPs Pronominalized in the Database

Role of Definite and Referential NP	Tokens in Pronoun Form (%)	Tokens in Lexical Form (%)
A	100	0
S	93	7
O	70	30
LM	25	75

unlikely to be pronominalized even when they are identifiable (table 6.4: 25% of the time, as compared with 100% of the As, 93% of the Ss, and 70% of the Os).

This strong dispreference for pronominalization suggests unequivocally that landmarks are not used for discourse tracking. Even LMs that are clearly identifiable and are mentioned several times in a given stretch of discourse do not tend to become pronominalized. An example of such an LM from the present data is AT&T, in conversation R. This referent is mentioned many times by name and remains discourse-active (or evoked) throughout a long sequence about long-distance telephone systems (as reflected by occasional "antitopical" stress-marking on its preposition; see chapter 8). However, AT&T is pronominalized only once, as "them," referring to AT&T lines:

(4) It's 'based off of AT&T's ''calling card .

　　　(. . . . . .)

　　　They can't call out ,

　　　. .'from ''Germany ,

　　　. .''on AT&T lines ,

　　　'we can just call ''in on them .

　　　(. . . . . .)

　　　'you know where they 'introduce ''competition ,

　　　''to AT&T ,　　　　　　　　　　　　　　　　　　　　　　　　　　(R:6–8)

It is as if the "continuity of identity is ignored" for LMs — like AT&T — which exactly describes the situation for Du Bois's discourse prop.

As mentioned, Du Bois distinguishes between a prop and a participant. In his 1980 study, he focuses on props in the O-slot, which are mostly of the predicative, pear-picking type. Thompson (1997) also mentions props that are used to classify in such phrases as "It's a celebration" and "when I was a kid." These kinds of predicative props may also be found as LMs in the present corpus.

(5) a. I've got . .''two 'cousins who are . . . out of 'work at the moment .　　　(R:5)

　　　b. The 'book is 'based on a sixth grade ''reading level ,　　　　　　　　(C:1)

　　　c. The 'phone system has 'gone through a ''lot of 'changes .　　　　　　(R:8)

However, these are not the kinds of props most commonly found in LM-roles in the present corpus. Predicating and classifying props are usually nondefinite, as in (5);

they have no identity beyond the predication that defines them. But, as we have already seen in table 6.1, 65% of LMs are coded definite.

At first glance we might think that this aligns LMs fairly closely with O-referents, which are similarly likely to be definite (60% of the time in table 6.1). But we know from table 6.4 that the definite Os in this corpus are highly likely to be pronominalized while LMs are not. We also know, from table 6.2 and from the literature (Du Bois, 1980, 1987), that O-slots may be used to encode participants as well as props, which is rarely the case for LMs.

Since definiteness and pronominalization are both associated with participant-tracking, we can reasonably infer that most of the definite NPs in O-roles refer to participants which do get tracked to some extent, though not as centrally topical as those in A- and S-roles.

In contrast, the LM-role is clearly not a participant-tracking slot. Its dispreference for pronominalizing even definite and referential NPs (table 6.4) distinguishes it from the O-role in this respect. Like O, the LM-slot encodes props; but unlike O, it does not also track participants.

Since we cannot tag the high percentage of definite LM-referents as participants, we are left with the conclusion that even these definite NPs encode some kind of discourse props.

What kind of prop is likely to be definite, but unlikely to be pronominalized? I would suggest that it is one whose identity is independent of discourse tracking. Whether or not its continuity of identity is ignored in the discourse, it is identifiable in its own right to the hearer.

This would apply, for example, to unused referents such as AT&T, Atlanta, and AIDS, which are independently known to the hearer on their mention. It would also apply to inferrable referents that can be recovered logically from our world knowledge schemata or our mental representations of familiar scenarios. These schemata allow us to infer part-whole relationships — for example, that drivers on race tracks tend to be associated with cars. Thus, we can infer the underlined referent on its first mention in (6), once we know that he refers to one of a group of drivers on a race track.

(6)   And he 'takes his ''helmet an ,
       ''CLUNK it 'goes on 'top of the ''car .   (A:11)

Notice from table 6.1 that inferrable and unused NPs are found almost exclusively in LM slot (these properties are explained in more detail in Appendix A.9). Furthermore, an informal data count reveals that proper nouns such as AT&T or Atlanta, as opposed to pronouns and common nouns, are also almost exclusively found in this slot: out of fifty proper nouns in the whole database, 68% are LMs, with only 32% distributed across the other slots.

What LM seems to represent is a slot for independently identifiable referents. It was explained in the last chapter (sections 5.1 and 5.2) that orientation is as conceptually basic in discourse as it is in the physical world. We can now see that discourse landmarks perform the same kind of orientation function as physical landmarks. The identification of independently known reference points is as crucial for discourse navigation as George Psathas finds it for physical navigation through space.

A second and even third trip through Oxford Circus, even after ... I had learned the name, did not enable me to associate the name with that particular place. But once having made the connection of the name to that place, my subsequent travels could make use of that knowledge. I could use Oxford Circus as a destination or starting-point for further travels; I could use it as a landmark to provide orientation "along the way" to other destinations, and I could use it to re-orient myself if I became lost. (1989:145)

For Psathas, the continuity of identity of Oxford Circus is not important. He is only interested in it as a reference point. But for this very purpose it must be independently identifiable. Examples (7a)–(7f) illustrate the same property of independent identifiability for some LMs in the database. Their referents are not topical, and they are identified not by discourse tracking but by access to shared knowledge and schemata.

(7)   a. It's 'based off of '<u>AT&T's</u>~~ ''<u>calling</u> 'card .   (R:6)

      b. 'Especially if you're in <u>the ''medical 'profession</u> ,   (C:3)

      c. You have all these little ''stickers on <u>our 'phones</u> saying ,   (R:9)

      d. You can't look 'up an ... give a funny 'look <u>on</u> <u>your face</u> and 'have the 'author change
         the ''<u>wording</u> .   (R:14)

      e. And on '<u>Sunday</u> they 'run ''<u>obstacle</u> .   (A:21)

      f. So we'll be ''using 'this , 'in ''<u>class</u> ,   (C:1)

In summary, the properties displayed in tables 6.1 to 6.3 construct a compelling picture of LM-referents as contextual elements. Semantically, they refer to circumstances. Pragmatically, they work as discourse props rather than participants. Furthermore, the data findings suggest that this discourse interpretation of LMs as contextual elements is more satisfactory than any explanation based on semantic or morphological properties alone, because it regularizes inconsistencies in these properties.

6.4.   Semantic Class as an Exception to the Pattern

First, we can consider some semantic exceptions to the pattern identified in table 6.2. There we saw that the LM-slot favors the place/time semantic class. This makes sense since a great deal of what we talk about refers to the physical world, where space and time provide orientation for the entities and events that become our topics of conversation.

But discourse orientation involves more than spatiotemporal reference. As mentioned in section 6.2, everything that we refer to in discourse has to be constructed intersubjectively. Everything that speakers talk about — physical entities, events and attributes, abstract ideas, and even discourse itself — depends on the negotiation of shared meaning. For this reason, we have such complex discourse strategies as topic identification, tracking, foregrounding and backgrounding, and so on. One strategy for constructing reference is by establishing links to already established meanings. In this way, interlocutors can build meaning from meaning and define new situations by predicating new contexts for pre-established information or by predicating new information in pre-established contexts.

If we look again at the examples in (7), we can see how this works. Although LM-roles favor space/time referents, they are not confined to this semantic class. Only two of the examples (7e and 7f) refer to the place or time semantic class, yet all of them provide contexts to situate another element of information.

Examples (7a) and (7b) elaborate information about their topics in terms of a new context: in the former, the topic is a special telephone line service; in the latter, the speaker is trying to identify the participants of the CPR class, whom she is meeting for the first time.

In (7c) and (7d), a pre-established context is used to introduce a new idea. In (7c), the stickers are introduced in terms of their situation, defined by our phones (the pre-established topic of conversation being phone systems and lines). In other words, the stickers are introduced and defined as "phone-stickers." Similarly, look in (7d) is defined more narrowly as a "face-look" (in other words, a facial expression).

In (7e) and (7f), whole propositions (expressed by the clause) are situated spatiotemporally. The propositions predicate events that are framed by the context-landmarks. In (7e), Sunday projects the hearer into a new temporal setting for the racetrack events and routines that the speaker is describing. In (7f), class reinforces the frame of reference shared by the speaker and hearers. This frame of reference warrants the proposition: since the speaker is the CPR instructor, class provides an appropriate setting to motivate her explanation of upcoming events.

We can see then, that, although place and time referents such as Sunday and class are particularly well-suited for the expression of contexts, it is not the semantic class of the landmarks that determines their use but their relevance as elements that help interlocutors to link meanings together. Thus, technological concepts, professional occupations, and inanimate objects can be used, as well as place and time referents, to establish contexts. Their contextual meaning emerges from *how* they are used in conversation, rather than from their semantic content.

6.5.   Pronoun Landmarks as an Exception to the Pattern

A similar situation obtains morphologically. As shown in table 6.3, LMs tend not to be pronominalized, and this makes sense if we define LMs as elements whose identity is established independently of discourse tracking. Nevertheless, 14% of the LMs represented in table 6.3 *do* appear as pronouns. This seems to suggest that LM overlaps with A, S, and O as a slot for participant tracking. However, if we examine the conversational use of these LMs, we see that, in these particular cases, they are being manipulated as contexts not as participants.

While there are 32 pronouns (out of a total of 231 LMs) in this corpus, they tend not to persist for more than one or two mentions. *Persistence*, or multiple contiguous mentions of a referent, is taken as an indication of topical status, so pronoun LMs do not seem to qualify as topical participants.

In addition, about half of the pronoun LMs refer to things, a semantic indication that they are used more as props than as participants since table 6.2 shows that things may occasionally occur in O-slots, but rarely in A- and S-slots. One example is underlined in (8).

(8)   They 'can't call ''out ,

  'from ''Germany ,

  ''on 'AT&T lines ,

  'we can just call ''in on <u>them</u> .   (R:7)

The underlined LM (<u>them</u>) does indeed serve as a prop — not the indefinite, activity-defining kind of prop that Du Bois finds in the O-slot with "pear-picking" but a definite condition in terms of which the proposition (<u>we can just call in</u>) makes sense. The antecedent of <u>them</u> (<u>AT&T lines</u>) refers to this condition, so pronominalization works very locally here to refer back to a contiguous referent rather than to track a participant. In (9), another pronominal prop uses a thing as a reference point: the CPR instructor is directing the hearers' attention back to the page before page six, which they are currently looking at:

(9)   Page right 'before <u>it</u> page ''one ,

  talks about the ''EMS 'system ,   (C:5)

Clearly, <u>it</u> is not a participant. The instructor is not talking about page numbers, but using them as reference points to direct her hearers. In this case, pronominalization comes from deictic accessibility (everyone is already looking at the page) rather than from discourse tracking.

  Another 25% of pronominal landmarks denote place, with the forms <u>here</u> and <u>there</u>. Interestingly, if we look at these place pronouns, we see that their NP-referents, semantically, are sometimes things not places (10).

(10)   It doesn't ''go too good on '<u>there</u> 'does it .   (R:29)

  It is conversational use rather than semantic class that defines a referent as a contextual prop. In this case, <u>there</u> refers to a concrete surface: a tabletop, covered with a tablecloth, on which a child is trying to run a toy car. But this surface — a thing — is pronominalized by <u>there</u> rather than <u>it</u>. In other words, this thing is coded as if it were a place because it is represents a defining context — the context in which the toy car "doesn't go so good." And here, as in (9), pronominalization results from deictic accessibility rather than from tracking.

  Now we are left with eleven LM pronouns that refer to person. Person is an ideal candidate for participant status. Nevertheless, I would suggest, using the following examples, that person in the LM-slot is referred to as a prop not a participant.

(11)   a. If you ''use 'CPR, it's 'probably gonna be on <u>someone you ''know</u> . (C:2)

  b. 'You all will have to 'carry on ''without <u>us</u> for a minute . (A:16)

  c. . .but I 'think er it's . . .it's . .to 'help you learn by ''<u>yourself</u> yeah . (C:2)

  d. ''Then I um . .became a ''lot less uh 'worried or 'challenged by <u>him</u> . (E:7)

  All of the underlined LMs provide defining contexts. In (11a–c) the CPR instructor defines certain activities in terms of new conditions. In (11a) <u>someone you know</u> is a specific condition narrowing the activity of CPR. Since the instructor does not go on to identify this "someone," it is clear that the LM refers to a condition rather than a participant. Once again, the pronoun here does not reflect tracking. <u>Someone</u> is a special, indefinite form used to refer to entities that have no specific lexical antecedent. The underlined LMs in (11b) and (11c) do refer to topical participants, but not *as* participants. In (11b), the speaker is talking about you, not us; us is only relevant here because without us defines a changed condition for you. In (11c), by yourself also defines a changed condition; in effect, it predicates you as the only person related to you. In both (11b) and (11c), pronominalization is again a result of deictic access rather than of tracking since us and you are physically present.

Example (11d) is interesting because its prepositional phrase is grammaticized: it is required by the Passive construction as an agent-marker. M.A.K. Halliday (1985:150) argues that this agentive passive construction marks the agent as a circumstance rather than a participant, a position that directly supports the one being proposed here. If we look at this example, him (referring to the person who was previously challenging and worrying the speaker) is definitely topical, but the whole purpose of representing this event in a passive rather than an active construction is to recast the him referent as a circumstance: the condition provoking the worry. Therefore, invoking Halliday, we can interpret the passive construction as a syntactic strategy for fulfilling the pragmatic purposes of orientation.[2]

In summary, LMs tend not to be pronominalized, since pronominalization is associated with identity-tracking, and tracking is irrelevant for independently identifiable contexts. However, this morphological tendency is a reflection rather than a predictor of the LM's function as a contextual prop. Some LMs *are* pronominalized. When they are, the pronoun form is used, not to establish and track discourse identity, but more often to show that the referent is already deictically identifiable. What remains consistent in the LM-slot is conversational use of referents as contexts, whether or not these referents are tracked as participants in other slots.

Thus, this analysis confirms Thompson's observation (1997) that LMs differ from other NPs. But it also provides an explanation for the difference: that LMs function as a special kind of prop, a contextual prop.

6.6. Prepositional Phrases and Intonation Units

Having established that the semantics, information status and morphological forms of LMs all reflect their function as contextual props, we can return to the entire prepositional phrase as a syntactic unit. Here we find a prosodic reflection of the same function — namely, a tendency for prepositional phrases to be set off from the main clause in separate intonation units.

The unit form of P-units was coded in this corpus. As explained in section 4.4.3, P-units are intonation units containing P-prepositions and particles. Unit form reveals whether these units occur as whole clauses, clause fragments, or some other recognizable constituent.

In general, the unit form findings overwhelmingly fulfill the predictions of the literature (Halliday, 1967; Chafe, 1986, 1987, 1988), since 81% of P-units correspond to clauses or multiples of clauses (one unit may frequently contain as many as three clauses). This percentage includes repairs and truncated utterances that are recognizable as clauses since they have a subject and a full verb.

Beyond this clausal pattern, only two other clear patterns exist: P-units occur as prepositional phrases 12% of the time, and as isolated predicates (usually following long or complex subjects) 3% of the time. These results seem to indicate that prepositional phrases have some kind of special status prosodically; they are by far the most likely constituent, after complete clauses, to be set off as independent intonation units.

According to Halliday, prepositional phrases represent independent assertions. Halliday calls them "minor processes" with the preposition as a "mini-verb" and its landmark object as a "circumstantial element" (1985:142).

The unit form findings suggest a prosodic parallel to the syntactic "separateness" proposed by Halliday. John Haiman (1985) has pointed out that syntactic forms often mark pragmatic functions iconically, and here we seem to have a clear case of iconicity. Both the prosodic and the syntactic separateness of prepositional phrases can be viewed as iconic responses to their pragmatic function, which is to provide independent defining contexts for situations. We can see how syntactic and prosodic signals alert the hearer to the staging of contextual information in example (12).

(12)   They 'can't call ''out,

   'from ''Germany,

   ''on 'AT&T lines,

   'we can just call ''in on them .   (R:7)

In explaining how the long-distance calling system only works in one direction, from the United States to Germany, this speaker carefully stages his information, progressively elaborating the situation with prepositional phrases in separate intonation units. First, from Germany provides a reference point to establish the source of the calling. Then, on AT&T lines specifies the enabling conditions for the calling from Germany. Each of these units, in effect, provides a new layer of contextualization to situate the previous unit.

6.7.   Conclusion

This chapter has argued from the P-corpus data that landmarks are used differently in conversation from other NPs. LM-referents are used not as participants but as contextual props. These props, unlike those found in the O-slot, tend to be definite and independently identifiable. Just as physical landmarks help us find our bearings in physical space, discourse landmarks help navigate our way through discourse. The pragmatic function of LMs is reflected in their semantic, informational, and morphological properties, and by the prosodic marking of prepositional phrases as independent syntactic units.

This evidence from P-landmarks strongly supports the proposed definition of P-prepositions as orienting elements in discourse. Prepositions link to contextual information which defines situations for other elements. The next task in this study of prepositions and particles is to discover the conditions under which landmarks become sublexicalized—in other words, to identify the contexts where orientation is performed by P-particles alone and those where it is performed by P-prepositional phrases.

7

Prepositions, Particles, and Pragmatic Focus

The last two chapters explained how particles situate and prepositions link to contextual props. Chapter 5 also explained that adpreps combine both situating and linking functions in the same element. But we have not yet established *why* alternation takes place — that is, what motivates speakers to situate without linking or to use P-forms as intransitive particles. In this chapter, I argue that the motivation is a conversationally strategic one and that the transitivity of P-forms is ultimately determined by considerations of pragmatic focus. Empirical evidence for this argument is provided once again by the findings from the conversational corpus. Theoretical support comes from current models of pragmatic assertion and focus.

7.1. Preposition or Particle? Cognitive-Semantic Motivations

Sue Lindner's (1981) account of the meanings of <u>up</u> and <u>out</u> characterizes particles as prepositions with sublexicalized landmarks. Although Lindner gives relatively little attention to what motivates sublexicalization, she does suggest that landmarks are expressed when they are relatively salient according to the perspective taken on the utterance. For example, in the following pair of sentences (1a, b), Lindner attributes the semantic difference to a difference in "the relative salience imposed on various objects present in each scene" (1981:184).

(1) a. Mary washed the spot out.

    b. Mary washed the shirt out.

In (1a), the trajector of <u>out</u> (<u>the spot</u>) is represented as more salient than the implicit landmark (<u>the shirt</u>). Therefore, the trajector is lexicalized and the nonsalient landmark is not. In contrast, Lindner explains that in (1b), <u>the shirt</u> is represented as salient by its lexicalization.

Unfortunately, Lindner does not define salience and the examples given can be misleading. Dictionary definitions of "salient" suggest such properties as "noticeable, conspicuous," or "prominent." In the physical world, salient objects are easily seen. In discourse, however, we have to construct every object we conceptualize and we have to impose salience on objects as we see fit. Lindner's account of the sentences in (1) seems to suggest that we do this by lexicalizing referents that we want to represent as salient, and sublexicalizing those that we view as nonsalient.

But under what conditions would speakers consider a referent nonsalient? The examples in (1) would seem to suggest that the relevant factor is semantic-pragmatic recoverability (or accessibility), either from the discourse context or from our knowledge of the world: if the identity of the landmark is recoverable without specific lexical mention, then it can be sublexicalized. This situation obtains with the "shirt" example in (1b) and also in Lindner's explanation for the "toothpaste" in example (2).

(2)   He squeezed some toothpaste out.   (1981:63)

Lindner legitimates the sublexicalization of the landmark <u>tube</u> in (2), as follows:

> Given that a LM object is sublexically specified . . . how is it possible to understand that, for example, the LM . . . is a TUBE? Recall the TOOTHPASTE is a profiled object in a base that will include information about other objects and relations typically associated with it, notably, that it bears an IN relation to a tube, that it is applied to a brush, that it may or may not have fluoride, etc. . . . the object TUBE is a likely candidate to match up with the sublexical LM in OUT. In general, then, knowledge of the world . . . (. . . as well as objects and relations present in the discourse context) will narrow the range of possibilities for the identity of the LM object, sometimes fairly exclusively. (1981:64)

However, accessibility alone does not work as a reliable predictor of sublexicalization. There are several cases in the present data where an obviously accessible landmark *is* lexicalized. We already saw two of them in the previous chapter (repeated here as 3 and 4).

(3)   They 'can't call ''out ,
      'from ''Germany ,
      ''on 'AT&T lines ,
      'we can just call ''in on <u>them</u> .   (R:7)

The referent is clearly accessible from the discourse context: <u>them</u> = "AT&T lines." However, the landmark is mentioned twice in two contiguous P-units.

(4)   ''Then 'I um . .became a ''lot less uh 'worried or 'challenged by <u>him</u> .   (E:7)

Furthermore, the speaker's choice is not free in these contexts. It would be unacceptable to sublexicalize the landmark for either (3) or (4), as we see in (5).

(5)   a. *You can just call in on.
      b. *I became a lot less challenged by.

Once the P-form <u>on</u> or <u>by</u> is mentioned in these examples, the speaker is apparently constrained to mention the landmark, too. The only possible alternative would be to drop the whole prepositional phrase in both cases, as in (6).

(6)   a. We can just call in.

      b. I became a lot less challenged.

It seems, then, that accessibility alone neither accounts for sublexicalization nor explains the constraints on it. If salience is indeed the motivating factor, then this notion needs to be defined in clearer terms.

A slightly different solution comes from studies of null-complementation and transitivity. However, these studies complicate the issue further since they associate sublexicalization not with salience but with the properties of phoricity and specificity.

7.2.   Cognitive-Semantic Motivations for Transitivity

Charles Fillmore's (1986) and Sally Rice's (1988) accounts of null-complementation, like Lindner's, come from a Cognitive Grammar perspective. Although they are directly concerned with the objects of transitive verbs rather than the landmarks of prepositions, their analyses are relevant here, since, like Lindner, I interpret particles as prepositions with null complements — or, in traditional syntactic terms, as intransitive prepositions.

The question asked by both Fillmore and Rice is why some verbs can be used both transitively (with mentioned complements) and intransitively (with null complements), while others cannot. Fillmore argues that verb complements may be zero-realized when they are definite or have phoricity. Phoricity may be defined as "identification with some known referent," according to John Du Bois (1980:226). For example, if we are being questioned about an accident, it is possible to answer *I didn't see* because the implicit complement of <u>see</u> is definite and anaphoric from the discourse context: we can recover it as something like "the accident" or "the details of the accident."

Rice takes Fillmore's explanation further, to explain how indefinite complements may also be zero-realized. The speaker's decision, she says, depends on "lexical knowledge ... a dynamic, interconnected network" of considerations, which involves an understanding of the pragmatic environment (1988:211). It also involves understanding the meaning of the verb; Rice suggests that the more generic this meaning is, the more likely the verb is to be used intransitively.

Therefore, according to Rice, we can say *Mike studied* but not *Mike perused*. We can say *Moses spoke* but not *Moses uttered*. The null complements of all these verbs are indefinite: we don't know exactly what Mike studied or what words Moses spoke. But Rice's point is that <u>study</u> and <u>speak</u>, as basic-level activities, invoke a generic scene with generically predictable participants. Within these scenes, we can infer that Mike studied his assignment and Moses spoke words. In contrast, <u>peruse</u> and <u>utter</u> are much more specific verbs that do not invoke a generic scene (you have to specify your meaning "à la carte," as it were, rather than ordering the basic combination).

Both Fillmore's and Rice's analyses are helpful in accounting for certain transitive phenomena, but they do not account for the data in examples (3) and (4). In both examples, the underlined landmarks have definiteness and phoricity but they cannot be zero-realized, as shown by the unacceptable examples in (5). Moreover, this constraint is not attributable to semantic specificity or to any other inherently transitive property of the P itself, because we have another example in the present data where one of these P-forms (<u>on</u>) is used intransitively.

(7)   OK, 'pressure's ''<u>on</u>.   (C:1)

And even though the data offer no examples of <u>by</u> being used intransitively, we can certainly think up grammatically and semantically acceptable examples such as *Time goes by* without much trouble. So we know that there is no semantic principle that requires complements for <u>on</u> and <u>by</u> as are required for <u>peruse</u> and <u>utter</u>.

These accounts of sublexicalization (or null-complementation) not only propose very different motivations for the phenomenon but also fall short of explaining the constraints observed in the data presented here.

7.3.   Proposed Discourse Motivations

7.3.1.   *Attention-Worthiness*

I believe that a more satisfactory account of sublexicalization, which explains the constraints in (3) and (4) and which unifies the accounts by Lindner, Fillmore, and Rice can be proposed as the following discourse-pragmatic principle:

(8)   Elements are lexicalized in a predication when the speaker wants to draw attention to them as definitive for the situation being predicated.

That is, lexicalization imposes discourse salience on an element when the speaker uses it to define a situation in a particular way. Thus, sublexicalization does imply nonsalience, as Lindner suggests; however, nonsalience is determined not by semantic recoverability but by relative attention-worthiness in the perspective that the speaker is constructing for a given situation. For example, in (3), the landmark <u>them</u> is recoverable from a previous mention. But it is nonetheless salient. The speaker is using it as a defining context: a condition that narrows the situation of <u>call in</u> to a specific set of cases (namely, calls using AT&T lines). In other words, it is not only the event that is being predicated but also the specific context that enables that event.

We can contrast the lexicalized landmark <u>them</u> with the sublexicalized landmark of <u>out</u> in the first line of the same example (<u>They can't call out</u>). The implicit landmark of <u>out</u> is the path of exit, as in *throw them out the window*, for example (see section 8.7 for a more detailed discussion of the semantics of <u>out</u>). The speaker's concern in this utterance, however, is not with the path of exit but with the source of the call (<u>from Germany</u>) and the enabling conditions (<u>on AT&T lines</u>), since these are the two significant contexts that make the calling impossible. Both of these contexts are introduced in separate prepositional phrases.

The landmark <u>him</u> in (4) is lexicalized for the same reasons as <u>them</u> in (3). Although accessible as a participant in the preceding conversation, <u>him</u> is nonetheless salient in its new role as a defining circumstance, the cause of the situation predicated by <u>challenged</u>. The principle proposed in (8) explains why it would be semantically and pragmatically unacceptable to sublexicalize the landmarks for (3) and (4), as we saw in (5).

If the landmarks are being introduced as defining contexts, then presumably the function of the preposition in each case is to link them to the discourse. If the speaker decides that there is no need to mention these defining contexts, then there is logically no need for the linking preposition and its appearance without the landmark would make no sense. In this case, we should simply expect the whole prepositional phrase to be omitted, as in (6).

If we go back now to Lindner's "toothpaste" example (2), we can see that the sublexicalized landmark (<u>the tube</u>, according to Lindner) is probably nonsalient, not because it is recoverable but because the speaker has no reason to direct the hearer's attention to it. Of course, since this example is invented rather than naturally occurring, we cannot say for certain what perspective the speaker intends to construct or how it relates to any specific discourse context. Nevertheless, assuming that the intention is simply to predicate an everyday, "toothpaste-squeezing" situation, and given the familiarity of <u>the tube</u> as a defining context, then presumably we can take the landmark for granted. Unlike <u>AT&T lines</u> in (3) or <u>him</u> in (4), <u>the tube</u> contributes no special definitive information to this particular discourse context, so there is nothing to warrant its mention.

7.3.2. *Attention-Worthy Complements*

We can also go back and apply the principle in (8) to Fillmore's and Rice's invented examples in their accounts of transitivity. Fillmore justifies the intransitive use of a verb in terms of the definiteness and phoricity of its complement: if someone asks you about an accident, it is possible to answer *I didn't see* because the complement of <u>see</u> refers anaphorically to a definite referent (the accident). Rice argues that we can say *Mike studied* or *Moses spoke* because both verbs invoke generic scenarios, complete with generic, inferrable complements. Although Fillmore's and Rice's interpretations seem to be offering different semantic explanations, they in fact point to a common discourse motivation for null-complementation, defined in (8): that the speaker is not directing attention to the complement as an attention-worthy definitive element.

The local semantics of each situation may vary. The complement may be definite and anaphoric, as in Fillmore's example, or indefinite but schematically invoked by familiar scenarios, as in Rice's examples. But these semantic facts are contained by a larger discourse-pragmatic fact: that the null complement brings no salient information to the speaker's subjective definition of the situation. In all the previous invented examples, we are to understand that the speaker intends simply to predicate an event: toothpaste-squeezing, seeing, studying, or speaking. In each case, the hearer can infer predictable complements which define these events: a tube containing the toothpaste, and so on. If the mention of these predictable complements adds no special definitive information to the predication, then lexicalization is not pragmatically warranted.

Returning to Rice's contrastive examples, *Mike perused* and *Moses uttered*, we can see how semantics interacts with pragmatics to confer discourse salience and hence transitivity. Again, it is difficult to ascertain speaker intentions with invented sentences such as these, but I would argue that any speaker who chooses to use these rather unusual verbs does so with a salient complement in mind. Rice's evaluation of these verbs as nongeneric seems to capture the fact that the verbs <u>peruse</u> and <u>utter</u> contribute an extra semantic-pragmatic feature over the more common verbs <u>study</u> and <u>speak</u>; that is, they express a particular attitude to and effect on their complements.

In fact, the etymological structure of these verbs suggests as much, since they each have an original P-prefix which directs the hearer's attention to their complement. The Latin prepositional prefix <u>per</u>-, meaning "through," suggests that the object of perusal is worthy of careful study — that it will be "gone through" or "used thoroughly" rather than just read. The Old English prefix <u>ut</u>-, meaning "out," confers a resultative state on its complement: we understand that to <u>utter</u> means to put words out, so our attention is directed to the output, as well as to the act, of speaking.

Similarly, to cite another example from Rice, "*Fred devoured" is unacceptable because the verb <u>devour</u> implies a salient complement. <u>Devour</u> contains a Latinate prefix <u>de</u>- (meaning "down," "from," or "away") which originally added a completive aspectual sense to the verb. To *devour* means to "seize on and destroy" something. Thus, Rice's example suggests a certain rapaciousness in Fred's attitude to whatever he was eating. The verb prefix predicates a state of total consumption on the complement; therefore, in choosing this verb, the speaker is drawing the hearer's attention to the complement.

For all these "inherently" transitive verbs, then, transitivity follows logically from the fact that they all define an activity in terms of its effect on or attitude toward the complement. Seen from this point of view, both the syntactic property of transitivity and the semantic property of "specificity" noted for these verbs by Rice are natural effects of the pragmatic principle in (8). These properties emerge from the use of a lexicalized complement that helps to define the situation being predicated.

This conclusion converges with that reached independently by Paul Hopper and Sandra Thompson's (1980) study of transitivity. The authors examine the semantic features of elements in transitive constructions cross-linguistically in an attempt to establish the discourse function of this property. Noting that transitivity marking is determined in some languages by semantic "individuation," "affectedness," and "specificity" of the verb complement, they interpret such semantic features as natural effects of a discourse-pragmatic foregrounding strategy. Foregrounding is apparently a notion that reflects the principle in (8), insofar as foregrounded elements display these "attention-worthy" semantic features.

7.3.3. Attention-Worthy Landmarks

Prepositions, like transitive verbs, have lexicalized complements, which help to define the situation being predicated. But prepositional landmarks define situations in a rather different way than do verb objects. It was shown in chapter 6 that landmarks can be distinguished from object NPs in their semantic, informational, and prosodic properties. Although certain object NPs — namely predicative ones — do serve as props to define situations, their referents are not viewed as independent arguments. Rather, they are centrally involved in the verb's predication. In fact, predicative objects in several languages are morphologically attached to the verb in a strategy known as noun incorporation (Lee, in Hopper and Thompson, 1993:359). This strategy is perhaps best paraphrased in English in such compound verb constructions as pear-picking and knife-sharpening. The semantic properties of these attached objects reflect their involvement in the verb's predication: objects of transitive verbs are highly likely to be affected by the situation being predicated.

In contrast, prepositional landmarks have the semantic and informational characteristics of independent circumstances, as was shown in chapter 6. Syntactically, too, they stand apart from the verb, their "distance" marked iconically by the preposition. And we have also seen that prepositional phrases are more likely to be set off prosodically from the clause than any other recognizable syntactic unit. In short, prepositions have a different type of transitivity than do verbs—a transitivity that marks the relative independence of their complements. This independence reflects that fact that landmarks define situations not by involvement in the situations being predicated but by contextualizing them.

7.4.   Contexts for Particle-Preposition Alternation

The motivation for sublexicalization and null-complementation formulated in (8) can now be illustrated in particular conversational environments from the database.

It was explained in chapter 5 that particles situate and prepositions link. In terms of transitivity, this means that particles predicate states without referring to the contexts defining those states, whereas prepositions introduce the contexts. In that chapter several conversational sequences were presented which involved particle-preposition alternation. If we reconsider some of them in (9) and (10), we can identify certain strategic reasons for a speaker's decision to use either a P-particle or a P-preposition.

(9)   a. M: And you know 6:30 in the morning . .guns you know .
           Cause there's farms over there .
           R: What's 'bad is they could send a 'bullet right <u>through</u> the "window .   (R:32)

     b. Hondas have these-have a real big windshield and so-and so ,
         if you roll an animal onto your hood I'm sure that it would   . .come 'roaring ''<u>through</u> .   (R:33)

(10) a. M: Wyncha just throw em <u>out</u> the window .
              (. . . . . .)

     b. C: I'm gonna put eh <u>out</u> in the yard .
              (. . . . . .)

     c. J: Throw the goddamn things <u>out</u> in the street !
              (. . . . . .)

     d. M: Put food <u>out</u> every day .

     e. J: [damn? cats] , just throw em <u>out</u> !   (U:78–94)

In (9a) and (10a), <u>the window</u> defines the situation from a particular perspective. It may be a matter of spatiodirectional definition, as in (9), where <u>the window</u>, as the path of the <u>bullet</u>, orients R's hearers by directing their attention back to the <u>farms</u> mentioned in M's utterance. Or it may be a more rhetorical kind of definition, as in (10). Here, <u>the window</u> is not needed for spatiodirectional definition: M's hearers could presumably infer the exit path of the kittens that are being thrown out. But in this particular sequence, <u>the window</u> marks M's utterance as a radical suggestion. M's interlocutors have been discussing the possibility of taking the kittens to the Humane Society and M, growing impatient, cuts in with a "no nonsense" alternative. By predicating <u>the window</u> as a rather unexpected route of exit, the speaker is expressing his attitude rather than simply making a practical suggestion.

In (9b) and (10b–e), the same P-forms, <u>through</u> and <u>out</u>, are used again with similar meanings, to predicate similar states. But now they are used as particles rather than as adpreps because the speakers are directing their hearers' attention to the states themselves rather than to any defining context. In (9b), unlike (9a), the previous mention of <u>windshield</u> provides an implicit landmark for <u>through</u>, so it is not needed for spatiodirectional definition. With the definitional context already "staged," so to speak, the speaker is able to focus the hearers' attention on the motion event and the endstate resulting from it.

In (10b–c) also, the speakers are less interested in defining the <u>out</u> path (which can be inferred spatiodirectionally) than in predicating the changed state and location of the kittens. The particle <u>out</u> predicates the state, and the prepositional phrase <u>in the yard</u> or <u>in the street</u> predicates the location. The final suggestions offered by M and J are again more concerned with predicating states than with introducing contexts: M wants the <u>food</u> to be <u>out</u> (implicitly, following the cats) and J simply wants the cats <u>out</u>.

Examples (9) and (10) juxtapose the alternation of particles with adpreps for a single P-form. Examples (11) and (12) juxtapose the alternation of particles with simple prepositions (rather than postverbal adpreps) for a single P-form, showing neatly how these uses separate the dual function of adpreps into situating and linking functions, respectively.

(11)   Well it 'sure is ''fun ,

to be ''moved '<u>in</u> ,

. .<u>in</u> our ''own 'place ''again .   (R:1)

By staging the utterance in (11) in two P-units, the speaker makes two separate predications with the same P-form. The first unit predicates his new state, using <u>in</u> as a directional particle. The second unit repeats the P-form <u>in</u> but now as a preposition which introduces a setting, <u>our own place</u>. This landmark is lexicalized not for locational definition (since that can be inferred from <u>moved in</u>) but to specify what is different about this location — that it is their *own* place.

Another interesting example of preposition-particle juxtaposition is found in (12).

(12)   Now 'those are a lot of ''fun ,

shittin '<u>around around</u> the ''track .   (A:21)

The contiguous repetition of <u>around</u> demonstrates the use of particle and preposition for different purposes. The speaker is talking about driving cars around a race track. As a particle, <u>around</u> first contributes a continuative aspectual sense: it predicates a state of aimlessness or nondirectedness on the activity. Then, as a preposition, it introduces the landmark in a separate P-sequence. Here, <u>around</u> has a more literal spatiodirectional meaning and links the <u>shittin around</u> to the explanatory context of the race track. This utterance demonstrates the speaker's intuitive differentiation between the two P-functions, using the same P-form first as a particle to situate and then as a preposition to link.

As a final example of the strategic interplay between prepositions and particles, consider example (13). Here, the speaker (the CPR instructor) does not use the same P-form for alternative functions, but she juxtaposes several prepositions and particles in the same instructional sequence. Notice her careful prosodic use of pauses as she demonstrates how to expel an object from the air passage of a choking victim.

(13)   ... go '<u>underneath</u> her ''a=rms ,

and ''then ,

''<u>between</u> ,

the ''navel ,

and the ''rib cage ,

'<u>on</u> an ''adult .

''<u>Up</u> ,

''<u>in</u> ,

and <u>out</u> .

'Wrong 'angle! I -I'm ''aiming ,

for a ''point .

''<u>Between</u> ,

the ''shoulder blades .

'<u>Up</u> and ''<u>in</u> .   (C:32)

The speaker has her arms around the "victim," a trainee sitting in a chair and bent over, with her back to the speaker. As the speaker demonstrates the positions and movements for CPR, she uses particles and prepositions for different purposes. The first two prepositions, <u>underneath</u> and <u>between</u>, introduce landmarks as explicit reference points to define the direction and position of movement. These landmarks are visually obvious from the physical context, but as Emanuel Schegloff (1972) points out in his analysis of place formulation, the physical world involves an infinite number of possible places, only some of which have conditional relevance for a speaker's immediate purposes. In the physical context of example (13), there are many possible landmarks for <u>underneath</u>, all equally accessible and true for this situation: the victim's sweater, her sternum, or her body in general (she is bending over); but only one of them (her arms) is conditionally relevant as the precise location for the action being demonstrated. Since precise location is crucial in this CPR context, the speaker takes no chances.

As if to emphasize this point, the speaker goes on to isolate the preposition between from its landmarks, the navel and the rib cage, in three intonation units separated by pauses, a highly unusual prosodic pattern. In this way, she uses between as a linking word to introduce the important locations, without distracting attention from its rhetorical force as a situating word with its own significant spatiodirectional content.

The next prepositional phrase, on an adult, frames the whole situation in a clarifying context; the previous instructions apply specifically to adults, and not necessarily to children. Since on serves mainly to link rather than to predicate location in its own right, there is no reason to isolate it for the hearer's attention, so this prepositional phrase follows the conventional prosodic pattern.

Once reference points and locations are clearly defined, the speaker is ready to describe directional movements. She does so through the use of simple P-particle predications, each set off for emphasis in its own P-unit: up, in, and out. Landmarks are not needed for these predications of direction and are therefore sublexicalized.

But next, as the speaker realizes she has hit the "wrong angle," she decides to reorient herself and her hearers spatiodirectionally. Once again, she splits the P-predication prosodically, using the P-form between to predicate the situation in one P-unit and its landmark the shoulder blades to predicate the defining location in another. Then, with reference points clearly established once again, she finishes the sequence with two simple particles predicating direction: up and in.

To summarize, the examples in this section have illustrated the choice between prepositions and particles as a strategically motivated one. Both prepositions and particles provide orientation but particles do it by predicating situations — or states — without reference to contextual landmarks. Prepositions do it by introducing the landmarks that define the states. The choice between preposition and particle depends on whether the context itself is salient or attention-worthy for definitional purposes. Contexts have salience for several reasons: to move the discourse into a new setting, to clarify the frame of reference; or to add an attitudinal, affective dimension.

In the world of discourse, just as on a theater stage, new realities are constructed through the manipulation and highlighting of significant props. These props are effective to the extent that speakers and audiences understand and participate in the construction. They are used strategically: props support but do not distract from the plot as events and relationships are elaborated on the stage. When they are not needed and contribute no significant information, they are omitted.

We have thus supported the conclusion reached in chapters 2 and 3 about the problem of P: that the distinction between preposition and particle is not an a priori categorial one. In the contexts shown here, at least, the choice between preposition and particle use of a given P-form seems to be determined locally by the pragmatic importance of the landmark in a particular utterance — in other words, whether the speaker is using that P-form to situate or to link.

We have also motivated Leonard Talmy's (1985) and Dwight Bolinger's (1971) intuitions that the adprep is a "coalescence" or "fusion" of both adverbial and prepositional forms, without having to resort to underlying levels of syntax. Their representations of underlying adprep meanings in sequences such as *I went past, past him* and *He drove off the chickens off the lawn* are in fact very similar to the naturally occurring sequences in (11) and (12).

The difference between my interpretation and that of the previous studies is that the duality expressed by the adprep lies not in its underlying structure but in its use as a prototypical orienting element. A P-form only becomes an adprep when it is used postverbally to perform both situating and linking. Examples (11) and (12) support this interpretation by showing how and why the dual adprep function may be divided into separate situating and linking functions.

So far, my arguments for the difference between prepositions and particles have been driven by evidence from the conversational data in this study. This evidence may now be recast in the light of an independent theory, which accommodates my own interpretation of salience, or attention-worthiness, within a more comprehensive model of pragmatic focus. The theory, formulated by Lambrecht (1994), not only supports my account of P but also gains some explanatory force from it, as we will see in section 7.5.

7.5.   Pragmatic Focus

7.5.1.   *Stress Marking*

Pragmatic focus is defined by Lambrecht as "the unpredictable or pragmatically unrecoverable element in an utterance. The focus is what makes an utterance into an assertion" (1994:207). "Focus" is very close to the notion of attention-worthiness. We would naturally expect that interlocutors pay more attention to what is unpredictable and unexpected in an utterance than to what they can already take for granted. In effect, the argument presented in previous sections is that particles focus states and prepositions focus their defining contexts.

In Knud Lambrecht's theory, prosodic stress, or accent-marking, is claimed to be the primary indicator of focus in English. The theory predicts that, in sentence-level utterances, primary stress or sentence accents will "fall on the last accentable constituent" of the sentence" (1994:251). Accentable constituents are those capable of bearing a focal status.

Lambrecht's stress placement predictions are primarily concerned with phrasal categories rather than with independent words. I will come back to this point shortly, to show how Lambrecht's constructional approach fits with my own approach, which has so far examined P-forms as individual lexical elements rather than as elements in larger constructions. For the moment, however, we can propose that if accentability is an index of focal status and if particles and landmarks are found to receive more sentence stress than prepositions in the present data, then Lambrecht's theory is relevant to differentiation between focal particles and nonfocal prepositions.

This pattern is confirmed in the data. Table 7.1 represents the results of stress placement coding for particles and prepositional phrases. We see that landmarks receive sentence (or primary) stress in 70% of their occurrences while particles receive primary stress in 51%; however, primary stress is placed on prepositions in only 5% of the cases. (For details on coding procedures for stress placement, see Appendix A.4.)

Table 7.1: Stress Placement Patterns for P-Particles,
P-Prepositions, and P-Landmarks in the Database

Element	Primary Stress	Secondary Stress	No Stress	Total Uses
Particle	51%	15%	34%	490
Landmark	70%	13%	17%	627
Preposition	5%	7%	88%	627

Notice that table 7.1 represents codings of both secondary and primary stress, which have been coded and included in order to obtain as much information as possible about P's prosody, on the premise that secondary stress is also pragmatically motivated. This premise comes from Bolinger's (1971) analysis of phrasal verbs and from Chafe's (1993) analysis of prosodic function. Chafe notes that a given intonation unit (IU) may consist of more than one accent unit, each with its own "domain of activation" and its own pattern of stress placement, where the information status of content words may be examined (1993:39–40). It would seem, then, that secondary stress placement within these subunits is pragmatically significant. Furthermore, as Bolinger points out, speakers have considerable choice in deciding how to distribute accent throughout an utterance (1971:45). For example, in the following utterance from the present corpus (14), the speaker could as easily have accented the verb hook as the particle up, so presumably his choice was pragmatically motivated.

(14)   I wanted to hook 'up my ''computer,   (R:8)

In fact, it turns that secondary stress is distributed in the same way as primary stress. We see from table 7.1 that secondary stress, like primary stress, is about twice as likely to be assigned to particles and landmarks as to prepositions in these conversational data.

Thus, when we combine the primary and secondary stress placement findings, we find that prepositions are not only dispreferred as candidates for sentence stress but also seem to be unaccentable in general: they receive no accent 88% of the time in these data. In contrast, particles usually receive some accent (66% of the time), as so do landmarks (83%). This pattern is consistent even for clause-medial elements such as those in (14), where, even though not sentence-final, the particle receives some accent. Apparently, even when accentable elements are not in a position to receive sentence stress according to Lambrecht's predictions (for example, when another accentable constituent such as an adverb or direct object occurs sentence-finally), they are still accented to some degree.

In short, the findings in table 7.1 strongly suggest that particles and landmarks tend to receive the accent marking that Lambrecht associates with pragmatic focus while prepositions do not. However, before we can draw any useful conclusions from this suggestion we must first examine some issues associated with Lambrecht's theory.

7.5.2. *Focal Status of Prepositions and Particles*

Within Lambrecht's theory, the findings in table 7.1 would not be taken as direct evidence for the differentiated functions of particles and prepositions. This is because stress is claimed to be structurally assigned, or "filtered through the machinery of grammar" (1994:247). The stress placement patterns shown previously would be seen as resulting from structural rules, rather than from the informational properties of individual words, for the following reasons.

First, in Lambrecht's theory, sentence stress is assigned not to a word but to a focus domain. Focus domains must be phrasal categories — verb phrase, noun phrase, prepositional phrase, and so on — rather than lexical categories.

> This is so because information structure is not concerned with words and their meanings ... but with the pragmatic construal of the relations between entities and states of affairs in given discourse situations. Entities and states of affairs are syntactically expressed in phrasal categories, not in lexical items. (1994:215)

Second, in the unmarked case (the most common), phrasal accent is assigned to "the right boundary" of the focal domain (247). Since landmarks normally constitute the right boundaries of prepositional phrases while particles often constitute the right boundaries of verb phrases, the theory would predict that both primary and secondary accents should be placed on these elements but not on prepositions. Third, sentence accents "fall on the last accentable constituent" of the sentence (251). Since landmarks and particles often occur sentence-finally, their candidacy for sentence stress placement seems to follow uncontroversially from stress assignment rules. Thus, the theory of pragmatic focus would predict the results in table 7.1 as a natural consequence of its grammatical rules, or word order stipulations, for stress placement.

However, such a prediction begs an important question: *Why* do speakers construe prepositions as the first element in prepositional phrases and particles as the right boundary in verb phrases? We have already seen in our analysis of categoriality tests (section 2.1.2) that this is not an easy question to answer. We have also seen that adprep prepositions belong equally to the verb and to the landmark in such sequences as *send a bullet through the window*. So there is no obvious reason on semantic grounds for this syntactic construal.

Furthermore, stress placement rules alone do not satisfactorily explain why speakers systematically avoid stress marking on prepositions even when these prepositions appear sentence-finally. This is the case for stranded prepositions, as seen in example (15).

(15) a. . .and 'that's . .pretty much . .the 'hard thing that you need to ''care <u>about</u> .   (C:2)

   b. Y'know it wasn't at 'all what she had ''planned <u>on</u> .   (R:1)

We see that even though these prepositions constitute the rightmost boundary of their phrasal category and the last constituent of the sentence, they are still unaccentable. It seems that in some way speakers know this, even when the syntax tells them otherwise and places the preposition in a place where, if it were a particle, it *would* be accented, as in (16):

(16) 'Okay , 'pressure's ''<u>on</u> .   (C:1)

Stranded prepositions are not discussed in Lambrecht's theory of focus, but presumably their ineligibility for stress placement would be explained by their status as purely relational elements. This status is attributed to prepositions generally in

Lambrecht's discussion of focal domains. Even though a preposition might denote the information point of a sentence, it cannot constitute a focal domain. For example, in Lambrecht's example (repeated here as 17), he explains that, even though TO contains the only new or unpredictable information in the sentence, "nevertheless the predicator *to* cannot by itself be the focus constituent of that clause. Since its denotatum is *purely relational*, it cannot supply an element of information whose addition to a presupposition would result in an assertion" (1994:215; emphasis mine).

(17)   and then, when we'd finished talking about pigs, we started talking TO the
        pigs,   (1994:215)

This stipulation, that prepositions are incapable of bearing focal status, is unconditional. In fact, even in those marked cases where a preposition may be accented by speakers, as it is in (17), Lambrecht explains the phenomenon as a special instance of "antitopical" marking, or "default accentuation" (1994:248ff), which shifts the accent from a constituent that would normally receive it (in this case, the landmark the pigs) when that constituent is discourse-active or topical. In other words, the strategy serves more to remove the accent from the pigs than to add it to to.

In effect, the theory of focus lumps prepositions together with other sentence elements "whose meaning (or lack thereof) does not seem to be compatible with focus status." These include grammatical morphemes such as the negative enclitic form n't and the infinitive verb marker to (Lambrecht, 1994:254). The function of prepositions is considered purely relational even though their semantic contribution may be substantial. In contrast, particles seem to be considered uncontroversial as accentable elements: for example, in the following example of predicate focus (18):

(18)   What happened to your car?
        It broke DOWN   (1994:223)

The particle, as an adjunct to the verb, is presumably interpreted as the right boundary of its focal domain (the verb phrase) and the last accentable constituent in the sentence. It therefore receives sentence stress.

But the theory does not explain *why* prepositions should be treated as purely relational when particles are not. After all, particles and prepositions can have the same semantic content, as is clearly illustrated by their juxtaposition in (19).

(19)   (It sure is fun ,)
        to be ''moved 'in,
        in our ''own 'place ''again .   (R:1)

Furthermore, a preposition *can* represent unpredictable information, as we see for Lambrecht's "default" example in (17) and in examples (20) and (21) from the data:

(20)   'Just kinda ''tiptoe ,
        because you 'have to go 'right ''by them .   (C:12)

Even in unmarked cases, prepositions (at least, P-prepositions) often make an independent semantic contribution (21):

(21) a. Whyncha 'just 'throw em <u>out</u> the ''window .   (U:78)

     b. 'I'm gonna 'throw him <u>in</u> the 'goddamn ''boiler .   (U:95)

In (21), the meaning of the prepositions <u>in</u> and <u>out</u> make quite a difference to the meaning of the utterance since they predicate opposite directions of motion. In fact, Lambrecht, as well as several other scholars, classes prepositions as predicators. Why, then, are they not as accentable as other predicators, such as verbs and verb particles?

Within Lambrecht's theory, the simple answer to this question might be that prepositions are construed as the first elements in prepositional phrases whereas particles are the last elements in verb phrases — and the last element of the phrase is the one to which stress gets assigned. But this brings us back to the first question: Why should the preposition be construed with the following landmark and the particle with the preceding verb?

In short, the theory of pragmatic focus does not tell us what it is about particles and prepositions that should cause them to be viewed as so pragmatically different from each other that the difference is grammaticized in stress assignment rules. The judgment that prepositions are relational and unaccentable seems to rest on a pretheoretical assumption that distinguishes prepositions from particles but that is not explained.

I propose that this assumption can now be theoretically justified by my own thesis that particles specialize in situating while prepositions specialize in linking. It is this distinction that speakers "know," and it is grammaticized in the stress-marking rules of English, which override semantic considerations and mark prepositions as relational even in cases where they contribute substantial meanings.

As situating elements, postverbal particles copredicate states with the verb. This explains why they may be viewed as the rightmost element in a verb phrase construction. Prepositions link to landmarks, which explains why they may be viewed as the first elements in prepositional phrases. It is this functional difference between prepositions and particles that produces the different syntactic groupings revealed by the constituency tests presented in table 2.1 of chapter 2.

Viewed from this perspective, my own account of prepositions and particles as being pragmatically different is reinforced by its accommodation within the theory of pragmatic focus. The findings in table 7.1 fulfil Lambrecht's predictions by showing that particles and landmarks systematically receive the marking associated with focal status while prepositions do not. Furthermore, the present analysis, which labels these elements as lexical items (rather than elements in phrasal categories) lends explanatory force to Lambrecht's constructional theory by motivating his stress rules for prepositional or verb-particle phrasal constructions.

It is taken as a well-known premise in the grammaticization and discourse-functional literature that "grammars are shaped by the way people talk" (Hopper and Thompson, 1993:358). Grammaticization is viewed as the regularization of patterns that have emerged naturally in discourse. Thus, if stress-marking is indeed the grammaticization of focus, then the structurally assigned stress patterns discussed by Lambrecht can be seen as a reflection of speakers' tendency to use prepositions as nonfocal elements and particles as focal ones.

Another line of support for this pragmatic account comes from Givón's (1984b)

Table 7.2: Assertion Status of P-Particles, P-Prepositions, and
P-Landmarks in the Database

Lexical Element	Asserted (%)	Presupposed (%)	Uninterpretable (%)	Totals
Particle	84	15	1	490
Landmark	86	14.5	0.5	627
Preposition	49	51	0.5	627

analysis of presupposition and assertion in discourse. His study complements Lambrecht's by providing a set of criteria by which we can establish the focal status of prepositions and particles as individual lexical items.

7.5.3. Assertion Status of Prepositions and Particles

Focus is defined by Lambrecht as the pragmatically unrecoverable element that turns an utterance into an assertion (1994:207). In the present discussion, this would mean that speakers must somehow use prepositions less "assertively" than particles. However, Lambrecht's theory, as I explained above, does not define "unrecoverability" or "assertion" in terms that can be operationalized for individual lexical items. These terms are provided by Givón's independent study (1984b) as a set of specific epistemic properties that can be coded for individual lexical items. When prepositions, particles, and landmarks are examined in these terms, the findings do indeed suggest that prepositions are used much less assertively than particles and landmarks, thus providing direct support for the thesis proposed here and indirect support for the theory of pragmatic focus. Table 7.2 represents these findings and is accompanied by an explanation of the properties coded.

Table 7.2 codes assertion status in binary terms, following Givón's distinction between "asserted" and "presupposed." The counts show that from a total of 627 P-prepositional phrases and 490 P-particle tokens, particles and landmarks are highly likely to be asserted (84% and 86% of their tokens, respectively), whereas prepositions are only asserted about half the time (49%). In other words, there is a clear pragmatic difference between the information contributed by particles and landmarks, and that contributed by prepositions.

At this point, Givón's criterial properties for presupposition versus assertion status should be elaborated and illustrated so that the reader can more clearly interpret the meaning of these results. (For more details on coding categories, and explanations of how intermediate cases were handled, see Appendix A.5.)

Presupposed Information

Presupposed Information constitutes "uncontested knowledge" for Givón. Knowledge may be uncontested for several reasons, three of which are relevant for the present data.

7.5.3.1. DEICTIC OBVIOUSNESS The information contributed by the lexical element is "held in the immediate perceptual field" of the interlocutors (1984b:503).

This category includes landmarks whose referents are physically present (you in example (22).

(22)   The 'Good ''Samaritan Act -um , ''protects you ,

... against 'any kinda ''legal action ,

that 'might be . . . 'inflicted ''upon you .   (C:3)

Deictic obviousness also applies to P-forms whose spatial reference is grounded in the discourse context (over, the deictic particle in 23).

(23)   And 'then they'll come over to ''this field over here .   (R:32)

In (23), the first mention of over is asserted because it predicates an unpredictable "contestable" change of state. But the second, underlined mention is presupposed because it serves simply as a deictic marker to orient the hearer spatially, pointing out the path between the old context (presumably another field) and the new one (this field). There is nothing contestable about this path since it has already been established in the first mention of over.

Note that in (22) the preposition upon receives primary stress. This stress marking represents the default accentuation strategy that Lambrecht associates with discourse-active landmarks (see explanation for 17). It may be that the small number of prepositions (5%) shown to carry sentence stress (table 7.1) generally represent such default cases.

Note also that in (22) the particle over (in the first mention) carries no accent even though it is asserted. In this case, the verb-particle construction is followed by a prepositional phrase (to this field) whose landmark carries the sentence stress, consistent with Lambrecht's predictions, while secondary stress is carried earlier in the predication by the temporal adverb then. This example illustrates the fact that stress placement cannot be predicted from assertion status even though both properties reflect pragmatic focus. The word order rules for stress placement, and the fact that several focal elements may compete for accentuation in a single utterance, will influence a speaker's prosodic choices in any given utterance.

7.5.3.2.   SHARED PRESUPPOSITION   Information has been "shared previously" (1984:503) and is now taken for granted. This category includes topical referents (e.g., the landmark you in example 22) and also repeated information (e.g., on in example 24).

(24)   M: Did you 'turn it ''o=n ?

R: 'Turn ''what on .   (R:2)

In (24), the only element asserted by R is what (assertion includes interrogation, for both Lambrecht and Givón). Everything else in R's utterance is repeated from M's and is therefore presupposed.

7.5.3.3.   ANALYTIC TRUTH   This information is presupposed by the interlocutors' subscription to "the same mode of thought, logic or rules of various games" (1984b:503). In this category I would include grammar as a kind of linguistic "game" with its own conventional rules; that is, if a preposition is conventionally construed with a certain element or in a certain sequence, then it may be considered a presupposed element in a lexicalized collocation. This is the case with such verb-preposition sequences as believe in and depend on (see section 3.2), where certain prepositions *always* appear with those verbs. An example of this kind of analytic truth is given in (22), where the verb inflict is conventionally constructed with the preposition upon (or on), and also in (25), where the idiom get on your case allows only one prepositional choice.

(25)   R: They ''never'get on your ''case.

       J: Elementary teachers do . <LAUGH>

       L: But 'she wouldn't get on ''my case , because 'I was her ''daughter-in-law but . (R:2)

Although the preposition on is presupposed analytically in (25), the landmark is asserted since my case contrasts specifically with your case.

Having given examples of asserted and presupposed elements, we can now more clearly interpret the results in table 7.2 to mean that particles and landmarks are far more likely to assert information (an average of about 85% of the time) than prepositions, which assert information only about half the time in this corpus.

In those cases where prepositions *are* asserted, they usually share the scope of assertion with the following landmark. In other words, they both situate and link. This situation obtains for adpreps, as has been demonstrated, and also for other prepositions that may contribute relevant spatiodirectional or temporal information. In (26), for example, after asserts a causal and temporal relation between the previous clause You'd be out and the landmark that; the landmark asserts a summarizing frame for a series of events previously mentioned, encapsulating them in a single pronominal reference and asserting them as a single circumstance. Together, preposition and landmark situate the previous clause in a clarifying context.

(26)   You'd be ''out ,

       after ''that .   (R:24)

In contrast, very few prepositions (an informal count reveals only 4%, or 27 tokens from a total of 627) are asserted by themselves — that is, with presupposed landmarks. This finding directly supports my own claim that prepositions link to definitive, attention-worthy landmarks. Landmarks refer to contextual props. If a prop were already presupposed and taken for granted, there would presumably be no need to lexicalize it and thus no need for a linking P-form. P-forms that are asserted by themselves occur as particles not prepositions.

Thus, we can see that the assertion status findings in table 7.2 correspond with the stress-placement findings in table 7.1 in marking prepositions as pragmatically less focal than particles or landmarks. However, it is clear that stress placement cannot be predicted from the assertion status of individual elements. If we compare the two tables, we see that 84% of particle tokens are asserted, but only 66% of particle tokens carry any stress marking (a percentage reached by adding the "primary" and "secondary" stress categories together). Landmarks are very likely to be both asserted

(86% of their tokens) and stressed (83%). And even though prepositions are asserted 49% of the time, only 12% receive any stress.

These findings support Lambrecht's claim that prosodic marking is "filtered through the machinery of grammar" (1994:247). This claim means that accent is structurally assigned to fall on particles, landmarks, and other accentable constituents. Except in special cases such as default accentuation, it is not assigned to fall on prepositions, even when they contain asserted information.

However, I have argued that the grammatical machinery is itself fueled and driven by many repeated conversational instances where prepositions are used for linking rather than focusing purposes; that the grammaticization pattern that appears to override word-level pragmatic considerations is itself motivated by such pragmatic considerations.

Let's summarize this section on pragmatic focus. Lambrecht's and Givón's theories converge to provide independent support for the pragmatic interpretation being presented here of particles as situating elements and prepositions as linking elements. The stress placement findings of table 7.1 bear out the predictions of Lambrecht's theory, revealing a focal status for prepositions different from that for particles and landmarks — a difference which is assumed by that theory, but explained by my own. The "assertion" findings summarized in table 7.2 offer independent evidence for this difference in focal status and help explain what it means, following Givón's epistemic criteria for assertion and presupposition.

We can now see more clearly the reason for the putative syntactic attachment of particles to preceding verbs and prepositions to following NPs. Postverbal particles focus states on preceding verbs or their arguments while prepositions bring following landmarks into focus.

In light of these insights on stress-marking, focus, and constituency, we can now more fully account for a well-known syntactic teaser in the problem of P: that of particle movement or NP-insertion.

7.6.   Particle Movement: A Focus-Marking Strategy

As we know, verb-particle constructions may vary their word order, with the direct object coming either before the particle (*I took my hat off*) or after it (*I took off my hat*). This phenomenon has been addressed in several different ways (see sections 2.1.2 and 3.1). Some studies view the first order as basic and posit an option of rightward NP-movement to produce the second. Others view the second order as basic and posit a strategy of rightward particle movement (or NP-insertion) to produce the first. Most of them concentrate on the properties of the direct object as the key issue determining the alternation. They explain that heavy, new, or unpredictable NPs are relegated to sentence-final position, whereas pronominal, familiar, or topical NPs are constructed more closely with the verb.

Bolinger (1971), however, considers the role of the particle itself in determining the word order of verb-particle constructions. He considers the particle an "important semantic feature" in the verb complex, whose movement to sentence-final position has the following strategic importance.

[The coupling of accent and position] ... retains something for English that the grammaticizing of word order might otherwise have destroyed: the freedom to put the transitive verb, or at least some significant part of it, at some other point than before its complement. Grammaticizing made it impossible to say *He the man ousted, but with the phrasal verb there is no trouble with He threw the man out. ... the prosody benefits in that the important semantic feature, contained in oust or out, erase or off, and the like, can be put in the normal position for the nuclear accent. (1971:49)

Bolinger's strategic interpretation of particle movement heralds Talmy's (1985) later decompositional account of motion events in several languages. Talmy points out that certain semantic features, such as manner or path, can be separated out from the verb nucleus and lexicalized as independent "satellites." He suggests that this strategy has the effect of foregrounding the lexicalized element (which is the path, in the case of particles).

Both Bolinger's and Talmy's insights support the present account of particles as pragmatically focused elements. The separation of the particle from the verb allows it to be foregrounded in sentence-final position, where it receives the nuclear accent.

We can now answer a question that remains unaddressed by previous studies of particle movement: Why do only particles, and not prepositions, display this syntactic versatility? If particles can be separated from the verbs to which they attach and be foregrounded sentence-finally, why can't prepositions be separated from the landmarks to which they attach and be foregrounded in the same way?

To answer this question, we need to ask, echoing Bolinger, "what it is that end position confers" (1971:41). The answer is that, when coupled with nuclear stress, it confers focus. And under the present account, landmarks, rather than prepositions, are the focal elements in verb-preposition sequences. Thus, their utterance-final position is warranted even when they carry familiar or pronominal information. In contrast, particles may compete with direct objects for focal status. Familiar or pronominal object referents are unlikely to have the assertion properties associated with focal status, and thus concede end-position to the particle. Heavy, new, or unpredictable referents, on the other hand, are more likely to have focal status and to occupy endposition themselves.

Thus, Bolinger's insights, synthesized with my own account of P, explain not only the peculiar strategic value of particle movement but also the constraints on prepositional movement, as a grammaticization of their relative focal status.

They also give an explanatory purpose to Lambrecht's "last accentable constituent" rule for sentence stress-marking. By Bolinger's account, it is no arbitrary rule that assigns stress to elements in sentence-final position but, rather, the "coupling" of stress and word order to foreground certain constituents as focal.

7.7. Conclusion

In this chapter, I have argued that preposition-particle alternation is driven by considerations of pragmatic focus. Particles focus states while prepositions introduce focal contexts that define those states. This interpretation adds explanatory value to

Lindner's (1981) interpretation of particles as prepositions with sublexicalized land-marks, by revealing why prepositions get sublexicalized.

I have also argued that the stress placement patterns of the present data reflect the grammaticization of this pragmatic distinction between prepositions and particles. I have explained how the distinction can be formulated within Lambrecht's theory of pragmatic focus, to answer some unaddressed questions in that theory.

In the process, I have defended the proposal set out in chapter 5 that P-forms are orienting elements. It is their orienting function that unifies them in the adprep function, but it is their situating and linking subfunctions that distinguish them as focal particles or nonfocal prepositions. These subfunctions also explain why particles seem to construct with preceding verbs (as co-predicators) and prepositions construct with following landmarks (as linking elements).

However, in solving these basic problems of categorial overlap and differentia-tion, we still have not solved the whole problem of P. We are still left with several questions from chapter 1 concerning P's semantic versatility and syntactic constraints. These questions will be answered in the next chapter, which examines P-forms as elements in construction.

8

P in Construction

The task set for this study in chapter 1 was to account for P's categoriality, semantic productivity, and syntactic constraints. The task was elaborated as a series of questions that language scholars or learners are likely to ask about P's complexity of forms and functions.

Previous chapters have now addressed the question of P's categoriality and have argued for a new definition of P as an orienting element that unifies prepositions and particles and also explains their differentiated functions in pragmatic, semantic, and syntactic terms.

From this definitional perspective, I now address several of the more specific questions, recapitulated here from chapter 1 (sections 1.1 through 1.2.1). We will get to the remaining introductory questions in chapter 9.

1. *Categorial extension*: How can a single word such as <u>up</u> function not only as a particle and a preposition, but also as a nonpostverbal "adverb" (<u>there used to be a place up in Toledo</u>) and even as an adjective (<u>a bunch of high up people</u>)?

2. *Phrasal verbs*: What is the difference between inseparable and separable phrasal verbs?

3. *Nonspatial meanings*: What is the meaning of nonspatial P-forms in such phrasal verbs as <u>depend on</u>, <u>talk about</u>, <u>burn up</u>, and <u>burn down</u>?

4. *Idiosyncratic patterning*: Why can we say *I threw it out the window* but not *I threw it out the room*?

To answer these and related questions, we need to examine P-forms not as independent words, but as elements in situating and linking constructions. In this chapter, I examine P-constructions in detail, synthesizing the insights of many previous studies within a data-driven analysis. I propose a network of orienting functions at all syntactic levels, both to capture P's polysemy and to account for the constraints on its syntactic patterns. This network contains principled answers to these questions.

8.1.   Constructional Meaning

Constructions are defined in the theory of Construction Grammar as form-meaning correspondences, most often consisting of phrasal patterns where "something about their form or meaning is not strictly predictable from the properties of their component parts or from other constructions" (Goldberg, 1995:4). Adele Goldberg claims that constructions often represent certain *gestalts*, or familiar scenarios grounded in our knowledge of the world (1995:152).

Many gestalts and scenarios are likely to be associated with such a basic experiential concept as orientation (see discussion in chapter 5, sections 5.1 and 5.2), so it is not surprising that P-forms participate in a wide variety of constructions. However, here I adopt an informal definition of "construction" that is less theoretically driven than Goldberg's: a construction is any distinct pattern in which P combines predictably with other elements to produce a special type of meaning. We will see that many of these patterns are highly productive and that they carry their own special syntactic constraints.

The notion of P as a constructional element has already been introduced. The notion has been important, for example, in identifying the attachment of particles to verbs and prepositions to following landmarks (chapter 2). In chapter 3, Lindner's account of alternative "composite scenes" for verb-particle constructions helped explain why a single sequence such as <u>clean up</u> could have two very different meanings; as well, Vestergaard's syntactic hierarchy, anticipating the role and reference grammar model, helped explain why a single preposition could have similarly different meanings.

However, as I explain in the early chapters in this book, the previous literature has produced only fragmentary solutions to the problem of P, leaving important issues unresolved. What is needed is a coherent model to unify preposition and particle constructions at all levels of constituency — a grammatical framework within which P-constructions may be slotted.

The skeleton for such a framework is suggested by the Role and Reference Grammar (RRG) theory of "layered clause structure" (Foley and Van Valin, 1984; Van Valin, 1993; Jolly, 1993). As pointed out in chapter 3, while RRG does not satisfactorily account for the similarities and differences between prepositions and particles, the basic model may be developed and modified for this purpose. The next section briefly summarizes these modifications, and the remaining discussion elaborates them, as appropriate.

8.2.   The Layered Structure of the Clause

Within the layered structure of the clause, elements are identified according to their syntactic and semantic scope of operation. Thus, the RRG model captures form-

Table 8.1: Summary of P-Constructions under Different
Syntactic Scopes

	Orientation Function	
Scope	Linking	Situating
Core	1. Adprep	
	2. Case-marking	3. Focal predicator
Nuclear	4. Verb-preposition	6. Aktionsart
	5. Qualifying	
Peripheral	7. Subordinator	9. Deictic marker
	8. Text-transition	
NP	10. Postmodifying	11. Premodifying
Particle	12. P-compound	

meaning correspondences more clearly than is possible by traditional grammar models or other theories that describe grammar in autonomous terms. To recapitulate briefly, the main constituents of the clause in RRG are the nucleus (usually the verb), the core (nucleus plus NP arguments), and the periphery (adjuncts to the core, such as adverbial phrases).

Most of the P-constructions identified in the present corpus operate under the scope of these constituents, especially the core. I will subsequently propose two other scopes of operation, not discussed in RRG but consistent with the model, as explanatory for certain P-constructions: NP-scope and P-scope.

Another significant modification to the RRG model is that I have combined particles and prepositions in a common set of P-forms whereas RRG represents them as categorially distinct, as "operators" and "predicators," respectively. This is a theoretically motivated decision based on the observation that this categorial distinction collapses in many cases — most notably in adprep cases (see chapter 3, section 3.2.3). More importantly, the distinction obscures the interrelated functions of prepositions and particles as orienting elements.

With these modifications in place, I now propose a framework that maps out the constituency and function of P-constructions within the layered structure of the clause. Table 8.1 represents this framework and names the constructions generated within it.

The following sections define and explain the constituency, meanings, and patterning constraints of these constructions. In all cases, we will see that particles consistently serve to situate other constituents while prepositions consistently serve to link them to defining contexts.

8.3.   Core Scope Constructions

Core scope constructions involve basic clause types where P construes with the verb and its arguments. They are semantically the most compositional kinds of constructions in that their meanings can usually be derived from the sum of their parts and that P-forms usually predicate states or contexts in the spatiodirectional domain of reference.

Here we find adprep constructions, which perform the generic orienting function of both situating and linking; but we also find case-marking prepositions and focal predicator particles.

8.3.1. *Adprep Constructions*

The adprep construction has already been analyzed in some detail in previous chapters. It involves a P-preposition that constructs with a verb to denote a physical change of state on one of the clause arguments. When the verb is transitive, the state is predicated on the direct object, as in (1a–1c); when the verb is intransitive, the state is predicated on the subject, as in (1d–1e).

(1)   a. Whyncha 'just throw em ''<u>out</u> the window .   (U:78)

       b. I 'knocked it <u>off</u> the ''bed, 'right ?   (U:24)

       c. 'Throw him <u>in</u> the 'goddamn ''furnace ,   (U:94)

       d. So we 'kinda went '<u>through</u> the ''country.   (R:33)

       e. She'll cl-'try to ''climb <u>up</u> your ''leg man .   (U:83)

Semantically, the adprep construction may be defined as one in which the verb and preposition together take a core argument as their trajector and an oblique argument as their landmark, typically in a motion event. The verb normally denotes manner or motion while P denotes the direction or resulting state of that motion. Thus, in (1b), <u>it</u> is the trajector which moves <u>off the bed</u>, and in (1d) <u>we</u> is the moving trajector. Syntactically, word order will vary according to whether the trajector is the subject or object of the verb. Consequently, the clause predicate in (1a–1c) has the structure (V+NP+P+NP), and (1d–1e) has (NP+V+P+LM). Pragmatically, they both situate and link.

The key point about adpreps is that they allow sublexicalization of the landmark. The choice, as explained in the previous chapter, is constrained by the speaker's pragmatic focus: by whether he or she wishes to focus state or context. Thus, the above utterances could presumably be rendered in an alternate form, as in (2).

(2)   a. Whyncha just throw em <u>out</u>?

       b. I knocked it <u>off</u>, right?

Sublexicalization produces a focal predicator sequence, which I will discuss next. Adprep constructions with transitive verbs include "caused motion" sequences, which Goldberg (1995) introduces as a separate construction (3).

(3)   Pat <u>threw the metal off the table</u>.

Goldberg defines the caused motion construction as one in which "X causes Y to move Z" (1995:152). The verb crucially contains a causative feature while the preposition denotes a resultant change of state on the object of the verb. However, Goldberg's analysis does not attempt to unify the caused motion construction with others involving intransitive verbs or nonresultant, evolving states, as in (1d–1e), and she does not relate it to the corresponding focal predicator construction. Therefore, I believe my own account of adprep constructions has the explanatory value of mapping out all of these sequences in relation to one other, as subcases of a larger motion event gestalt.

Goldberg does discuss the apparent overlap between caused motion events and resultative constructions, as in examples (4) and (5).

(4)   Pat threw the metal off the table.   (caused motion)

(5)   Pat hammered the metal flat.   (resultative)

Goldberg argues that the resultative construction is a metaphorical extension of the caused motion construction, where change of state (i.e., flatness) can be metaphorically viewed as a change of location.

I would suggest that the basic distinction between (4) and (5) is in the presence or absence of orientation: <u>off</u> predicates a change of state which is definable only in terms of the changed relation between the metal and the landmark (the table); in other words, it predicates a situation. In contrast, <u>flat</u> predicates a change of state that is definable in terms of some property contained in the entity (the metal) itself; in other words, it predicates a new attribute.

8.3.2. Case-Marking

Case-marking involves an essentially linking prepositional construction under core scope. Bernard Comrie (1981) defines case typologically as a morphosyntactic strategy for marking relations between core clause arguments (e.g., agent, subject, and patient), or between clause and oblique arguments (oblique arguments mark such relations as possessive, benefactive, or comitative). In many languages, case is marked morphologically by inflectional affixes; but in English, an analytic language, relations between core clause arguments are marked syntactically by word order. Relations between core clause and oblique arguments are usually marked by prepositions: <u>for</u> marks benefactive case, for example, and <u>with</u> marks comitative.

Case-marking is grammaticized in English for several non-P-prepositions, such as <u>to</u>, <u>for</u>, <u>with</u>, and <u>of</u>— that is, these prepositions are structurally assigned to mark specific case relations. Used in this way, they have very little situating capability: they do not predicate states by themselves, and we do not see them used as particles, except in a few rare, idiomatic cases (*Let's take it <u>with</u>; push the door <u>to</u>; etc.*).

But P-prepositions may also mark case relations, most notably locative relations, as in (6).

(6)   a. I had my ''weight,
         my 'head and 'shoulders ''<u>over</u> my 'hands ,   (C:22)

      b. Sit out <u>in</u> the sun .   (A:20)

      c. R: . . . 'even if you live <u>in</u> ''Boulder ,
         M: Anyone can . .even residential .
         R: But you if you 'live <u>in</u> ''Boulder ,
             You 'pay a lot ''more .   (R:11)

      d. He was ''up <u>on</u> the= . . . ''trailer hh , or 'up <u>on</u> the 'back of his ''pickup truck .   (A:20)

      e. You're 'right ''<u>o=n</u> him ,   (C:22)

    f. Okay we're <u>in</u> a restaurant ,   (C:32)

In all these examples, the underlined P-prepositions link the landmark to a core clause argument. Unlike non-P-prepositions, they do contain spatiodirectional information, so they have some situating potential. But the case-marking function is primary, as shown by the syntactic constraint against sublexicalization. It would not be grammatically possible to omit the landmark from any of the examples in (6). Note, for example, that in (6c), the speaker repeats the landmark <u>Boulder</u>, even though it is discourse-active and accessible from his previous mention. Particle alternation is impossible for case-marking prepositions, and this constraint is what distinguishes them from adpreps under core scope.

    This syntactic constraint showed up in the previous chapter (section 7.3), where it was pointed out that the following sequence did not allow sublexicalization for the underlined landmarks.

(7)   ''Then 'I um . .became a ''lot less uh 'worried or 'challenged by <u>him</u> .   (E:7)

In that discussion, I explained the constraint pragmatically, in terms of the attention-worthiness (or focal status) of the linked landmark. We can now explain it more clearly, as an effect of the case-marking pattern, which prohibits sublexicalization in this essentially linking construction.

    Actually, example (7) reveals a special grammaticized case-marking sequence where <u>by</u> specializes as agentive marker for the passive construction. Passive constructions place the semantic patient (<u>I</u>) in the subject slot normally associated with agents and moves the agent (<u>him</u>) into the oblique slot normally associated with landmarks. Comrie (1981:121) explains that special case markers are used for such "unnatural combinations" and "unexpected relations." For passive constructions in English, this special case marker is the P-form <u>by</u>. M.A.K. Halliday (1985; see chapter 6, section 6.6) claims that the passive construction recasts the agent as a circumstance rather than a protagonist in an event. In other words, the passive construction represents a special instance of case-marking, which requires a specific P-form to perform the necessary link.

    Note that the last three examples in (6) involve the verb <u>be</u> as the main-clause predicator. In these sequences, which lack any substantive verb predication, the focal status of the situation is highlighted: it is the main — in fact, the only — predication in the clause.

    I argued in chapter 5 that orientation is as basic in our construction of the discourse world as it is in our comprehension of the physical world. Location is a fundamental orientational concept or gestalt. Therefore, it is not surprising that locative relations should be represented by a predictable constructional pattern in the grammar, since grammars code "what speakers do most" (Du Bois, in Hopper and Thompson, 1993:358). Certain non-P-prepositions mark other fundamental relations such as possession, partition, and so on. The main difference between them and locative P-forms is their degree of grammaticization: unlike P-forms, prepositions such as <u>from</u> and <u>with</u> can only function as case markers. The reasons for their greater grammaticization will be taken up in chapter 9.

8.3.3. *Focal Predicator*

Under core scope, focal predicator particles construct postverbally to predicate a state on a trajector. They may co-predicate with semantically substantial verbs, as in (8a)–(8d), or they may serve as the only predicator, following the copular verb <u>be</u> (as in 8e–8g). The sublexicalized landmark can usually be inferred from the spatiodirectional domain.

(8) a. it would . . . come 'roaring ''<u>through</u> .   (R:33)

    b. [damn cats] ,
       just 'throw em ''<u>out</u> !   (U:94)

    c. You 'wanna 'hand stuff . . . ''<u>over</u> ?   (R:27)

    d. [It's really nice just to sit down and stop] . .lifting ''<u>bo=xes</u> | and 'moving things
       ''<u>around</u> .   (R:17)

    e. . .'Okay, 'pressure's ''<u>on</u> .   (C:1)

    f. You'd be . .eh ''<u>ou=t</u> ,
       [after ''that].   (R:24)

    g. . .and by ''then it was so far ''<u>along</u> that ,   (R:24)

In traditional grammar, particles such as those in (8a)–(8d) are often labeled directional adverbs. This term, although reflecting their postverbal constructional status, obscures their close connection with adpreps, of which they are, basically, sublexicalized versions. Like adpreps, focal predicators often co-predicate motion events with verbs, as in (8a)–(8d). The only difference is pragmatic: focal predicators focus states for core arguments whereas adpreps focus both states and contexts for them.

Particles such as those in (8e)–(8g) are often labeled predicate adverbs. Again, this traditional label obscures their close connection with adpreps and directional adverbs, with which they share the same function of predicating states on core arguments. They differ only in that they serve as the main predicator in the clause after a copular verb rather than as co-predicator with a verb of motion.

These postcopular particles may even sometimes be labeled predicate adjective because of their co-occurrence with adjectives in this clause-predicative slot. For example, compare <u>pressure's on</u> in (8e) with the alternative "pressure's intense." Both renderings predicate something about the core argument, <u>pressure</u>; since the particle does not look like a prototypical adverb in this postcopular sequence, it can easily be interpreted as a simple noun-modifier: in other words, as an adjective.

What distinguishes the particle from the adjective, however, is once again its orienting function. The particle predicates a state which is relationally defined (in terms of the sublexicalized landmark, inferrable as <u>you</u>, perhaps). But the adjective predicates an attribute, a self-contained quality of intensity.

8.4.   Nuclear Scope Constructions

8.4.1.   *Rationale*

Under nuclear scope, P-forms refer only to the verb nucleus and not to the core arguments of the verb. The verb itself is the trajector which gets situated by particles and linked to landmarks by prepositions. For this reason, nuclear P-constructions often do not express the same kind of spatiodirectional meanings that we associate with core-level constructions. Under core scope, we "see" core arguments — most often as physical entities — being situated in relation to other entities. Under nuclear scope, however, the domain of reference is metalinguistic rather than physical: particles and prepositions situate linguistic entities (verbs, which refer to activities, processes, events, etc.) rather than physical ones.

Although the distinction between nuclear-level and core-level prepositions is not developed in the RRG model, it is a legitimate one, which follows logically from the definitions contained in that model. Furthermore, it turns out to be a very useful one for the present study since it allows us to identify verb-preposition constructions, which are noted for their idiosyncracies as "inseparable phrasal verbs."

Several special-purpose constructions may be identified under nuclear scope in the present study, including verb-preposition and qualifying constructions, which link, and Aktionsart constructions, which situate (see table 8.1). All are semantically productive in generating new meanings, and all impose their own patterning constraints.

Before turning to these specialized constructions, however, we should first consider some more transparently compositional P-sequences, exemplified in (9).

(9) a. . . .they 'can't call ''<u>out</u>,
          'from ''Germany ,
          ''on 'AT&T lines ,
          'we can just call ''<u>in</u> on them so .   (R:7)

     b. and breathe <u>into</u> the ''tube ,   (C:7)

     c. and they 'breathe '<u>under</u> the ''diaphragm .   (C:8)

     d. You 'need to 'look <u>on</u> the ''recording .   (C:26)

     e. . . .it was so beautiful I couldn't believe it .
          Looked like you could- you know 'shave <u>off</u> the~ ''fenders .   (A:27)

These sequences are compositional in the sense that the P-forms are semantically independent (not required in any lexicalized sense by the verb) and refer in the spatiodirectional domain. But in each case, they orient a verb rather than a core argument. In (9a), for example, <u>they</u> are not <u>out</u> and <u>we</u> are not <u>in</u>; in (9b) and (9c), the breathers are not moving <u>into the tube</u> or <u>the diaphragm</u>; <u>you</u> are not <u>on the recording</u> in (9d), nor <u>off the fenders</u> in (9e). Rather, it is the *calling* that goes <u>out</u> or <u>in</u>, the *breathing* that goes <u>into the tube</u> and <u>under the diaphragm</u>, the *looking* that is <u>on the recording</u>, and the *shaving* that is <u>off the fenders</u> (the speaker here is talking about the shiny paintwork of a car). In other words, the activity, rather than the actor, is the trajector that gets situated by the particle or linked by the preposition.

Note that the underlined particles in (9a) look very much like core-scope focal predicators (i.e., directional adverbs). The only difference, in fact, is their level of constituency. Similarly, the prepositional constructions in (9b)–(9e) perform a specific kind of case-marking but, unlike the core-scope case markers in (6), they express locative relations for verbs rather than for core arguments.

We can now look at other P-sequences under nuclear scope which do not refer in the spatiodirectional domain. The first of these are verb-prepositional constructions and, as the label would suggest, we find that they are exclusively linking in their function.

8.4.2. Verb-Preposition Sequences

Verb-preposition sequences are lexicalized collocations which hook up a particular verb with a particular preposition. They are exemplified in (10).

(10) a. if 'you believe <u>in</u> ''that ,   (U:31)

b. 'I'm not ''talking <u>about</u> 'that man ,   (U:2)

c. It 'depends <u>on</u> if it's a 'partial or a ''full ,   (C:21)

d. It wasn't at 'all what she had ''planned <u>on</u> .   (R:3)

Verb-preposition sequences, sometimes called prepositional verbs (Jacobs, 1993: 245–247) are often listed in grammar textbooks as inseparable phrasal verbs (Azar, 1989). This term is misleading because it implies a connection with separable phrasal verbs which, as we will see below, involve particles rather than prepositions and perform a very different function. But the term does capture a clear syntactic constraint that distinguishes this construction from separable phrasal verbs — namely, that no element can be inserted between the preposition and the following NP (see table 2.1, the NP-insertion test). In other words, verb-preposition constructions are exclusively prepositional.[1]

Another distinguishing characteristic of verb-preposition sequences is the semantics of their verbs, which typically denote nonmaterial (i.e., cognitive, verbal, or attitudinal) processes and activities. To explain the specific linking function of the landmark, we can invoke Halliday's (1985) notion of verbal Range.

Halliday claims that certain processes construct with certain arguments that "define [their] co-ordinates, so to speak"; these arguments he calls range elements. A range element "specifies the range or scope of the process" (134). Processes may be "material, behavioral, mental and verbal" and the range element may or may not refer to a real-world entity. Halliday's examples include *climbed the mountain, sing a song, play the piano, take another quick look*, and *ask a silly question* (1985:134–137).

Nuclear scope landmarks have the same defining function as Halliday's range elements. They define the coordinates of the verb by providing contexts that circumscribe its domain of reference. Halliday's range elements are very similar to John Du Bois's "predicative objects," discussed in chapter 6 (section 6.3). But as explained in chapter 4, the difference between a predicative object prop and a contextual prop is one of orientation. Object props are represented as entities subsumed by the verb. Landmark props are represented as independent circumstances or reference points.

Halliday's notion of range seems to capture this independent property of landmarks and their special case-relation to the verb.

For material processes, or physical activities, the nuclear scope construction is likely to express spatiodirectional meaning and the range landmark is likely to refer to a concrete entity. We can see this in the examples in (9). There, P-prepositions predicate some directional or locational state for the activity (*breathing*, *looking*, or *shaving*), and the state is defined in terms of some delimiting object (the tube, the recording, or the fenders).

However, the verb-preposition construction usually refers to nonmaterial processes: for example, believing, talking, depending, and planning, as in the examples of (10). The preposition, therefore, refers in an abstract, nonspatial domain, and the landmark is also likely to refer to an abstract entity, such as a proposition, a hypothetical condition, or a plan.

In short, the nuclear scope verb-preposition construction, like other case-marking constructions, represents a basic experiential gestalt. But this gestalt is grounded in the cognitive, rather than the physical, domain of human experience. It provides speakers with a conventional way of defining and mapping out the referential domain of mental processes.

We are now in a position to address certain issues which have not been clearly explained in previous accounts of P. These are, first, the perception of verb-preposition sequences as somehow transitive; second, their status as two-word or inseparable verbs; and third, the apparent arbitrariness of lexical choice for prepositions in these sequences.

The issue of transitivity was raised in chapter 2 as part of the syntactic "problem of P." It was explained there (section 2.1.2) that passivization did not work very well as a test for preposition versus particle categoriality, since some prepositional phrases could pass the test and others could not. In Chapter 3 (section 3.2.2), Torben Vestergaard's analysis of semantic roles for landmarks was invoked to address this problem. On his continuum, the sequence impose on (which patterns like believe in, depend on, etc.) involves the prepositional object in a central participant role. This account, which effectively represents the prepositional object as an argument of the verb, would explain the apparent transitivity which allows the sequence to be passivized. Thus, we could say *you shouldn't be imposed on / depended on / talked about*, and so on. This transitivizing effect has been noted as a persistent phenomenon for verb-preposition collocations throughout the history of English (Visser, 1984:390).

Although Vestergaard's account is helpful in explaining the transitivity of verb-preposition sequences, the label central participant is less helpful. It seems strange to assign a label normally reserved for subjects, agents, and patients to prepositional objects, which in both the contemporary and traditional literature would normally be labeled oblique or peripheral. In other words, it obscures an important distinction between patients, which are not case-marked in English, and obliques, which are. At the same time, Vestergaard's label does reflect the transitivizing effect of the preposition, which has also been noted by F. Visser (1984:390).

I think, however, that this transitivizing effect can be explained less controversially as an effect produced by the characteristics of the verb-preposition construction itself. As a nuclear scope sequence, it brings the preposition into tight construction with the verb; and as an essentially linking sequence, it brings the landmark along with it. Furthermore, these sequences are lexicalized to some extent; certain verbs are conventionally constructed with certain prepositions, so that depend is usually followed by on, talk by about, and so on. These prepositions do not contribute much independent semantic content since their function is essentially to link.

The syntactic effect is that of a two-word verb (consisting of the verb itself and a predictable, semantically insubstantial P-form), which requires a following argument. That argument, as a range element, contributes specificity to the verb, and specificity, as Paul Hopper and Sandra Thompson (1980) point out, is a semantic feature that increases the transitivity of a predication. Thus, the verb-prepositional construction has the syntactic and semantic characteristics of a transitive sequence, and passivization will be possible in those contexts where it is pragmatically appropriate (see Shibatani, 1985, for a pragmatic analysis of the passive construction).

Hopper and Thompson argue that transitivity is a continuous rather than binary property for clauses, and this argument is supported by the verb-preposition construction, which seems to share the low transitivity that Halliday assigns to middle clauses with range objects. Note that, in some cases, the linking preposition can be dropped in a verb-preposition construction, which produces a more prototypically transitive sequence and renders the following argument a direct object rather than a landmark.

(11)   If you believe in that
       → If you believe that

(12)   It wasn't at all what she had planned on
       → It wasn't at all what she had planned

Even in these invented utterances (11 and 12), however, the direct object is not a central participant of the clause. It still functions semantically as a range element, defining the referential domain of the verb, and does not carry the patient-like semantic feature of affectedness typically associated with transitive objects. Although I hesitate to base any arguments on invented utterances (an introspective procedure which I have previously criticized as dangerous), I would point out an interesting distinction between the meanings of the transitive and prepositional alternatives in (11) and (12).

In Roget's Thesaurus, one finds synonyms for the verb plan that are different from those for the verb-preposition sequence plan on. Plan has such synonyms as "intend," "resolve," and "aim," while plan on has synonyms such as "figure on," "count on," "bank on," and "bargain for." The feature captured by the first set of synonyms, which is missing in the second, is clearly one of volition. Intend, resolve, and aim all suggest a certain imposition of the actor's will on the situation at hand. In contrast, figure on, count on, and bargain for all suggest a more reactive process — a response to circumstances. Volitionality, like specificity and affectedness, has been proposed by Hopper and Thompson (1980) as a semantic feature that increases transitivity. However, the authors do not explain what it is about the addition of a preposition that adds volitionality to a verb.

I believe the question can be answered quite simply from the perspective of the present study. What the preposition contributes is an orientational dimension. It defines the process (of planning, in this case) in a particular way, which represents the range element as an independent circumstance. In an iconic sense, the prepositional sequence marks a separation between the activity and the circumstances defining it. In contrast, the more transitive construction represents the range element as a predicative object, incorporated by the activity. Actors may naturally be assumed to have more volitional control over their activities than over the surrounding circumstances. The semantic feature of volitionality therefore emerges naturally from the speaker's choice of a transitive verb construction over a verb-preposition construction. This choice is determined by the speaker's subjective perception of the activity involved.

Returning to the problem of P, we can also now address the perception of verb-preposition sequences as inseparable phrasal verbs. This perception is evident in several studies, including Betty Azar's notion of "inseparable phrasal verb" (1989), Arthur Kennedy's "verb-adverb combination" (1920), W.P. Jowett's "phrasal verb" (in Sroka, 1972), Visser's "verb-preposition" compound (1984), and Roderick Jacobs's "prepositional verb" (1993).

The perception is problematic because, as I mentioned previously, it suggests some functional commonality with verb-particle sequences, which have also been called two-word verbs, phrasal verbs, verb-adverb combinations, polyverbs, and "multi-word verbs" (Vestergaard, 1977).

The problem is that these studies do not explain why verb-preposition sequences are inseparable. Even more problematical, Jowett includes verb-preposition sequences such as <u>look at</u> in the same category with verb-particle sequences such as <u>pick up</u> on the grounds that both display a common "lexical indivisibility" (in Sroka, 1972: 182:4); but he does not address the point that the two kinds of sequences pattern quite differently (see chapter 3, section 3.2).

I propose that the indivisibility of verb-preposition sequences is imposed by their construction under nuclear scope and by their lexicalized nature. Both of these characteristics bind them as transitivizers to the verb.

But this kind of indivisibility is very different from that of a verb-particle construction, where the particle either co-predicates with the verb under core scope (as a focal predicator) or situates the verb itself (as an Aktionsart marker; see section 8.4.4). Like verb-preposition constructions, certain particles tend to collocate with certain verbs in semilexicalized sequences such as <u>pick up</u>. But these particles have a focal status in the verb phrase and contribute their own predicative meaning. This is precisely why they are separable or movable. As we saw in the previous chapter (section 7.6), particle movement is a pragmatic strategy for focusing the particle in isolation from the verb complex. This is why they pass the NP-insertion test and verb-preposition sequences do not (see table 2.1).

Finally, the present account of the verb-preposition construction sheds some light on the issue of apparently arbitrary preposition selection. Learners of English tend to be frustrated by this arbitrariness. They can find no meaningful principle to help them remember, for example, that <u>believe</u> must be followed by <u>in</u> rather than <u>on</u>, or <u>depend</u> by <u>on</u> rather than <u>in</u> — or <u>of</u>, or <u>from</u>, for that matter.

Although the present analysis may not make the learning task any easier, it can at least reassure learners that, in fact, the choice of preposition really doesn't matter very much. Semantically, the preposition carries little meaning. Its main function is to link; in fact, an erroneous choice would make very little communicative difference.

This point is supported from a historical perspective by the fact that verb-preposition collocations have changed frequently over the last few hundred years. Obsolete uses include <u>depend of/in</u>, <u>yearn to/towards/after</u>, and <u>think to/on/upon</u>, among many others (Visser, 1984:392–393). What remains constant over time, however, is the function of these prepositions: to link the verb to a range landmark.

One more prepositional construction remains to be identified under nuclear scope, which I will label the qualifying construction.

8.4.3. *The Qualifying Construction*

This highly productive construction can actually be identified as a subset of the verb-preposition construction, but it has a very specialized function and generates meanings that extend beyond those normally associated with P-forms. Some examples are given in (13).

(13) a. If you're <u>spending in the ''hundreds of 'dollars a 'month</u>   (R:9)

  b. <u>'spending under ''300 dollars a 'month</u> ,   (R:9)

  c. [C: They go how fast?]
   G: <u>Over a 'hundred miles an ''hour</u> .   (A:37)

  d. . .Usually it <u>takes about a ''teaspoon</u> ,   (C:6)

This construction also links the verb to a range landmark: <u>spending</u> is delimited by <u>hundreds of dollars</u>; <u>go</u> by <u>a hundred miles an hour</u>, and so on. What distinguishes the preposition as a qualifier is simply that the range landmark refers to an expression of quantity or measurement.

I identify this type of sequence as a distinct construction because of its great productivity as a template for unusual P-meanings, all associated with quantities and measurements. Thus, the landmark of <u>over</u> denotes a minimum amount, the landmark of <u>under</u> a maximum amount, and the landmark of <u>in</u> a sort of "ballpark" estimate.

Particularly productive in this template is the preposition <u>about</u>, which is now far more frequently used as a qualifier than as a spatiodirectional preposition. In fact, I will argue in the next chapter that <u>about</u> has become syntactically reanalyzed in this function and is no longer recognized as a preposition but as a sort of qualifying adverb. This element can be constructed with almost any expression of quantity or measure, in any syntactic slot under any scope of operation, to express a sense of uncertainty and approximation about that quantity or measure, as in (14).

(14) a. . .'Usually it 'takes <u>about</u> a teaspoon ,
   That's <u>about</u> all the 'water they can ''get in their 'lungs ,   (C:6)

  b. 'She said 'they're <u>about</u> . . . fifteen years ''behi=nd ,
   in their ''medical 'literature ,   (R:24)

  c. 'Took you <u>about</u> ''fifteen 'seconds ,   (C:27)

Note, however, that despite its apparent reanalysis, one thing remains constant for <u>about</u>, as well as for other P-forms used as qualifiers: its function of linking to a range landmark. Much more attention will be given to the reanalysis of <u>about</u> in chapter 9.

So far, we have considered only linking constructions under nuclear scope. I now turn to a significant situating construction: Aktionsart marking. This verb-particle construction has received a great deal of attention in the literature because of its peculiar meanings and constraints.

8.4.4. *Aktionsart*

Aktionsart is defined by Brinton as "the character of a situation named by the verb" (1988:3). Aktionsart constructions, often referred to in the traditional literature as separable phrasal verbs, are illustrated in example (15).

(15) a. 'Took her ten 'stitches to sew the ''arm up .   (U:19)

b. . .I 'checked the ''ashtray out 'first .   (U:85)

c. When we 'clean up the ''table it'll˜˜   (R:34)

d. I'll 'find out in a ''second .   (U:8)

e. 'helping out with this other department that 'needed [help] ,   (R:18)

f. . .an you can ''open it [*"it"* = *dummy's shirt*] ,

. .open 'up an make 'sure so you can ''feel ,   (C:13)

In this construction, the particle takes the verb as its trajector and situates it in a metalinguistic domain of reference. The particle does not refer to a core argument; thus, the arm is not predicated as up, the ashtray is not out, and the table is not up, in any sense. Rather, these states are predicated on the verb itself, to denote a sense of goal orientation or accomplishment.

Like verb-preposition sequences, Aktionsart sequences involve certain types of verbs with certain particles in conventional collocations. But they are only semilex-icalized: the selection of the correct particle is more semantically significant for particles than it is for prepositions in verb-preposition collocations. For example, clean up in (15b) would make no sense as clean down; *it's burning up* is not in-terchangeable with *it's burning down*; and, even though up and out are both said to express a sort of perfective, completive meaning known as "telicity" (Brinton, 1988:182), we cannot assign them freely to any verb: fade out is acceptable, for example, but *fade up is not.

Much attention has been given to the meanings of telic particles, and several studies have attempted to map their meanings as semantic extensions from the spa-tiodirectional domain (see especially Kennedy, 1920; Bolinger, 1971; Lindner, 1981; Brinton, 1988). Kennedy, for example, assigns a sense of "motion to a certain posi-tion or standard" to up, a sense of "diminution" to down, and a sense of complete "removal" or "exhaustion" to out (1920:19–24). These differences would explain the subtle attitudinal differences between burn up, burn down, and burn out. Such se-mantic extensions will be traced more fully in chapter 9. The main point here is that Aktionsart particles, although removed from the physical spatiodirectional domain, do have semantic content: they predicate different kinds of states for the verb.

The Aktionsart template is highly productive in generating new meanings from the construction of particles with different verbs. The most frequent type of Aktionsart meaning is telicity, and its markers are overwhelmingly up and out. In the corpus for this study, <u>up</u> is used as a particle 132 times in total, and <u>out</u> 114 times, as compared with the next most frequent particle <u>over</u>, which is used only 71 times. Many of these particles occur in Aktionsart constructions. In this corpus, the sequences in (16) are produced by combining a verb with only one Aktionsart particle — <u>up</u>; all of these sequences generate a new meaning for the verb complex.

(16)   hook up, end up, wake up, sign up, divide up, open up, break up, cover up, crack up, fix up, wise up, screw up, mess up, fuck up, heat up

The productivity of the Aktionsart construction is also evident from Mario Pelli's (1976) statistical analysis of verb-particle combinations in American literature written over the last two hundred years. Pelli's counts show that, after core scope adverb sequences such as <u>walk in</u> and <u>climb up</u>, Aktionsart sequences are by far the largest verb-particle group (see also chapter 5, 5.6.1).

Brinton very carefully defines a telic situation as one in which "there is a process leading up to a goal as well as a goal" (1988:26). It must involve both durativity and goal orientation. Brinton suggests that the prototypical Aktionsart construction involves a telic particle added to an activity, turning it into an accomplishment by adding a necessary endpoint:

> In its two-way structure of simple verb (naming an activity) and telic particle (equivalent to an achievement) the phrasal verb in fact provides evidence for the bipartate semantic structure of the aktionsart category *accomplishment*. (1988:184)

However, in the present data there is only one example that matches Brinton's prototypical description (15a). All the other instances of telic particles seem to be constructed with verbs of achievement (referring to punctual events) or accomplishment (referring to processes with inherent endpoints), as in the sample listed in (16).

This finding appears to tell us something significant about the semantic contribution of the telic particle. It suggests that directional extension rather than endstate is central to the meaning of the telic particle. A punctual achievement verb such as *hook* has no inherent feature of extension, but the particle <u>up</u> contributes this extension, in effect, turning a punctual event into a goal-oriented process. For an accomplishment verb such as <u>clean</u>, which already implies goal orientation, the particle makes this orientation explicit or makes a covert endpoint overt (Lindner, in Brinton, 1988:174–175). This property of directional extension will be examined more fully in chapter 9.

Telic particles, then, situate the verb in a very specific way. Much as the verb-preposition construction maps out the verb's domain of operation by linking it to a range element, the particle situates the verb in a sort of teleological space of directed purpose. The particle predicates an extended, evolving state on a verb that would not otherwise be understood in this extensional way.

For example, the verb <u>clean</u> by itself would not necessarily communicate the sense of a process being carried out to satisfaction, but <u>clean up</u> does, thereby imposing the speaker's subjective evaluation on the semantics of the situation. The following conversational sequence in (17) shows how this works.

(17)   An ''I'm goan <u>clean up</u> the 'm=ess ?
       (. . . . .)
       So ''now ,
       'after he ''left ,
       I'm <u>cleanin ''up</u>, right ?
       (. . . . .)
       I 'left my 'garbage pail in his ''hallway ,
       I <u>cleaned</u> and I 'left my 'garbage pail in the ''hallway .   (U:2)

In this sequence, the speaker's first two mentions of <u>clean</u> come shortly after a sequence where he has been belaboring the point that it wasn't *his* job to clean up. Therefore, *cleaning up* here is represented as a significant process requiring some time and effort. The particle helps to make this covert message clear, by giving the process more space, as it were. But his third mention of <u>clean</u> merely represents a summary of his preceding actions, a sort of transition to the next part of the story. In this context, the internal structure of the cleaning process is irrelevant, so it is simply represented as a punctual event, with no directional extension; there is no need for an Aktionsart construction.

In its two <u>clean up</u> mentions, the sequence in (17) offers a perfect example of what Paul Hopper would call a MAVE, a multiply articulated verbal expression. Hopper's discourse-functional analysis of eventhood defines a MAVE as comprising

> an open-ended array of ideas closely associated with the verb and serving, not to report an "event" in any simple way, but to combine an account of what is being reported with a set of epistemic attitudes and perspectives, in other words to *construct* an account of "what happened" with a view to coopting the listener/reader into the narrator's perspective. (1995:146)

Although Hopper's study does not deal explicitly with verb-particle constructions, they have clear potential as MAVEs. In particular, the verb-situating capabilities of the Aktionsart construction are custom-made for the subjective construction of events from the speaker's point of view.

In the literature, Aktionsart constructions have sometimes been lumped together with caused motion events as resultative sequences. Dwight Bolinger, for example, claims that Aktionsart particles have "simply traded their full resultative meanings for the bare meaning of 'result achieved' " (1971:96). Laurel Brinton disagrees with this interpretation for at least two good reasons. First, it doesn't work with nonspatially referring particles, since "*to chop up mushrooms* [does not mean] 'to cause mushrooms to be up by chopping.' " Second, result is only expressed "when the particle is in semantic 'focus' or 'predicative' position" — thus, *he wiped the window off* "seems marginally more resultative" than *he wiped off the window* (1988:179–182).

Brinton's account ties in neatly with my own arguments presented in chapter 7 (section 7.6) about the focal significance of particles in end position; however, I would disagree with the interpretation of her second example as "resultative." After all, *the window* is in no sense *off* as a result of wiping. The apparent incongruity between verb-particle constructions that express result and those that do not can be explained more simply as a difference in their syntactic scope of operation.

Resultative and caused motion events operate under core scope, and Aktionsart particles operate under nuclear scope. The function of the former is to predicate states on core participants, which are likely to undergo a change of physical state as a result; but the function of the latter is to predicate states on the verb, where no such resultant state is visible in any physical sense. This distinction between nuclear and core scope construction thus allows us to clarify one more apparent idiosyncracy of P's meanings, not as an incongruity but as a principled consequence of P's participation in this construction.

Moving on from telic particles, we find an essentially nontelic kind of meaning contributed by Ps such as <u>on</u> and <u>around</u>.

(18) a. . .there isn't that . . . I 'guess that 'joking ''around ,   (R:21)

     b. . .and it 'keeps ''on .   (U:12)

Brinton states that technically, particles contribute continuative aspect rather than durative Aktionsart. The distinction between the two meanings need not be entered into here. The main point is that these particles (Brinton adds <u>along</u>, though it does not occur as an Aktionsart particle in the present corpus) fit within the Aktionsart template to generate a special extensional meaning to the verb. In these sequences (18), extension is added to typically unbounded activities: <u>joking</u> is represented as an ongoing, iterative process in (18a), while <u>keeps</u> works as a semantically unspecified verb denoting nothing but an ongoing event. The general sense is one of nonpurposefulness.

<u>Around</u> is particularly productive as an Aktionsart particle. It can transform the meaning of a wide variety of verbs into a general sense of non-goal-oriented activity. Combinations found in this database include <u>fooling around</u>, <u>shitting around</u>, <u>traveling around</u>, and <u>goof around</u>.

<u>On</u> also predicates extended activity, but it lacks the explicit aimlessness of <u>around</u>. It tends to refer more to temporal than to teleological space and to apply to activities that may be purposeful but which are extended beyond the expected endpoint. In this database we find <u>keep on</u>, <u>carry on</u>, <u>hang on</u>, and <u>go on</u>.

What both telic and continuative particles have in common is their orienting function. They situate the verb metalinguistically by extending its reference over an implicit frame. The frame may represent teleological space (i.e., purpose-space), as with telic particles, or temporal space, as with continuative particles. But the frame is always subjective, representing the speaker's attitudes and expectations rather than external perceptions. And it is always implicit; it is never lexicalized as a landmark.

8.5.   Peripheral Scope Constructions

P-sequences under peripheral scope situate a whole clause rather than a clause element. The clause is construed as the trajector of P. The domain of reference is therefore metalinguistic, expressing orientation for linguistic "chunks" rather than physical entities. The components of these chunks may refer in the spatiodirectional domain or to temporal and logical relationships. The general function of these sequences is to provide text-level orientation by connecting pieces of text together or by directing the interlocutors from one frame of reference to another.

Special P-constructions under peripheral scope include subordination, text-transitional phrases, and deictic marking. But first, we will consider some sequences where P's independent meaning is more easily recoverable.

Most of the peripheral sequences in the conversational corpus are linking sequences that require prepositions. Their landmarks typically frame a clause within a spatial, temporal, or evaluative-subjective setting. To the extent that the P-preposition has semantic content, it may also situate. In fact, since these sequences operate under peripheral scope and do not construct with a verb, the P-form is the main predicator. But, as with case-marking constructions, they have a crucial linking function and therefore prohibit sublexicalization of the landmark. They include the following examples.

(19) a. [and] . .'lock themselves in a 'stall ,
          and ''die !
          In the ''bathroom .   (C:32)

      b. And then they moved in , with my Dad's parents] ,
          ''i=n ,- in ''Atlanta .   (R:4)

      c. Y'know in an 'emergency 'situation 'it's a 'lo=ng ''time .   (C:5)

      d. 'You know, ''we'd been 'married three 'years by then and˜˜ .   (R:22)

      e. 'You'd be . . . eh ''ou=t ,
          after ''tha=t ,   (R:24)

In (19), single clauses or clusters of clauses are linked by the underlined P-form to some kind of setting or reference point. The landmark offers a defining context which is somehow focal for the speaker's meaning. For example, the bathroom in (19a) defines the type of event that the CPR instructor is warning her trainees about. Her point is that they should never let a choking victim escape to a remote place. It is *because* the victim is in the bathroom that she dies.

In (19b), the landmark Atlanta, as a newly introduced setting for the narrative, moves the discourse from one frame to another, much as a television or cinematic plot is moved from one episode to another by camera shots of new settings and locational frames. In this way, the speaker is able to construct the steps of the story about his mother's immigration to America.

An emergency situation in (19c) is a subjective frame, expressing the speaker's evaluation of the situation. It provides an explanatory condition that justifies the proposition in the main clause.

Finally, in (19d) and (19e), the landmarks summarize a series of events and situations that the speaker has just recounted, in a single temporal reference point — then or that. These sequences therefore have multiclausal trajectors that are contextualized metalinguistically.

Notice that all these landmarks have the interesting syntactic option of fronting to the beginning of the P-unit, as in (19c). The discourse-pragmatic effect of fronting is to give the prepositional phrase a pivotal function, similar to that which Cecilia Ford

(1993:65) points out for utterance-initial adverbial clauses: the phrase links back to a previous proposition and forward to the framed one.

It is under this scope that we most often find prepositional phrases set off in separate intonation units, as in (19a) and (19b). In chapter 6 (section 6.6), I interpreted this prosodic pattern as an iconic strategy for marking landmarks as independent circumstances. Prosodic separateness is especially appropriate for these clause-peripheral constructions. They operate as global discourse orienters, lumping episodes together into contextual frames or moving us from one setting to another.

A special subset of peripheral linking sequences is represented by the subordinating construction. Here, the preposition takes whole clauses as both its trajector and its landmark.

8.5.1. *Subordinator*

In this construction, the preposition functions as a subordinator by situating one clause in relation to a temporal, enabling or otherwise circumstantial clause.

(20)   a. But 'I was there ''<u>before</u> 'he was ,   (U:26)

   b. 'One thing we ''do need to find out '<u>before</u> we watch the ''film ,   (C:3)

   c. Okay ? You're checking for unresponsiveness ,
       And '<u>after</u> you 'call for ''help ,
       ''Remember ,
       'Major 'force on the ''forehead .   (C:8)

   d. . .they ''learn <u>by</u> 'looking at the 'lights ,   (C:21)

   e. . .'He's being 'ethnocentric <u>by</u> ''doing that .   (E:10)

   f. It's 'no=t just <u>in</u> . . . 'laying people ''o=ff ,   (R:20)

The construction may involve either finite clauses (20a–20c), or nonfinite clauses (20d–20f), as its landmark. In the former case, the landmark would traditionally be labeled a subordinate clause construction, with the preposition as a conjunction. In the latter, the landmark would be called a gerundial complement to the preposition. These dichotomous labels, however, do not capture the functional and syntactic parallel between the two kinds of sequences. Nor do they suggest any explanation for the use of the same word as a preposition and as a conjunction. By interpreting subordinating uses of P as a logical consequence of P-construction under peripheral scope, we can solve this particular problem of categorial indeterminacy for P-forms.

For finite-clause landmarks, the most prevalent pattern involves the P-forms <u>before</u> and <u>after</u> as temporal prepositions. The prepositional phrase may come after the trajector (20a) or be fronted (20c). For nonfinite clauses, a variety of prepositions may be used, including <u>through</u>, <u>about</u>, and <u>on</u>, as well as those exemplified in (20d)–(20f).

Although these P-forms and landmarks refer to the external world of time and circumstances, the type of orientation achieved here is once again metalinguistic: P links linguistic elements like clauses and propositions rather than externally referring entities. The purpose is to organize propositions in relation to each other, to assist discourse navigation.

P-forms co-occur in the subordinating construction with adverbial conjunctions. Several of these conjunctions also establish links with circumstantial clauses and double as prepositions in other syntactic contexts (e.g., since, as, like). Therefore, these forms also contribute orientation, athough their meanings do not originate in the spatiodirectional domain. The rhetorical, discourse-cohesive functions of these conjunctions are discussed in detail by Christian Matthiessen and Sandra Thompson (1988) and Ford (1993).

Other subordinating constructions have a nonorienting function: for example, the complementizer that, which represents the subordinate clause as a participant rather than as a circumstance (Givón, 1980). Thus, the present model for P-constructions helps us see more clearly their relationship, not only to each other but also to other, nonorienting constructions that co-occur with them and may sometimes be confused with them under a single label such as "subordinator."

A more abstract type of metalinguistic meaning is generated by P-prepositions in the text-transitional construction, which refers entirely to text relations.

8.5.2. *Text-Transitional Phrases*

Text-transitional prepositions link to a clause that defines logical text relations rather than space and time relations. The trajector may be a single clause or an episodic cluster of clauses. The specialized function of this construction is text-cohesive. It generally takes the unit-initial, pivotal position, since the landmark provides a textual bridge between the previous discourse and the following situation. We can see how this works in example (21).

(21)　. .In ''particular ,
　　　 this ''one kid I 'remember was ,
　　　 . . . he was in a (. .) ''road 'accident ,　　　　　　　　　　　(C:20)

The landmark, expressed by particular, bridges the previous discourse episode with the upcoming anecdote. In this way the speaker helps his hearers see the logical connection between what has been said and what he is going to say, by framing the anecdote within a context of particularity.

Notice that in this example the landmark particular is not a noun, as we normally expect. This phenomenon is not unusual for text-transitional sequences — we also find, for example, in short, in brief, and others. The interesting thing is that, within this constructional template, the appearance of an adjective as a landmark is acceptable — no native speaker would consider the sequence ungrammatical. Goldberg (1995:159) claims that the syntactic template of a specialized construction can "coerce" meaning for semantically incongruous elements, allowing, for example, a locational word to be interpreted as a directional one. It seems, however, that the construction can also coerce categoriality for a syntactically incongruous element, allowing an adjective (in this case) to be interpreted as a noun.

Other conventional text-transitional collocations include on the other hand, in fact, in a sense, on reflection, and so on. Interestingly, very few of them appear in the conversational corpus for this study. I will return to explain this point shortly. In traditional grammar, these sequences would be labeled adjunctive phrases, disjuncts, and conjuncts (Quirk et al., 1972).

Although the text-transitional construction itself is productive, the sequences within it tend to be lexicalized: each of the preceding examples represents a well-known formula, of the type that might be defined as a *transition* in any composition textbook. Each of them expresses a specific discourse purpose for the speaker: to establish a contrast, to elaborate a point already made, or to evaluate it. The preposition, as a purely linking element, carries little semantic content. The significant meaning of the phrase is carried by the landmark.

The rhetorical significance of this construction is well established. In composition textbooks, several pages are likely to be devoted to text transitions and the kinds of logical relationships they express. Any academically oriented speech class for learners of English is likely to emphasize the importance of these transitional phrases in text cohesion for showing our hearers "where we are going" in our construction of meaning. Thus text-transitional constructions perform discourse orientation at the syntactically highest, supra-clausal level of rhetorical organization.

However, my data suggest that this construction is less common in conversation than in written composition. In fact, the example in particular (see 21) is the only clear instance identified in this corpus. Most of the peripheral linking sequences involved spatial or temporal setting landmarks rather than textual ones.

Even more surprisingly, I could find no examples at all of text-transitional particles. Yet we know from experience that they exist, at least in written discourse — most commonly to refer to preceding or following paragraphs, as in the invented examples in (22).

(22)   a. Consider the exmaple which I gave above.

       b. I will explain this phenomenon below.

In these examples, the particles above and below have the text-cohesive function of situating the preceding clause (the example which I gave or I will explain this phenomenon in relation to the surrounding text.

It may seem odd that my data reveal such a scarcity of text-transitional prepositions and particles. But these findings, though not initially obvious to our intuitions, make a lot of discourse sense. Text-cohesive P-forms are necessarily more significant in written discourse than in conversation because written discourse is constructed in a very different way.

First, writing is a solitary exercise. Writers have primary responsibility for managing information flow since they cannot rely on their interlocutors to finish their sentences, elaborate their points or otherwise participate in the co-construction of meaning. Furthermore, their "turns" are much longer, so internal cohesion needs to be very explicit. Their readers cannot ask clarifying questions about logical connections or the direction of the argument. Even at the sentence level, coherence needs to be planned; writers cannot resort to repairs, new starts, or truncated utterances if they sense that a sentence is somehow getting out of line. Therefore, the need for special-purpose text-orienting devices is fundamental in written discourse. Text-transitional phrases serve this need: they allow the writer to specify and focus significant logical frames which package ideas in relation to one other.

Second, written text is visible. We can see it on the page and refer to its spatial dimensions, which are neatly delineated by means of sentence punctuation and paragraph layout, with titles and numbered headings as signposts. Therefore, spatially referring particles such as above, before, and below can be used as convenient directional devices to point the reader from one piece of text to another.

In speech, meanings are constructed on-line and interactively. Interlocutors may switch topics, insert digressions, and build on one other's utterances at any point. Text cohesion is still important, especially in narration; we need to signal shifts to a new episode or refer back to a previous one. But this kind of orientation is more likely to be performed in the predication of new spatial or temporal settings, as in (19). Just as the watcher follows a movie plot from one visual frame to another, so the hearer follows a narrative plot from one discourse frame to another, assisted, where necessary, by the prosodic signaling of separate P-units. Therefore, the specific pragmatic requirements of conversation as opposed to written text explain the different types of peripheral constructions employed by these genres.

The only productive particle construction to be identified under peripheral scope in my data is deictic marking.

8.5.3. *Deictic Marking*

Deictic marking sequences direct the hearer's attention from their present position or location in the discourse to another. The most productive type of deictic marking in these data was identified under peripheral scope, in the spatiodirectional domain of reference. However, I did find one example of a temporally referring deictic particle (23).

(23)   um . .so it 'sounds like most of you guys have ''ha=d , CPR ,
     . . . ''before ,   (C:2)

The effect of the particle before is to situate the preceding clause in the past, to predicate a state of anteriority on it. Though I could find no examples, afterpresumably serves a corresponding function by predicating posteriority. Both these P-forms were used more often as prepositions than as particles, however, which perhaps attests to the significance of framing and contextualizing at this global level of discourse organization.

A far more common use of peripheral-level particles in these data is illustrated in (2).

(24)   a. An=d she got 'stationed in ''Germany ,
       . .where my ''Dad was 'stationed and ,
       . .<LAUGH> they got ''married .
       Over ''there .   (R:3)
     b. He got 'barred from running ''go karts,
       over in ''Tiffen .   (A:14)
     c. One guy came out and 'bet him twenty dol-''bucks , he could 'beat his ''snowmobile .

... On 'dry ' 'la=nd .
'Out on the 'damn ' 'blacktop .   (A:35)

   d. Can 'you guys ' 'see <u>over there</u> ?   (C:7)

Notice that these underlined examples juxtapose the situating function of the deictic particle with the linking function of a preposition, and refer in the spatiodirectional domain. The effect is to direct the hearer's attention away from the present (implicit) context toward a new one that is being introduced by the prepositional phrase.

These P-particles (<u>over</u> or <u>out</u>) situate their clause trajectors directionally, by designating a path over a sublexicalized space from "here" to "there." In each example, the situating particle is followed immediately by a prepositional phrase or a pronominalization of a prepositional phrase (the pronoun <u>there</u> in (24a) means "in Germany" and "in that corner" in (24d). The preposition shares the same clause-level trajector with the particle but links it to a defining or framing context.

Thus, the syntactic relation between the particle and the prepositional phrase is one of apposition or parataxis — both elements operate under peripheral scope. Notice, however, that the particle seems to assist the linking construction as an optional elaboration. In each case, the speaker could conceivably drop the particle: *they got married there, he got barred in Tiffen,* and so on. But then a certain degree of orientation would be lost and the new settings would seem rather incongruous. The speaker seems to judge in each case that his or her hearers need a pointer to clarify the contextual shift from "here" to "there."

The prepositional phrase, in contrast, is not optional. The sequence could not occur grammatically without it (e.g., *They got married over*). The main focus in each utterance is on the new context being introduced, not on the deictic particle.

Although the deictic marking construction occurs most frequently under peripheral scope, where it is particularly useful for higher-level discourse organization, it may also operate under core scope and NP scope (NP scope will be defined and explained in the following section.

(25) *Core Scope*:

   (a) You're ' '<u>over</u> there 'visiting ,   (R:3)

   (b) Of course 'he has to 'take it ' '<u>down</u> there .   (A:32)

   NP Scope:

   (c) There 'used to be a 'place <u>up</u> in ' 'Toledo that'd 'make em for you .   (A:31)

   (d) And 'then they'll come over to ' 'this field <u>over</u> here .   (R:32)

In (25a)–(25d), the deictic particle situates an argument rather than a clause. But it serves the same purpose as in the peripheral sequences of (24), redirecting the hearer's attention from "here" to "there," thus preparing them, as it were, for the introduction of a new context by a linking preposition.

By identifying this construction, we have resolved one more issue of categorial indeterminacy for P (see chapter 1, section 1.1). As far as I know, deictic particles have not been explicitly discussed in the P-literature. In traditional grammar, they would be categorized as "adverbs." But that label tells us little. It does not explain how forms such as <u>over</u>, <u>up</u>, and <u>out</u>, traditionally interpreted as verbal adjuncts, can end up in contexts where they do not modify a verb; it does not tell us why they always seem to be compulsorily followed by a prepositional phrase in these contexts. The answer to these questions is found in the syntactic versatility of P-forms, which allows them to perform orientation under any syntactic scope with almost any constituent.

8.6. NP Scope

Under NP scope, P refers narrowly to a NP-argument, which it takes as its trajector. Unlike P-forms in core scope constructions, this P does not co-predicate with the verb. Rather, its orienting function is contained within the structure of the NP. Linking sequences under NP scope postmodify the noun, and the corresponding situating sequences premodify it.

8.6.1. *Postmodifier*

The underlined sequences in (26) represent postmodifying prepositional phrases.

(26)   a. In fact this one woman we know just died of cancer ,
            . .who . .went to the doctor there , with <u>a-a ''lump , in her ''breast</u> .   (R:24)
         b. If they're 'all 'Keegans like <u>the ones around ''Greensprings</u> ,   (A:14)

The functional overlap between this construction and the category of adjective is readily apparent. We could rephrase both of the sequences in (26) as compound nouns with the landmark in prenominal, adjectival slot: "a breast-lump," "the Greensprings ones." This overlap comes about because, under NP scope, P-constructions elaborate the meaning of the NP-referent in some way, and this function is similar to that of the adjective (see Thompson, 1986, for a discussion of the predicative function of adjectives).

However, the difference is once again in the feature of orientation. The postmodifying prepositional phrase identifies the referent (<u>a lump</u>, <u>the ones</u>) by defining its situation in relation to a significant context (<u>her breast</u>, <u>Greensprings</u>). In contrast, the adjective defines an attribute, a self-contained property of the entity itself, such as size and color.

8.6.2. *Premodifier*

Corresponding to the postmodifying prepositional sequence, we find a premodifying particle sequence.

(27)   you know laid 'off a . . . 'bunch of . . . 'really high <u>up</u> ''people ,   (R:19)

This premodifying particle use looks even more adjectival than the prepositional use in (26), since it is represented by one word in adjectival slot. We could substitute "important" for <u>high up</u> and get away with it, perhaps. But, once again, we would lose orientation, which is particularly important in this context where the identity of the <u>people</u> is only relevant in terms of their superior position within a certain company.

It is fairly unusual to find a particle placed in front of the trajector it situates; in fact, I only found one example of a premodifier among the 132 instances of up in this database. But, in view of the common predicative function shared by particles and adjectives, it is not surprising that a particle should occasionally find itself in adjectival slot, when its function is to predicate a state under NP scope. Several conventional collocations exist to perform this function — for example, the in group, the out group, and the down side.

Therefore, the identification of P-constructions under NP scope helps once again to resolve an issue of categorial indeterminacy or overlap between the functions of P and the function of adjective.

Finally, the identification of a new scope for P-constructions — the scope of P itself — will help us directly to answer one of the teasers raised at the beginning of this chapter and explain why we cannot say *I threw it out the room.

8.7.   P Scope: The P-Compound Construction

This scope is not mentioned by the RRG framework. However, I identify it, following RRG principles, as one in which the trajector is a P-form itself. The construction identified here is the P-compound, where a prepositional phrase links the particle to a defining context. The result is a (particle+preposition+LM) sequence, as illustrated in (28).

(28)   a. I've got ... ''two 'cousins who are ... out of ''work at the 'moment   (R:5)

   b. and some languages just ... 'hang 'o=n to that ''tendency .   (R:16)

   c. 'I'll have it 'run up to ''five pounds 'pressure .   (U:95)

   d. I have 'two ''cats | I'd like to turn in to the ''Humane 'Society .   (U:81)

I identify these sequences as compounds because of the close construction between particle and preposition. The particle essentially predicates a direction or an endstate, and the following prepositional phrase defines the locational dimensions of that state. The linking phrase typically involves a non-P, case-marking preposition such as of or to, which cannot predicate direction by itself or occur as a particle. In a sense, then, its function resembles that of a core scope case marker or a nuclear scope range marker, except that it contextualizes a state rather than a core argument or a verb.

To my knowledge, no previous studies have offered this syntactic/semantic interpretation for sequences such as those in (28). Such sequences tend to be overlooked, or the particle-preposition collocations are simply labeled as "two-word prepositions." But they occur too frequently to be overlooked, and the label begs the question as to why two words should be required to form a preposition.

A more specific and intriguing question is why most uses of the P-forms out or up almost always require the insertion of a case-marking preposition. I found only one example of each P-form used directly as a preposition in my data, out of 132 occurrences of up and 114 occurrences of out. In other words, as I asked in the introduction to chapter 1: Why can we say *I threw the cat out the window*, but not **I threw the cat out the room/house/car?*

The semantic literature has not satisfactorily answered this question. Bruce Hawkins (1984) views <u>out of</u> as a preposition with a source-referring landmark and does not list <u>out</u> as a preposition at all; yet we know that <u>out</u> can be a preposition, from sequences such as the one in example (29).

(29)   Whyncha 'just 'throw em <u>out</u> the ''window .   (U:78)

Sue Lindner (1981) views <u>out</u> and <u>up</u> as prepositions that may sublexicalize their landmarks, and, like Hawkins, she suggests that the landmark of <u>out</u> refers to a source, constituting some kind of enclosed space. Thus, for *John threw the cat out*, Lindner suggests that the sublexicalized landmark refers to a source "capable of containing a cat, e.g. a house or a car" (1981:62).

However, this suggestion is problematic, for we cannot grammatically lexicalize the landmark and use <u>out</u> as a preposition in this context: **John threw the cat out the house* is unacceptable. We have to insert <u>of</u> after <u>out</u>. Furthermore, in those contexts where it would be acceptable to use <u>out</u> as a preposition, the landmark does not refer to a containing source. For example, in (29), the cat is not contained in the window before it gets thrown out.

A similar problem exists for <u>up</u>. Lindner suggests two different kinds of possible landmarks: a Path (as in *The cat climbed up the tree*) and a goal (as in *He rushed up and said hello*) (1981:112, 139). The path interpretation works for a prepositional rendering of <u>up</u> but the goal interpretation does not. We cannot say **He rushed up the stranger and said hello*. For a goal landmark to be expressed, we would have to insert <u>to</u> after <u>up</u>.

In a footnote, Lindner does suggest that, while prepositional and particle <u>up</u> sequences both have the "same potential landmarks," they differ in that path landmarks are more salient in prepositional phrases whereas goal objects are more salient in particle constructions (1981:196, n.7). However, salience is not defined (as pointed out in chapter 7, section 7.1) and the distinction does not explain why <u>to</u> should be required for the expression of goal landmarks.

For <u>out</u> constructions, Lindner claims that the source landmark may refer either to "an enclosed area or some opening in the boundary of the enclosed area" (1981:196). She says that <u>of</u> may be added to prepositions with the "enclosure" landmark to represent the trajector as a "subpart of the area enclosed" (1981:197). But again, this does not explain why <u>of</u> must be inserted in order to make the prepositional phrase grammatical, when other directional prepositions (e.g., <u>through</u> and <u>over</u>) may simply express their different types of landmark without any inserted element.

I suggest that this problem of necessary preposition-insertion may be solved by interpreting <u>up to</u> and <u>out of</u> as particles with case-marking prepositional phrases under their scope. There is no need to posit alternative types of landmark for <u>up</u> and <u>out</u>. Their landmark is, in each case, an extensional, directional path. When this landmark is required as a defining context, it will be lexicalized, as in the following adprep examples.

(30)   a. She'll cl-''try to ''climb <u>up</u> your ''leg man .   (U:83)

b. Whyncha 'just 'throw em <u>out the ''window</u>.   (U:78)

Goal referents do not serve as the landmark of <u>up</u>, nor do source referents serve as the landmark of <u>out</u>. Under this interpretation, some apparently idiosyncratic constraints become regularized, so that <u>up</u> and <u>out</u> resemble any other P that may occur with or without a following landmark. But since directions and paths, in human experience, are very often associated with sources and goals, it is not surprising that we frequently find these particles associated with source and goal landmarks. The preposition <u>of</u> has a specialized function as a partitive case marker for source landmarks, and <u>to</u> has a specialized allative case-marking function for goal landmarks. This explains why <u>out</u> is often collocated with <u>of</u> and <u>up</u> is often collocated with <u>to</u> in naturally ocurring discourse.

The data counts reveal, in fact, that <u>up</u> and <u>out</u> occur far more often with source and goal arguments in P-compound constructions than with their own path landmarks. Thus, we very rarely see them as prepositions. In chapter 9, I explain this phenomenon as an effect of their specialization as situating rather than linking elements. For now, however, we can simply identify the P-compound construction as a template for expressing a very basic experiential gestalt: exit from source, or progress toward goal. The particle situates the trajector directionally, and the preposition links it to the relevant starting-point or end-point.

<u>Up</u> and <u>out</u> are the most frequently occurring particles in the present database. But other particles may also construct with case-marking prepositions, as we see in the <u>on to</u> and <u>in to</u> sequences in (28b) and (28d). We are now in a position to address another interesting phenomenon: the tendency of certain P-forms to conflate with non-P-prepositions, into new prepositions (e.g., <u>onto</u>, <u>into</u>, and <u>upon</u>). These conflations emerge naturally from the P-scope construction. The particle in each case denotes direction, and the prepositional landmark denotes goal. These particular conflations are represented orthographically as one-word forms, but <u>up to</u> and <u>out of</u> could also be viewed as common conflations in conversation (together with, in some dialects, <u>off of</u>). This, no doubt, accounts for Hawkins's intuitive interpretation of <u>out of</u> as a two-word preposition.

The identification of the particle-scope construction allows us to regularize one apparently irregular P-pattern — the compulsory insertion of prepositions after many uses of <u>up</u> and <u>out</u> — and to unify these words with other P-forms. It also identifies an important morphological source for the generation of new prepositions.

8.8. Conclusion

The preceding discussion has elaborated the constructional framework summarized in table 8.1. That framework shows how linking and situating P-constructions generate new meanings at all levels of constituency, and how they are related to one other. In the course of the discussion, we have resolved many of the issues left open in the previous literature (see chapters 2 and 3), under a unified account of P-forms as orienting elements.

8.8.1.   *Syntactic Tests Revisited*

We can now explain the results of the syntactic tests presented in chapter 2 — both the tests that work effectively, and those that do not (see table 2.1).

Tests A1–A4, B3, and B5 are concerned with the tendency for prepositions to construct with following landmarks and particles to construct with verbs. Now we can explain the reason for these tendencies. Prepositions construct with following landmarks because their job is to link these focal landmarks to the clause; particles construct with verbs because they either predicate focal states on the verb itself (as in Aktionsart constructions) or co-predicate them with the verb on core arguments (in focal predicator constructions). The ungrammatical test sentences in A1–A4 and B5 fail because they break up the constituency of these constructions, separating landmark from preposition or particle from verb.

However, notice that A1 is a bad test. It does not work because we could produce a verb-particle sequence that would pass the conjunction reduction test: *We turned the blue lights off and the red lights on*. This sentence is grammatical because, as focal predicative elements, particles may be separated from their verbs and moved to sentence-final position, where they are stressed (see chapter 7, section 7.6). We see this pattern in B3. The conjunction reduction test is therefore misleading in suggesting that particles may not be separated from verbs. A better interpretation of its results would be to say that, if particles are to be separated from verbs in verb-particle constructions, then, as focal predicators, they should follow the elements which they situate (e.g., the stereo in A1).

The results of the other tests may also be explained as logical constraints on linking versus situating constructions. For example, in A5 we can sublexicalize the road (a landmark) but not the light (a trajector), because the light is the core argument that off, as a focal predicator, is situating. In contrast, the road, as the landmark of an adprep, may be optionally sublexicalized.

However, adpreps are the only prepositions allowing NP-ellipsis, or sublexicalization. The test will not work, for example, with case-marking prepositions (*I was sitting on*) or for verb-preposition constructions (*I believe in*). In contrast, many particle P-constructions will pass the test: it is quite possible to say *I cleaned up (the room)* or *They took over (the company)*, in any context where null-complementation (or direct object ellipsis) is appropriate.

Thus, the very examples intended to distinguish prepositions from particles in A5 reflect instead their functional overlap in the adprep category.

Passivization (test B1) is unusual for landmarks in adprep constructions such as the one here because of their function as defining circumstances rather than as clause participants (see chapter 6). This makes them unlikely candidates for topicalization in subject position, which is the purpose of the passivization strategy. However, as explained in chapter 2 (section 2.1.2), passivization is grammatically possible even for landmarks, depending on the pragmatic purposes of the speaker. It is particularly possible for verb-preposition constructions, which have a transitivizing effect on their verb. Therefore, this test is no more foolproof than the others in distinguishing prepositions from particles.

The verb-substitution test (B2) reflects diachronic phenomena, which will be examined in chapter 9, but we can explain here why it doesn't effectively distinguish prepositions from particles. It makes sense that we can often find simplex paraphrases for verb-particle constructions (e.g., "exit" for turn off), given the tendency for particles to co-predicate with verbs and form semantic units with them. But we can also find simplex paraphrases for verb-preposition constructions (e.g., "consider" for think about, or "investigate" for look into). This is because prepositions in these nuclear-scope constructions also form inseparable semantic units with the verbs they collocate with.

Finally, the stress-marking patterns of test B4 are explained by the focal status of particles versus the nonfocal status of prepositions (see chapter 7, section 7.5.2). The first example of on for this test involves a focal predicator particle, which situates the button. The second involves a preposition under nuclear scope, which simply links the verb sew to its range landmark dress.

In short, under an orienting account of P, these piecemeal syntactic tests of P's constituency, which have challenged linguists for so long, become as unnecessary as they are ineffective. There is no need to test posthoc the distinctions between prepositions and particles because these distinctions are predictable consequences of their respective situating and linking functions in different constructions under different scopes.

8.8.2. *Semantic Solutions Revisited*

We can also return to the unresolved issues from the semantic literature reviewed in chapter 3. As I concluded there, semantic accounts of P's constituency leave us wondering why prepositions and particles show different syntactic behavior. That question has now been answered.

For Lindner's (1981) account of verb-particle constructions, the present analysis has explained not only the reasons for landmark sublexicalization but also the constraints on it. For Vestergaard's (1977) hierarchical account of prepositional constructions, it has resolved his apparently arbitrary dismissal of particles from the hierarchy. For RRG's layered clause structure (Foley and Van Valin, 1984), it has elaborated additional scopes to accommodate P-constructions that the RRG framework has not accounted for. It has also recast the problematic RRG distinction between predicative and nonpredicative prepositions (Jolly, 1993) by showing how nonpredicative (i.e., purely linking) functions can be performed under all scopes.

8.8.3. *Summary*

Finally, the framework proposed in this chapter allows us to answer the tricky questions introduced at the beginning of this chapter.

1. *Categorial extension*: A particle such as up may overlap with an adjective or a predicate adjective when it performs the similar function of predicating a state on a noun, under NP or core scope. The difference is in what it predicates: a relatively defined state rather than an attribute.

2. *Phrasal verbs*: For inseparable phrasal verbs such as think about, prepositions collocate with verbs under nuclear scope. The linking function of the preposition has a transitivizing effect on the verb, which accounts for the inseparability of this verb-preposition construction. For separable phrasal verbs such as think over, particles co-predicate with verbs or predicate states on them, thus also forming semantic units with them. In addition, as elements with focal status, they can be moved to sentence-final position, which marks this status.

3. *Nonspatial meanings*: Inseparable prepositions function as Range-marking elements for nonmaterial processes and have little independent meaning of their own. Separable particles in Aktionsart constructions (e.g., burn up, burn down) predicate various perfective or telic states.

4. *Idiosyncratic patterning*: *I threw it out the window* expresses the path landmark of out. **I threw it out the room* expresses a source landmark, but this is not the landmark of out and must therefore be introduced by a separate preposition of.

Only a few questions remain from chapter 1. However, these questions raise the significant issue of specialization for certain P-forms in particle or preposition uses, which in turn opens a window to P's status as a constantly changing element. These considerations are the focus of chapter 9.

9

The Historical Picture:
P and Specialization

Chapter 8 mapped out a grammatical framework showing how P's many constructional meanings could be contained and its syntactic idiosyncracies explained, by its interactions with other constituents at different syntactic levels. The unifying principle for these interactions was that particles always situate and prepositions always link.

But one significant question remains from chapter 1: Why are all prepositions not P-forms? We have seen that pure prepositions such as <u>of</u> share the case-marking function with P-prepositions, and that pure particles (or directional adverbs) such as <u>away</u> share the focal predicator function with P-particles. But neither of these pure types of element ever shares the adprep function with P: <u>of</u> never sublexicalizes a landmark, and <u>away</u> never lexicalizes a landmark.

Related to this question is the one raised in chapters 3 and 8: Why do even P-forms seem constrained in their alternation as particles or prepositions? For example, we saw that <u>up</u> and <u>out</u> hardly ever function as prepositions, whereas <u>in</u>, <u>on</u>, and <u>by</u> rarely function as particles. This issue of skewed distribution has not been addressed by either semantic or syntactic "solutions" to the problem of P.

And — to return to a much smaller question from chapter 1 — we still have not seen why simplex paraphrases such as "extinguish" and "ascend" exist as formal alternatives for combinations such as <u>put out</u> and <u>climb up</u>. Nor have we found a motivation for the "lexical creativeness" (Bolinger, 1971:xi) that produces so many meanings for a sequence such as <u>make up</u>.

All these questions are essentially historical ones. To answer them, we need to examine P from a diachronic perspective, discovering how its meanings have evolved and specialized over time. The grammatical template of chapter 8 is explanatory, but only in a static sense. Like the semantic networks proposed by other studies, it maps out meanings but does not reveal how they emerged or how they are still changing.

This last, dynamic piece of the puzzle is presented in this chapter. It explains that P's semantic evolution is driven by the pragmatic requirements of situating and linking. It reveals prepositions and particles as elements in a constant state of extension from spatiodirectional meanings to progressively more specialized and (in some cases) grammatical types of orientation.

Chapter 9 begins with the problem of skewed distribution for certain P-forms and shows that the semantic structure of these P-forms offers a clue to their specialization as either particles or prepositions. In the light of universal grammaticization principles, it then hypothesizes a unidirectional pattern of semantic extension for P-forms.

This hypothesis is supported by four lines of argumentation: first, from the typological literature, which reveals a similar pattern for P's counterparts in unrelated languages; second, from the diachronic literature on P's Indo-European ancestors, which reveals the same; third, from the documented history of certain P-forms and (non-P), grammaticized prepositions; and fourth, from the synchronic variation found in the conversational corpus for this study (in chapter 8).

The last section of the chapter involves an internal reconstruction from the conversational data, which traces probable paths of extension step-by-step from core scope spatial meanings to more abstract meanings under other scopes. This reconstruction supports the unidirectional hypothesis, by illustrating it in these naturally occurring data and by revealing the pragmatic purposes and cognitive processes which facilitate the shift from one meaning to another.

My typological and diachronic approach in this chapter to the problem of P serves not only to answer remaining questions about English prepositions and particles but also to show how their orienting function fits into the big picture of language universals and language change.

9.1.   Particle and Preposition Specialization

We now turn to the skewed distributions of certain P-forms in the conversational data, originally presented in table 3.1 (in chapter 3).

9.1.1.   *Particle/Preposition Distributions*

As was noted already in chapter 3, before the detailed examination of the intervening chapters, P-forms do not occur randomly as particles or prepositions, even under core scope. They show a marked preference for either preposition or particle forms, occurring far more frequently as one than as the other, and indicating a specialization in either situating or linking functions.

A significant correlation was observed ($P = .002$) between these overall P-frequencies and the P-frequencies for each of the four longer conversations, according to the Spearman rank-order correlation coefficient. The correlations are summarized in table 9.1. The only conversation whose P-frequencies did not show a correlation with the overall rankings in table 3.1 was E, a very short sequence involving only twenty-six P-units and about five minutes of speech. Therefore, we can conclude that the same P-forms occur with much the same frequency across the four longer conversations in the present corpus.

Table 9.1: Correlations between Overall P-
Distributions (Table 3.1) and P-Distributions
per Conversation in the Database

Conversation	Total P-units	Correlation (r/s)
C	496	0.97
R	275	0.78
U	225	0.86
A	223	0.09
Total	1,219	

To confirm the representativeness of these conversations, the frequency rankings in table 3.1 were checked against W. Nelson Francis and Henry Kučera's (1982) word frequency analysis for American English. A significant correlation of .85 ($P = 0.002$) was found. As a second check, my rankings for P-forms in American conversation were compared with those of a word frequency analysis for British English words (Johansson and Hofland, 1989). A significant correlation of .78 ($P = .002$) was found between my rankings and theirs. Thus, we can be satisfied that the relative frequencies of P-forms in the present study are representative of the English language in general.

9.1.2. *Theoretical Implications of Distributions*

On examining the distributions of individual P-forms, we find some very interesting patterns, some of which are counterintuitive and none of which, as far as I know, has been addressed in previous accounts of P-forms.

As noted previously, *all* the eleven most frequently occurring Ps in this corpus are skewed, in some cases heavily, toward either prepositional or particle realization. Of the twenty Ps coded in this study, I have excluded nine from table 3.1 because their numbers were too small (fifteen tokens or less) to justify any generalizations about them.

A theoretical point raised by these results is that we can easily make false introspective guesses about how our native language is used. This issue was raised in chapter 4 (section 4.1), where it was explained that although by has often been treated in the literature as a noncontroversial particle (Live, 1965; Talmy, 1975, 1985; Dixon, 1982), both my frequency counts and those of Francis and Kučera reveal that it is hardly ever used in verb-particle constructions such as *pass by* or *go by*.

The same point is true for after. I had expected to find particle examples, as in the well-known nursery rhyme "And Jill came tumbling after." However, the real-life findings revealed that after is almost never used as a particle, according to both the 1982 findings and my own. The lesson to be learned is that corpus-based linguistic analysis may often reveal discourse realities that would not be revealed by intuitive analysis based on memory.

In fact, to my knowledge, the previous literature has not discussed this issue of specialization at all. In an early study, Anna Live's (1965) grouping system for P-forms implies that some are more likely to be used as either prepositions or particles;

but she does not explore the issue and, like later scholars, simply concludes that "most of the common prepositions double as adverbs" (1965:432).

However, I think that the pattern of P-specialization is a significant one for any cognitively oriented linguistic analysis. If our intention is to reveal insights into how speakers actually use language, we should not fail to consider questions of frequency and distribution. Without such consideration, any conceptual map of P's potential for polysemy would be abstracted from reality, telling us little about how that semantic potential is actually exploited or why.

The most frequent P-forms in table 3.1 are associated with a wide variety of constructional meanings in abstract as well as spatiodirectional domains: text-transitional phrases, range marking for nonmaterial verbs (in verb-preposition sequences), or Aktionsart (see chapter 8). These same P-forms are also among the most heavily skewed or specialized. This suggests that although these P-forms have the potential for particle-preposition alternation, the potential is channeled into constructions that perform either situating or linking functions, but generally not both. In other words, these forms reinforce either their situating or their linking function as they participate in specialized constructions beyond the spatiodirectional adprep construction.

In the next section, we will see that the semantic structure of certain P-forms facilitates their use in nonspatial meanings. I will propose that it is the situating or linking requirements of particular discourse contexts that drive and constrain these meanings.

9.1.3. *Semantic Structure and Specialization*

From a Cognitive Grammar perspective, Bruce Hawkins (1984) provides a detailed description of the semantic structure of English prepositions. His descriptive inventory includes most of the P-forms in this book. Hawkins identifies three basic parameters of variation within the meaning of any preposition: trajector configuration, landmark configuration, and the relational factors holding between them.

Trajector configurations involve "specific topological and geometric properties" (1984:64) — for example, directionality on a bounded or circuitive path for the trajectors of out and around. Landmark Configurations are less specific, and are defined in terms of their "relational potential" (64) — for example, the medium configuration denotes potential inclusion of the trajector by the landmark and is therefore a property of in. The two basic relational factors that may hold between trajector and landmark are coincidence and separation; thus, in has properties of coincidence and out has properties of separation. These three parameters are highlighted against a background, or base, which users understand implicitly. For example, by refers implicitly to a scale of distance in its connotation of proximity; and up and down refer implicitly to a domain of oriented physical space, with negative and positive polarity, respectively.

Hawkins's descriptive inventory provides a useful nomenclature for analyzing the semantic structure of the most skewed P-forms in table 3.1. We can start with those forms that specialize as particles.

9.1.3.1. PARTICLE PS   If we examine those Ps in table 3.1 that specialize as particles in terms of the semantic properties assigned to them by Hawkins, we find that

they all have one thing in common: they all highlight "significant extension" for a determinate trajector path (1984:89). Significant extension means that the trajector's state evolves in space rather than being confined to one point. This extensional property facilitates the expression of directionality, of temporary states and changes of state, of goal-orientation: in short, of all the meanings that are associated with the situating constructions in chapter 8 of this book.

Table 3.1 shows that the most specialized particle Ps are up, out, down, off, and (to a lesser extent) over and around. If we consider the constructions where these Ps are most often used, we can see how their situating potential is exploited.

First, all these particles may be used for Aktionsart marking. The first four mark telicity, over marks iterativity, and around marks continuation, as illustrated in example (1).

(1) a. (They'll) 'chew up all my ''material .   (U:94)

    b. I s-'checked the ashtray out 'first but ,   (U:85)

    c. and they 'keep breaking the 'building ''do=wn ,   (U:32)

    d. His 'wife ran 'off with 'Bill ''McCann .   (A:26)

    e. Just to goof around with .   (A:32)

Up and out, almost exclusively "particle Ps," are overwhelmingly the most productive in their Aktionsart meanings. These meanings are a popular subject of study in the literature (Kennedy, 1920; Bolinger, 1971; Pelli, 1976; Lindner, 1981; Lakoff, 1987; Brinton, 1988), although it is interesting to note that the extreme specialization of up and out as particles rather than prepositions has not been questioned in these studies. Similarly, Hawkins's study includes up unquestioningly as a preposition, with no mention of its improbable use in this form; and Sue Lindner (1981) offers such sentences as *the cat climbed up the tree* as prototypical instances of the use of up. Lindner points out that "the real differences" between particle and preposition collocations "lie at the level of the construction," in the way that its component elements are "'hooked up' to each other" (1981:195). However, she does not address the fact that up is almost exclusively "hooked up" as a particle, so that sentences like the prototypical one here are very unlikely to occur.

Some clues to this extreme specialization come from the semantic properties of up and out. Both P-forms qualify semantically as particularly useful elements for situating other constituents in discourse. For example, if speakers want to situate activities and events, they may exploit the positive polarity properties of up to express a sense of gradual progress toward an endpoint, as in (2).

(2) a. (They'll) 'chew up all my ''material .   (U:94)

    b. Don't 'wise her ''up,
      she's 'liable to ''do it .   (U:19)

In contrast, they may want to situate an event in a different way, exploiting the unadulterated separation property of out to express a sense of gradual differentiation from an original state, as in (3a), or a sense of exhaustiveness, a process being carried to its final stages, as in (3b).

(3) a. Because the ''super didn't put a 'bulb on the 'second floor ,
         and it's '<u>burnt</u> ''<u>out</u> ?   (U:1)

     b. I s-''<u>checked</u> the ashtray <u>out</u> 'first but ,   (U:85)

Different Aktionsart meanings are expressed in (4) by the other particle Ps: <u>down</u>, <u>off</u>, <u>over</u>, and <u>around</u>.

(4) a. and they 'keep breaking the 'building ''<u>do=wn</u> ,   (U:32)

     b. His 'wife ran '<u>off</u> with 'Bill ''McCann .   (A:26)

     c. 'clean out ''everything . .and start ''<u>over</u> again .   (C:6)

     d. Just to goof <u>around</u> with .   (A:32)

All of these Ps express significant extension in different ways. In (4a), <u>Down</u>, like <u>up</u>, contributes a sense of progress toward a goal, but with "negative polarity," adding a sense of reduction and destruction rather than of incrementation and construction, to the verbal process. <u>Off</u>, according to Hawkins, has an "initiative" path property as well as a relational factor of "separation"; together, these properties express removal from a state of contact or connection, as in (4b). <u>Over</u> expresses unbounded direction in relation to a horizontal surface. This property may be exploited to situate an event like <u>start</u> in (4c) as evolving over a path already followed: as George Lakoff explains, "the landmark is understood metaphorically as an earlier completed performance of the activity" (1987:435). Thus, the Aktionsart meaning is one of iterativity (or repetition). Finally, in (4d), <u>around</u> has a crucially nonrectilinear path property that allows the interpretation of unbounded, undirected activity in its function as a continuative aspect-marker).

Several of these particle Ps are also associated with another essentially situating construction: deictic marking. As explained in the last chapter (section 8.5.3), this construction often involves the juxtaposition of a particle with a prepositional phrase, as the examples in (5) illustrate.

(5) a. There 'used to be a 'place <u>up</u> in ''Toledo that'd 'make em for you .   (A:31)

     b. [He could beat his snowmobile] ,
        . . . On dry la=nd .
        '<u>Out</u> on the 'damn ''blacktop .   (A:35)

     c. [And they got married ,] <u>over</u> ''there .   (R:3)

     d. He's got a 'friend <u>down</u> in ''China ,   (R:28)

Since the discourse function of deictic constructions is to direct the hearers' attention to a new context, the crucial property shared by all these P-forms, other than extended path, is the relational factor of separation. This property is exploited to produce discourse pointers from "here" to "there."

Note that the exploitation of a P-form's situating properties in a special-purpose construction such as Aktionsart or deictic marking does not prevent the exploitation of its linking properties in another construction such as the adprep sequence. Table 3.1 shows that <u>over</u> and <u>around</u> are less specialized than the other particle Ps, occurring as prepositions 24% and 34% of the time, respectively. Hawkins's inventory reflects this, by indicating that these P-forms highlight certain landmark configuration properties in addition to their trajector paths. <u>Over</u> implies a horizontal surface configuration. <u>Around</u> implies a medium landmark configuration representing inclusion by the landmark, and also an indeterminate landmark configuration, representing the landmark as a nondimensional point rather than an extensional space.

Thus, <u>over</u> and <u>around</u> highlight some properties appropriate for situating and others that are appropriate for linking. This reflects their tendency to be used in adprep constructions under core scope. Even when used as particles to predicate Aktionsart-like states of telicity or continuation, the landmark is fairly recoverable, at least metaphorically, from the spatiodirectional domain.

(6)   a. So 'once you initiate 'care you 'need to 'follow ''<u>through</u> .   (C:3)

     b. [It's a lot of fun ,]
        shittin '<u>around</u> around the ''track .   (A:21)

The semantic structure of preposition Ps similarly qualifies them for linking constructions, as we will now see.

9.1.3.2.   Preposition Ps   Preposition Ps in table 3.1 include <u>in</u>, <u>on</u>, <u>about</u>, <u>by</u>, and <u>through</u>. With the exception of <u>about</u>, all these forms are tagged in Hawkins's inventory with landmark configuration properties which, I propose, facilitate their use in specialized linking constructions.

The most frequently occurring Ps in the database, <u>in</u> and <u>on</u>, both take prepositional form more than 80% of the time. They are associated with such linking constructions as verb-preposition sequences, postnominal modification, and text-transitional phrases. Two significant properties shared by these Ps are the relational factor of coincidence (as opposed to separation), and an indeterminate trajector configuration. Trajectors with an indeterminate configuration have no "significant extension in any dimension": in other words, this kind of configuration "is not really a configuration at all. It actually represents the absence of any configurational information" (Hawkins, 1984:89). I suggest that such a property is very appropriate for constructions like verb-preposition and text-transitional phrases. In such sequences, the landmark itself, rather than the preposition, defines the dimensions of the situation being predicated (chapter 8, sections 8.4.2 and 8.5.2). For example, if you *believe in* an idea, that idea defines the range of your belief; and for the transitional phrase <u>in particular</u>, the particularity of the upcoming idea is the circumstance that delimits its content. In both cases, the trajectors of the constructions (<u>believe</u>, or the upcoming idea) are viewed not as extending in space but as contained and framed by their landmarks.

The landmark configurations highlighted for <u>in</u> and <u>on</u> are "medium" and "surface," respectively. Medium denotes a potential for inclusion or containment, and surface denotes contact, contiguity, or support. Again, these properties facilitate P's function of expressing links with various kinds of landmark, such as the range landmarks in the following verb-preposition constructions, which metalinguistically support or contain the processes denoted by the verbs:

(7)   a. It wasn't at 'all what she had ''planned <u>on</u> .   (R:3)

     b. I=f 'you believe <u>in</u> ''that ,   (U:31)

Coincidence, inclusion, and contiguity are also important semantic features in postmodifying constructions, which often define part-whole relationships, as in (8a), or in case-marking, which introduces locative settings for core-scope arguments, as in (8b):

(8) a. [. .who . .went to the doctor there],
         with a-a "lump , <u>in</u> her breast .   (R:24)

     b. You're 'right ''o=n him ,   (C:22)

Thus, <u>in</u> and <u>on</u>, in their specialized linking constructions, exploit relational factors and landmark configurations rather than trajector configurations.

After these two forms, the most frequently occurring prepositional P is <u>about</u>, with sixty-six tokens. <u>About</u> presents an especially interesting case. First, it has no clear particle tokens in this corpus. As with <u>in</u> and <u>on</u>, <u>about</u> is often used as a range marker in verb-preposition constructions (9a and 9b) and also as a qualifier meaning "approximately" (9c and 8d) (see chapter 8, section 8.4.3 for an explanation of this construction).

(9) a. Well 'tell me <u>about</u> your ''classes .   (R:14)

     b. <OH> don't ''worry <u>bout</u> it .   (R:24)

     c. That's <u>about</u> all the 'water they can ''get in their 'lungs , (C:6)

     d. 'She said 'they're <u>about</u> . . . fifteen years ''behi=nd ,
         in their ''medical 'literatu=re ,   (R:24)

Despite clearly prepositional uses, as found in (9a) and (9b), Hawkins does not include <u>about</u> in his inventory. I believe this may be because <u>about</u> is so frequently used in its specialized qualifying function, as in (9c) and (9d), and so rarely for spatiodirectional meanings (in American English), that its lexical categoriality is not transparent. In fact, Francis and Kučera (1982) tag the qualifying use of <u>about</u> as adverbial. And yet, as we see from the preceding examples, <u>about</u> is a crucially linking element. All of its sixty-six tokens in the present corpus are followed by some kind of definitional landmark, whose sublexicalization would be ungrammatical. I will return to examine this P-form subsequently as a clear case of grammaticization and categorial reanalysis.

For the moment, however, I propose that the semantic structure of <u>about</u> involves an indeterminate landmark configuration (the landmark is viewed as a reference point rather than an extended path), together with a relational factor of either radial separation or radial coincidence (which Hawkins also posits for <u>around</u>), and a base implication of proximity.

These properties are exploited to express a variety of meanings, all of which involve the notion of general proximity ("more or less close") to a reference point. That reference point may be a range, as in the (9a–9b) verb-preposition constructions, a maximal limit, as in (9c), or a chronological point, as in (9d).

<u>By</u> is the most predominantly prepositional P-form after <u>about</u>, occurring as a preposition 89% of the time. This is the only P-form in the present data which more often occurs under peripheral scope (46% of the time) than under core scope (40% of the time), a phenomenon that reflects its specialization in text-cohesive

and metalinguistic meanings. As the following examples show, it typically provides extra-clausal links to (10a) nonfinite (gerundial) clauses, (10b) time phrases, (10c) passive agents, or (10d) text-transitional references to the discourse itself.

(10) a. 'He's being 'ethnocentric by ''doing that .   (E:10)

     b. and by ''then ,
        it was so far ''alo=ng that ,   (R:24)

     c. You know Coo-'Cooper got asked this 'question by this ''German guy ,   (E:4)

     d. 'This is an 'international sign of ''choking by the 'way .   (C:32)

The crucial semantic properties of by for all these meanings include, first of all, its indeterminate, "point-in-space" landmark configuration. This is appropriate for expressing landmarks as circumstantial reference points (see chapter 6, section 6.5 for M.A.K. Halliday's (1985) interpretation of passive agents as circumstances). Second, by expresses the relational factor of separation, with proximal distance in the base, thus facilitating the interpretation of landmarks as separate from but closely linked to the trajector clause. These properties are what distinguish by from other P-forms such as in and on, which represent landmarks as inclusive or contingent frames in their peripheral, text-cohesive meanings.

    Finally, through, also primarily prepositional (65% of the time in these data) is described by Hawkins as having the properties of unbounded trajector path and medium landmark configuration, with a relational factor of minimal coincidence. All these properties are commonly exploited in the present corpus, either in adprep constructions, where situating and linking are performed equally, or in focal predicate constructions, where the sublexicalized landmark is recoverable from the context. We see examples of both in (11). Even in (11d), where through contributes a kind of telicity to the verb follow, the landmark is more transparently recoverable (as, perhaps, *the procedure*) than in most Aktionsart constructions.

(11) a. What's 'bad is they could send a 'bullet right through the "window .   (R:32)

     b. It's a 'nice place to ''live . .and ''grow 'up , or . . . ''drive through 'you know it's ,
                                                                                (R:34)

     c. 'maybe you can 'hand them th- . .''through , 'I'll take ''one and˜˜   (R:10)

     d. so 'once you initiate 'care you 'need to 'follow ''through .   (C:3)

Through is therefore less specialized as either a situating or linking element than most of the P-forms examined to this point. It also tends to be used more in compositional, spatially referring sequences under core scope than in metalinguistic or text-cohesive constructions under nuclear or peripheral scope.

9.1.4. *Summary*

The preceding analysis shows that certain P-forms have certain semantic properties which customize them for use in either situating or linking constructions. These properties persist at all syntactic levels and in all semantic domains of reference.

    But semantic analysis alone does not explain the heavily skewed distribution of certain P-forms. It does not tell us why these potentially situating or linking properties should be abstracted, in effect, from the full range of properties in the semantic structure of one P-form and reinforced in special-purpose constructions where other, less relevant properties are trimmed or reduced. We know, after all, that particle Ps such as <u>out</u> can, in rare cases, link, and prepositional Ps such as <u>in</u> can predicate directional states (12).

(12)   a. Whyncha 'just throw em <u>out</u> the ''window .   (U:78)

      b. 'throw him <u>in</u> the goddamn ''furnace,   (U:94)

    I propose that the patterns of specialization shown in table 3.1 reflect a historical process of pragmatic strengthening. In this process, speakers, finding the semantic properties of a spatially referring P-form effective for a certain orienting purpose, exploit these properties again and again for similar orienting purposes in a wide variety of semantic domains. This collective and habitual exploitation over time fixes certain P-forms as either situating or linking elements, producing the skewed patterns of distribution reflected in the data of this study.

    The principle of pragmatic strengthening is well established in current grammatization theory. So is my interpretation of "synchronic language states as states in a diachronic process" (Svorou, 1994:62). Furthermore, if we examine English P-forms in the predictive light of grammaticization theory, we can form a reasonable hypothesis about the direction of their pragmatic strengthening.

9.2.   Grammaticization Principles

9.2.1.   *Synchronic Variation and Diachronic Change*

Grammaticization (or grammaticalization) is defined by Elizabeth Close Traugott and Bernd Heine as "the linguistic process, both through time and synchronically, of organization of categories and of coding" (1991:1). In the last fifteen years or so, in the search for universal principles of grammar and language change, typologists have uncovered a series of unidirectional paths of change for certain lexical elements from relatively unconstrained expression to increasingly constrained morphosyntactic functions, or from relatively concrete to progressively abstract meanings. These paths include such developments as tense, modality, and aspect markers from main verbs (Traugott, 1989, 1990; Bybee, Pagliuca, and Perkins, 1991; Bybee, Perkins, and Pagliuca, 1994; Lehmann, 1991), prepositions from body part nouns (Claudi and Heine, 1986), causal and concessive conjunctions from temporal conjunctions (Traugott and König, 1991), or discourse-deictic pronouns from physically referring locatives (Frajzyngier, 1991).

    Traugott and Ekkehard König summarize a large body of such cross-linguistic research into three general principles for grammaticization and semantic extension. These principles are presented as semantic-pragmatic tendencies 1, 2, and 3.

    1. Meanings based in the external-described situation [become] meanings based in the internal (evaluative/perceptual/cognitive) situation.

    2. Meanings based in the described external or internal situation [become] meanings based in the textual situation.

3. Meanings tend to become increasingly situated in the speaker's belief-state/
attitude toward the situation. (1991:208–209)

These semantic-pragmatic tendencies are motivated by communicative needs, in the
constant quest for greater specification of meaning. They are facilitated by certain
cognitive processes — primarily, the processes of metaphorical and metonymic inferencing.

Metaphor involves "representing members of one semantic domain in terms
of another" (Traugott and König, 1991:212) and facilitates the shift from concrete,
physical reference to progressively abstract, mental, or textual meanings — the kind
of shift represented by tendencies 1 and 2. An example of metaphorical extension
is given by the authors in the development of prefer (a Latin-based word meaning
"carry before") from a meaning that expresses spatially oriented action to one that
expresses mental evaluation.

Metonymy involves explicitly conventionalizing a meaning which was originally
implied or covert in a particular conversational context. For example, the development
of since from temporal to causal connective can be traced as a process of metonymical
inferencing in contexts such as those illustrated in (13).

(13)   a. I have done quite a bit of writing since we last met (= temporal)

   b. Since Susan left him, John has been very miserable (= temporal and causal)

   c. Since you are not coming with me, I will have to go alone (= causal)   (Traugott and
König, 1991:194)

A context like that in (13b), where temporal contiguity also implies cause, provides
the locus for the metonymic inference. The causal meaning becomes explicit and, in
fact, replaces the earlier temporal one in a context like (13c). Metonymy, according
to the authors, is the cognitive process which facilitates tendency 3, in the shift from
objective meanings to increasingly subjective ones that serve speakers' interactive
purposes in the negotiation of conversation.

When the inferences produced by metaphor or metonymy become pragmatically
strengthened or conventionalized, reanalysis takes place: the word has a new meaning,
which may coexist with the old one to produce synchronic variation. Metaphor and
metonymy are both considered problem-solving strategies which allow speakers more
precise specification of meaning (1991:112–113). Such tendencies are found to be so
regular cross-linguistically that, according to Traugott,

it is possible to develop predictive hypotheses that can be tested against historical
data. They are sufficiently predictive that one can take synchronic polysemies from
any period in any language and project change back into the past. In other words,
one can do internal semantic-pragmatic reconstruction. (1989:31)

This is, in effect, what Traugott and König do in their juxtaposition of meanings
for since in (13). Synchronic reconstruction is also the methodology applied by Joan
Bybee, Revere Perkins, and William Pagliuca (1994), as a procedure for discovering
the origins of grammatical meanings. In their cross-linguistic analysis of tense, aspect,
and modality, these authors claim that for a grammatical element (or gram) to have
two or more synchronic uses, "implies a diachronic relation between the meaning

labels in the adjacent uses, since it is reasonable to assume on the basis of our knowledge of documented cases that one use developed after, and probably out of, the other" (1994:53).

They posit a source determination hypothesis which interacts with Traugott's semantic-pragmatic tendencies to allow more precise predictions about how certain grams are likely to evolve. According to this hypothesis, grams have inherent semantic content that derives from their earliest sources in lexically independent elements, the flavor of which is preserved throughout subsequent meanings.

The lexical origin of a gram is therefore a predictive resource in helping us trace how certain semantic nuances develop through metonymic inferencing, and new semantic domains are referred to through metaphorical inferencing.

9.2.2.   *Hypothesis: The Diachronic Extension of P*

In light of these theoretical models, the synchronic variation and specialization of P's meanings may now be interpreted as a clue to P's diachronic evolution. These meanings display the progressive range of external > internal > textual > subjective meanings produced by tendencies 1 through 3. Furthermore, in at least some contexts, each P-form functions as a lexically independent element with inherent semantic content that refers to spatial relations. But most P-forms also have more abstract meanings and in some cases special grammatical functions, such as case-marking or Aktionsart. These functions retain some of the same properties or semantic flavor as we find in their concrete spatiodirectional uses.

Thus, we can apply the theoretical principles of source determination and unidirectional extension to form a specific hypothesis for the evolution of P-forms.

1. The basic, original function of P-forms is to orient in the spatiodirectional domain under core scope. In this function, P-forms may alternate as adpreps or particles:
   They could send a bullet right <u>through</u> the window.
   They could send a bullet right <u>through</u>.

2. P-forms extend their situating or linking functions into more abstract domains in constructions under different syntactic scopes:
   When we clean <u>up</u> the table . . .
   If you believe <u>in</u> that . . .

3. In these extensions, semantic properties associated with situating and linking become pragmatically strengthened, leading in some cases to reanalysis and grammaticization:
   They're <u>about</u> fifteen years behind. (= reanalysis)
   I became less threatened <u>by</u> him. (= grammaticization)

This hypothesis will be supported in the remainder of this chapter with evidence from four different sources: first, from the typological literature, which documents similar developments for P's counterparts in a variety of unrelated languages; second, from documented historical evidence of P's evolution in English; third, from the synchronic variation observed in the data; and fourth, from an internal reconstruction of P's synchronic uses in the present conversational corpus.

9.3.   P-Meanings in Unrelated Languages

The typological literature reveals that spatiodirectional elements in many languages are susceptible to the same kinds of alternation, constructional patterns, and diachronic extension as I am hypothesizing for P-forms; the literature supports my claim that these phenomena are pragmatically driven.

The adprep/particle part of my hypothesis is paralleled by a certain ambivalence between adverbial and adpositional functions that is noted as a cross-linguistic tendency by William Croft (1990). Croft invokes Bybee's principle of iconic distance, which claims that "elements that go together semantically tend to occur close together in the clause" (Bybee, 1985:11), to explain why directionals are grouped with nouns in some languages and with verbs in others.

> One ... example of a conceptually intermediate category is directional phrases, found in sentences that express motion along a path relative to an object. In these sentences, the path is conceptually linked to the action, because motion involves change in location; but it is also conceptually linked to the object, since the path is defined relative to the object ("in," "out of," "to," etc.). Typologically, this is manifested in variation as to whether the directional phrase forms a prepositional phrase with the object noun, or an adverb or directional affix with the verb. (Croft, 1990:182)

Croft's analysis matches my own account of particles as focusing states (which may be action-related) and prepositions as linking to focused contexts, and to the consequent tendency for these forms to construct with either verbs or following landmarks. Discourse-motivated processes of verbal and nominal attraction are also amply documented in English and other languages by John Myhill (1985).

The second part of my hypothesis — namely, the extension of spatiodirectional properties into more abstract meanings in special constructions — is paralleled in several non-Indo-European languages, where the serial verb or co-verb performs many of P's situating and linking functions with similar semantic versatility. Serial verbs, depending on the language, may express directional, temporal, case-marking, Aktionsart, or clause-linking meanings (Lord, 1973; Li and Thompson, 1974; Clark, 1978; Matisoff, 1991; Givón, 1991; Svorou, 1994). The following examples illustrate the use of serial verbs as a case-marking preposition in Thai (14) and as a focal predicator in Fijian (15).

(14)   *Thai*:

    Dèk khɨɨn nansɨɨ <u>hây</u> khruu.
    Boy return book <u>give</u> teacher
    'The boy returned the book to the teacher.'   (Foley and Van Valin, 1984:199)

(15)   *Fijian*:

    E viri-<u>tū</u>-ra   na duru na tūraga
    CM put-<u>stand</u>-TR ART post ART chief
    'The chief erects the post.'   (Foley and Van Valin, 1984:262)

Other studies have traced the development of directionals into aspect markers (Bybee, Perkins, and Pagliuca, 1994; Svorou, 1994) and adpositions into subordinators and complementizers (Genetti, 1991; Lichtenberk, 1991; Craig, 1991). These findings parallel my own identification of directional particles as Aktionsart markers and prepositions as subordinators (see chapter 8).

The phenomenon of reanalysis and grammaticization for spatiodirectional elements (the third part of my hypothesis) is well established in the literature, particularly, in the notion of grammaticization chains, where spatiodirectional elements, emerging from body part nouns, evolve toward more subjective, qualitative meanings. Such chains have been documented primarily in African, Tibeto-Burman, and Oceanic languages. (Heine and Reh, 1984; DeLancey, 1984; Claudi and Heine, 1986; Heine, Claudi, and Hünnemeyer, 1991a, 1991b; Carlson, 1991; Genetti, 1991; Bowden, 1992). For example, in Ewe, Bernd Heine, Ulrike Claudi, and Friedrike Hünnemeyer propose that, through metaphorical extension, a source noun referring to a body part (back) may become a preposition or adverb expressing space and time (behind, after) and finally, an attribute denoting the quality retarded (1991b:157–164). The progression of this chain from concrete to abstract semantic domains is represented in (16).

(16)   Person > Object > Process > Space > Time > Quality
                                            (Heine, Claudi, and Hünnemeyer, 1991b)

For English, we can readily plot certain P-forms along this scale. J.T. Shipley (1984) finds the source of the word down in an original object noun meaning "grassy upland country." Before, originally referring to the brow of a person, now denotes anteriority in both space and time; and in modern English, the synchronic meanings of behind include reference to the human anatomy, to spatial location, and to a quality meaning "retarded." We have also identified up as a prenominal modifier in the present corpus (17), expressing the quality of seniority or importance.

(17)   You know, laid 'off a ... 'bunch of ... 'really high up ''people ,   (R:19)

In short, there is plenty of evidence from the typological literature that semantic extension and grammaticalization for spatial morphemes follows the extensional paths being proposed here for English prepositions and particles.

9.4.   The History of Indo-European P-Forms

There is also ample evidence from the diachronic literature on English P-forms and their Indo-European ancestors that spatial morphemes have always displayed the categorial flexibility hypothesized for the English adprep (part one of my hypothesis) and that they have extended into the same kinds of situating and linking constructions (part two).

9.4.1.   *Indo-European Ancestors*

The original P-lexeme is identified in Proto-Indo-European (PIE) as a spatially referring element that can be interpreted as either an adposition or an adverbial element under core scope. Paul Friedrich notes that spatial elements "function variously as preverbs, adverbs, prepositions and postpositions." As such, they can "stand in immediate construction with a noun ... or in immediate construction with a verb ... or modify about equally both the noun and the verb." Because of this categorial indeterminacy, Friedrich proposes that "the term 'locative auxiliary' seems apt" for this element (1975:34–35).

In Homeric Greek, spatial elements are attached to nouns and verbs as separable prefixes or as lexicalized units. They may also precede and follow verbs with varying degrees of separation. One revealing example of this variation is given for amfi, the Greek lexeme meaning "around," "about," "on both sides." In one of its functions, corresponding to the English adprep, "the locative auxiliary functions as a relatively independent predicator that is in construction with both the verb and the substantive" (1975:36).

In another type of sentence, involving landmark sublexicalization (translated as "The fire played around [the tripod])," "the locative auxiliary is prefixed to the verb" (1975:36). This directional preverb-verb construction effectively corresponds to the focal predicator construction in modern English (see chapter 8, section 8.3.1).

The same word also extends into a third, perfective meaning ("they ate up all the cattle"). Interestingly, in this function, which corresponds to telic Aktionsart marking in English, amfi is separated from the verb by several words. Thus we see in Homeric Greek the same strategy — of particle movement toward the end of the sentence — that Dwight Bolinger (1971) notes as conferring focal status on particles in modern English.

Also interesting (Barbara Fox, personal communication) is the fact that around, the English counterpart of amfi, is decidedly nonperfective, that is, nontelic, in its Aktionsart meaning. This reinforces my earlier point that the semantic properties of a given spatial word may be extended in more than one direction; however, once that direction has become pragmatically strengthened as either a situating or a linking one, it persists.

Friedrich claims a similar syntactic and semantic flexibility for locative auxiliaries in Anatolian and Sanskrit as for Homeric Greek (1975:36–37). Thus, in ancient languages we see some evidence of the same sublexicalization and focal marking strategies associated with P-alternation today, as well as the extension from directional to Aktionsart meanings that we see for English particles.

Kuryłowicz (1964) posits a historical process of differentiation for locative elements in PIE, matching my own synchronic interpretation of the extension from adprep into distinct situating and linking functions. He explains that the originally autonomous locative element, when positioned between object and verb in a sentence with subject–object–verb (SOV) word order, functions as both postposition and preverb. The same element positioned between object and verb in a SVO-ordered sentence functions as both adverb and preposition (as the adprep does in English today). Kuryłowicz sees this dual-function situation as the locus for a syntactic shift toward either case-marking or verb-modifying (= focal predicator) functions: "within a construction [(verb + adverb) + oblique case] a syntactic shift ... may entail a new articulation [verb + (adverb + oblique case)]" (1964:171). Kuryłowicz points out that total grammaticization in one function or another does not occur for a locative element unless a new, independent morpheme is brought into its place, occasioning "the formal renewal of the old adverb" (1964:). I will suggest in the following section that this is exactly what has happened in English for such pairs as <u>of/off</u> and <u>to/too</u> and is happening in American English for <u>about/around</u>.

In later IE languages, P's counterparts are documented as covering the same range of constructional meanings as in modern English, apparently with the same kind of differentiation between linking and situating functions. In Latin, for example, according to W.B. Lockwood (1968:176), locatives occur both as prepositions and as separable verb prefixes, depending on whether they are construed with the verb or with the landmark. Thus, the directional form <u>ad</u> ('to') in the sentence *ad Capuam veni* ('I arrived at Capua') functions as an adprep. But with sublexicalization of the landmark, the same directional morpheme functions adverbially (<u>ad-venire</u>, 'arrive').

Latin spatiodirectional prefixes are also susceptible to lexicalization with the verb to form new, abstract meanings. For instance, <u>sub-placere</u> (literally "under-plead") becomes <u>supplicere</u> ("implore") and *ob-ire* (literally, "because of-go") becomes <u>obire</u> ("suffer," "undergo") (Lindsay, 1894). English preserves some of these Latin lexicalizations in many cognitively referring verbs today: for example, <u>supplicate</u> and <u>obey</u>. But it paraphrases many of them with inseparable verb-preposition sequences such as <u>investigate</u> ("look into"), <u>consider</u> ("think about"), <u>discuss</u> ("talk about"), or <u>address</u> ("talk to").

In contrast, other Latinate prefixes still predicate directional or telic Aktionsart meanings, such as <u>in-hale</u>, <u>ex-hale</u> ("breathe in, out"), or <u>sur-render</u> ("give up"). These lexicalizations parallel separable verb-particle constructions in English.

Besides Latin, several PIE descendents use locatives and directionals for semantically abstract meanings or in constructions similar to adpreps, adverbs, case-markings, or Aktionsart: Middle Iranian (Brunner, 1977:130); Balto-Slavic (Lockwood, 1968:101; Hill, 1977:16); Lithuanian (Schmalstieg, 1988:169–239); and Old Irish (Lewis and Pedersen, 1961:258–267). For Russion, Čerkasova attributes such extensions to the need for "finer and more differentiated connections" (cited in Hill, 1977:16) — in other words, for greater specification.

In the Germanic family, overlap among preverb, preposition, and original adverb (namely, adprep) is commonplace (Lockwood, 1968:177). Case-marking functions have been almost entirely taken over in German, the Scandinavian languages, and English by prepositions, many of which also perform focal predicator functions in constructions allowing particle movement (Lockwood, 1968:175–180; Haugen, 1982:167). For Scandinavian languages, the categorial ambivalence prompts Einar Haugen to define Scandinavian prepositions as transitive adverbs, a label mirrored conversely by Joseph Emonds's (1972:547) definition of English adverbs as intransitive prepositions.

Metaphorical extension from the physical to the psychological domain is documented by J. West (1982) in modern German for such sequences as <u>bei-standen</u>, which means "to stand by" (physically) as well as "to support" (psychologically); similarly, <u>zu-reden</u> means "to talk to" and "to urge." The occurrence of the spatial gram as a prefix or a postverbal particle depends on the syntactic environment and the type of meaning expressed. Thus, "German has kept alive an ancient syntactical device which enables it to register semantic and stylistic differences" (Lockwood, 1968:177).

English no longer has separable prefixes; the original situating and linking functions of these forms are performed today by particles or prepositions. But Latinate and Germanic lexicalizations (e.g., <u>advance</u>, <u>suffer</u>, <u>obey</u>, <u>understand</u>, <u>underlie</u>, <u>overcome</u>, and <u>oversee</u>) still attest to earlier patterns of construction with the verb in English.

A certain stylistic difference, matching the one observed by Lockwood for German, is expressed today in the alternation between Latinate prefixed compounds and Germanic verb-particle combinations. For example, <u>exit</u>, <u>exceed</u>, <u>investigate</u>, <u>infuse</u>, and <u>peruse</u> seem more appropriate for formal discourse modes than <u>go out</u>, <u>go over</u>, <u>look into</u>, <u>put in</u>, and <u>look through</u>. This stylistic alternation is a source of puzzlement for English learners but can be explained fairly simply as a historical phenomenon (interestingly elaborated, by the way, in the television documentary, "The Story of English").

After the Norman Conquest of England in the eleventh century, French (a Latinate language) became the language of the ruling class, the court, and the public or official domain. Latin also enjoyed prestige throughout Europe as a public and scholarly language. In contrast, Anglo-Saxon (a Germanic language) became the less prestigious language of the commoner, used for domestic and informal purposes. For this reason, Latin-based words came to carry a sense of prestige which persists today and provides a useful repertoire of alternative vocabulary for formal or written genres of modern English. The originally separable prefixes of Latin are now lexicalized in simplex verb forms but still express many of their original P-meanings, thus providing a set of alternatives for preposition and particle constructions that use Anglo-Saxon P-forms.

Interestingly, a similar pragmatic and stylistic distinction is noted for Scandinavian languages, where separable verb-adverb combinations are very common in speech while their "corresponding compounds" are "a marker of learned style" (Haugen, 1982:191).

9.4.2. *Prepositions and Particles in Earlier English*

For Old English, categorial flexibility under core scope among adverb, preverb, preposition, postposition, and prefix is well documented (Visser, 1984:668; Mitchell, 1985:440–448; Colman, 1991). The later rigidification of SVO order fixed some Ps in differentiated roles as prepositions or preverbs (Traugott, 1972), which became increasingly productive in construction with other elements.

In modern English, several relics of the old separable and inseparable prefixes survive in lexicalized compounds. In general, their meanings are metaphorically extended beyond the spatiodirectional domain. Some of them reveal a case-marking function (linking) and others an adverbial function (situating). For example, in compounds, both Germanic and Latinate (e.g., *underlie, understand, oversee, survey,* and *intervene*), the prefix exists in a case-marking relationship to the following NP: if you *overcome* your enemy, you are in a metaphorical sense positioned "over" that enemy. This relationship is documented by etymological dictionaries (Bosworth and Toller, 1872; Barnhart, 1988).

As mentioned in the last section, several of these compounds, in their metaphorical meanings, function very much like verb-preposition constructions in modern

English. Underlie, understand, and intervene, for example, denote cognitive or perceptual processes, with the following NP defining their range of activity. F. Visser (1984:390) points out the transitivizing effect of the prefix, which brings an otherwise intransitive verb into construction with the landmark NP. The prefix's inseparability from the verb in these abstract meanings is also matched in such verb-preposition constructions as depend on, believe in, and talk about. Visser applies syntactic tests similar to those proposed by modern English P-studies (cf. chapter 2), including stress, verb substitution, conjunction reduction, and passivization, to distinguish inseparable transitivizing prefixes from separable, adverbial ones.

The adverbial prefixes and preverbs in Old English are the ancestors of postverbal, focal predicator particles today. Their prefixation does not affect the syntactic transitivity of the verb: for example, ofer-fallen ("to fall over") retains the intransitivity of the simple verb, predicating a state on the subject; aen-hangen ("to hang up [a sword]") and under-putten ("to subjugate [an enemy]") retain their transitivity, predicating a state on the object. Prefixation for these words reflects the semantic unity of the verb-adverb combination in modern English. Note, however, that both earlier prefixed constructions and modern verb-adverb constructions have the separable property of allowing P-movement to a more focal position in the sentence.

Laurel Brinton (1988) describes in detail how many of these spatiodirectional prefixes develop into Aktionsart-marking phrasal verbs in Old English through metonymic inferencing in appropriate discourse contexts. For example, the original spatial meaning of through, with its feature of motion "into and out at the opposite end" covertly implies endpoint: "the locus for change from directional to telic is the kind of context ... in which the prefix may have both meanings, e.g. ... "to clean through" or "to clean to the end, completely, thoroughly" (1988:205).

When positioned postverbally as prepositions, Old English P-forms allow landmark sublexicalization, just as they do in modern English adpreps. Fran Colman (1991) explains that a preposition in Old English may be interpreted as an adverb in cases of prepositional object ellipsis. For example, the sequence com to may be interpreted as a verb-adverb combination (parallel to the Latin advenio, "arrive") "in the absence of an overt governed case-marked NP" (1991:82). But the same sequence can also be construed as a verb followed by a case-marking preposition, as in the sequence com to him.

Ellipsis occurs, according to Colman, when the object is an indefinite or a deictic referent. This account is reminiscent of those proposed by the null-complementation studies of transitivity (Fillmore, 1986; Rice, 1988), and by Lindner in her notion of nonsalience as the motivating factor for sublexicalization (see Chapter 7, sections 7.1 and 7.2).

In summary, Indo-European spatial grams, from PIE down to modern English, reveal the same categorial alternation, the same constructional versatility, and the same semantic extensions in situating and linking functions that we see in the synchronic variation of P-prepositions and particles today. If we now look more closely at the history of certain spatial grams in the history of English itself, we will find traces of the diachronic path toward reanalysis and grammaticization which have been proposed for P-forms (as part three of my hypothesis).

9.4.3. *Grammaticization Patterns in Earlier English*

The preceding section on PIE languages mentioned Kuryłowicz's claim that shift and reanalysis may occur from autonomous spatial adverb to grammaticized case-marker. The necessary conditions are explained as follows.

> Within a construction[(verb + adverb) + oblique case] a syntactic shift . . . may entail a new articulation [verb + (adverb + oblique case)], i.e. (preposition + oblique case). Such possibilities depend simultaneously 1. on an external impulse represented by the *formal renewal of the old adverb*; 2. on the previous existence of a secondary function (semantic or syntactical or both) of the old adverb. (1964:171)

I propose that a similar syntactic shift can be identified in Old English for the morpheme of. This morpheme, according to etymological dictionaries, occurs in Old English as both an independent word and a verbal prefix, expressing the directional meanings associated with off or away (Bosworth and Toller, 1972; Barnhart, 1988). These meanings are extended into abstract Aktionsart functions under nuclear scope: that is, ofgifan means "to give up, leave" (Brinton, 1988:206).

But of also specialized under core scope as a case-marking preposition, meaning "from" (Traugott, 1972:128). Later in Old English, a new form, off, emerged to take up the situating functions (i.e., directionality and Aktionsart marking), while of became grammaticized as a genitive and partitive case marker (Barnhart, 1988). In Jerzy Kuryłowicz's terms, the old adverb was formally renewed. In semantic terms, we might say the properties of significant extension that facilitate directional and Aktionsart meanings for off became siphoned off, so to speak, into a new P-form which now performs almost exclusively situating functions. At the same time, the relational and landmark configuration properties relevant for case-marking (namely, separation from source) were reinforced in of.

Similar patterns can be traced for other Ps in earlier stages of English. Another example is the original preposition/adverb to, which first meant "apart" and later presumably meant "toward." Its situating properties were extended to predicate a subjective state of excess (Mitchell, 1985:484), which in turn facilitated nuclear scope Aktionsart meanings of "to the limit," as in tobrecan ("break to bits"; Brinton, 1988:207).

But the linking properties of to were also extended under core scope, to the point where to became grammaticized as an allative case marker licensing goal landmarks. This development seems to have occasioned the formal renewal of the old adverbial functions. The situating properties of to were taken up in a new form, too, whose directional meaning is still expressed in idiomatic sequences such as come to and push the door to.

Even later, however, the subjective state of excess predicated by the adverb was metonymically extended in a different grammatical direction: William Walker (in 1655) lists too as an adverb meaning "over" in such sequences as *If you are too eager* . . . (interestingly, this meaning is carried by another P-form, over, today). Too is now completely reanalyzed as an adverbial modifier (as in *don't work too hard*). This adverb, no longer recoverable as a P-form, now specializes in situating (or predicating states) on adjectives rather than on verbs or clause arguments.

The same adverb has become reanalyzed in yet another situating meaning, that is, "also," a scope-free adverb that predicates a supplemental quality on clauses, arguments, and verbs — on any constituent, in fact, which the speaker considers "extra." Walker documents this use in sentences such as *I have need of your authority and counsel and favour <u>too</u>* (1655:chapter 52, unpaginated).

The linking meanings of <u>to</u> have also diverged in various directions, including its grammaticized use as an infinitive marker (<u>to eat</u>, <u>to go</u>, etc.). I interpret this use as a highly specialized kind of case-marking, since it licenses a following verb and also effectively nominalizes it by treating the verb syntactically as a landmark. In fact, its function as a nominalizer is grammaticized in this infinitive construction to the extent that the *to + Verb* phrase can be moved to other syntactic positions normally reserved for NP arguments, functioning, for example, as the subject of an English sentence (e.g., *to know her is to love her*). In this respect, <u>to</u> differs from subordinating prepositions such as <u>by</u> and <u>in</u>, which introduce gerundial verbs (chapter 8, section 8.5.1), in that gerundial prepositional phrases have not been fully reanalyzed as arguments; we cannot, for example, use them in subject position.

I would suggest that the shift from case-marking to infinitival marking involves metonymic inferencing from contexts where goal also implies purpose: for example, *I went to the movie* implies that I went *to see* the movie. If processes such as <u>see</u> become interpreted as purpose/goal landmarks and this interpretation becomes pragmatically strengthened, then a prepositional phrase such as <u>to see</u> may come to be interpreted as the complement of a verb expressing purpose or volition. In fact, many volitional verbs in English (e.g., <u>want</u>, <u>intend</u>, and <u>plan</u>) are followed conventionally by infinitive forms. Once reanalyzed as a nominal complement, the *to + verb* infinitival construction may be used under any scope in any appropriate NP slot.

Yet another specialized case-marking function for <u>to</u> expresses a dative, or benefactive meaning, after verbs of giving, showing, and telling. Again, it is fairly easy to reconstruct a metonymic shift from an allative, goal-marking use of <u>to</u> toward a benefactive meaning. For example, in *I sent a letter to my friend*, the landmark denotes both a physical goal and, secondarily, a recipient. This secondary sense becomes primary for benefactive verbs, whether or not physical motion toward a goal is involved.

The polysemous extension of <u>to/too</u> is clearly remarkable. However, as some meanings of <u>to</u> have proliferated, at least one has been lost. Walker (1655) lists an "obligation" meaning of <u>to</u> with verbal landmarks, as in "I am <u>to</u> go." While still familiar in literary contexts, this particular case-marking function, which actually involves a predicate-P construction (chapter 8, section 8.3.2) is archaic in modern conversational English. The closest meaning is perhaps expressed in an infinitive-marking construction with verbs already expressing obligation, such as <u>have to</u> or <u>need to</u>.

The formal renewal of <u>to</u> involved an etymologically similar form: <u>too</u>. But Kuryłowicz's study of syntactic shift notes (1964:172) that formal renewal of adverbial functions may also be performed by an unrelated form. This has apparently happened for another original adprep which is now a grammaticized case-marker: <u>with</u>. Talmy (1975:213) suggests that the adverbial sense of <u>along</u>, as in *he's coming along*, exists as a path counterpart to the comitative preposition <u>with</u>. Since <u>along</u> is in fact a new adprep, its introduction actually brings the whole diachronic process around full circle. In contrast, other, non-P forms such as <u>away</u> and <u>together</u> may simply take up the situating functions of such case-marking prepositions as <u>from</u> and <u>to</u>, without replacing them as adpreps.

For all these original P-forms, the linking specialization is complete at the point of grammaticization. They can no longer function as adpreps, but only as pure case-marking prepositions, with new forms taking up their situating functions.

Another type of formal renewal involves obsolescence of the old form and introduction of a completely new one. This happens when the linking or situating meanings of a word have proliferated to the point of confusion. Several P-forms have become obsolete (or lexicalized as nonproductive affixes) through the history of English. For example, the Old English prefixes <u>a</u>-, <u>be</u>-, <u>ge</u>-, and <u>ful</u>- have all fallen out of favor (Brinton, 1988:204–215). Each of these prefixes had developed a wide variety of situating meanings, including direction and Aktionsart. As a result, they became "seriously over-extended" and finally "semantically unclear and empty" (212). P-forms renewed these old directional meanings and have themselves extended into Aktionsart markers. Interestingly, though, in modern English the old strategy of prefixation, which is generally obsolete, has been recycled in a marginal but productive type of Aktionsart function.

> The preponderance of extended meanings, especially of 'superiority' and 'excess,' which derive from the idea of reaching a goal and surpassing it, may have contributed to the need for other, purer means of expressing direction and goal. These extended meanings are precisely those found in [modern English] *over-* and *out-* verbal compounds. (Brinton, 1988:213)

Notice that modern Aktionsart prefixes as found in <u>overburden</u> and <u>overinflate</u> have exclusively situating functions: they do not establish transitive links to a following landmark, as do older, lexicalized prefixes (as in <u>overhang</u>, <u>oversee</u>, and <u>override</u>). If I *override* your objections, then my action is metaphorically situated *over* those objections, as if to trample them. But if I *overinflate* a ballon I am not *over* the balloon. Rather, my action is viewed as reaching a state of excess beyond some implicit optimal limit. The modern prefix <u>out</u> also has an exclusively situating, telic function in verbs such as <u>outfox</u>, <u>outdo</u>, and <u>outrun</u>. It predicates, for certain competitive activities, a state of accomplishment — a quality of having surpassed the activity of the competitor. Thus, these recycled forms have been enlisted for exclusive service as nuclear scope situating elements, to provide greater specification for an Aktionsart function which has itself become overextended.

In its other nonspatial meanings, <u>out</u> has persistently functioned as a situating element. Walker (1655) lists seventeenth-century meanings which are now obsolete or at least archaic: "angry," as in *he is <u>out</u> with me*, and "appear," as in *it will <u>out</u>*. These meanings are more adjective-like or verb-like than P-like, but we have already noted this sort of categorial overlap for particles in focal predicator and premodifying sequences (chapter 8, section 8.6.2). As situating forms, <u>out</u> and <u>up</u> predicate states, a function which tends to produce semantic overlap with other predicative categories.

In short, the tendency for P-forms to perform specialized linking or situating functions has persisted through the history of English. Specialization may or may not result in their reanalysis and grammaticization.

The historical literature and etymological dictionaries provide another significant insight: that P's meanings are notoriously unstable, even in the spatiodirectional domain. We have already seen that to originally denoted a state of separation ("away") but now denotes approximation ("toward"). In Middle English, with meant "against" and for meant "through." According to Bruce Mitchell's (1985) inventory of preposition/adverb meanings in Old and Middle English, one P-form could encompass a remarkable range of meanings, some of which were antonymous. For example, of has at different times marked source (meaning "from," "out of"), agent (meaning "by"), instrument ("with"), partitive case ("of"), and dative case ("to"). Lindner describes a similar instability for the meanings of modern English up, down, in, and out in her study of "the ins and outs of opposites" (1982:305–323).

Nevertheless, despite their semantic inconsistency as spatial grams, P-forms are remarkably consistent in their directions of extension: as their meanings extend beyond the spatial domain, they tend to become more and more specialized in either a linking or a situating direction. Those which display great polysemy as linking elements show far less polysemy as situating elements, and vice versa. Mitchell's list of functions for of and my own list for to involve only case-marking functions; Lindner's (1981) network of meanings for up and out involves almost exclusively directional particles (or focal predicators). Similarly, my own constructional template in chapter 8 shows that certain P-forms (e.g., in and on) show up consistently in linking constructions under all scopes, whereas other P-forms (e.g., up and out) show up in situating constructions under all scopes.

What this tells us, I believe, is that the semantic properties of a spatial gram cannot by themselves determine its path of evolution. The inherent properties identified by Hawkins (1984; also section 9.1.3) have a certain predictive force, as we know from the source determination hypothesis. But these properties may be combined and exploited in many possible meanings, some of them antonymous. Most P-forms have the semantic potential to express a full range of meanings, from location to telicity, and do so in their earlier, less specialized stages of evolution. However, what constrains their polysemy over time and produces the skewed patterns in table 3.1 is their consistent use for either situating or linking purposes, along with the tendency for speakers to select the same P-forms again and again for these differentiated purposes.

9.4.4. Grammaticization Today: About and Around

More evidence for my hypothesis of adprep emergence, specialization, and possible reanalysis can be found in the ongoing evolution of the English P-form about.

According to the *Oxford English Dictionary* (1989), the Old English ancestor of about was ymbe-utan, meaning "by the outside"; Webster's (1981) also documents a-b-utan with the same meaning. A simpler form, ymbe, is documented for the eleventh century, meaning "around."

We know from Mitchell (1985:515–518) that ymbe became overextended semantically into a variety of spatial, temporal, and textual meanings, including "at," "after," and "concerning." Mitchell explains that this polysemy became confusing and motivated the replacement of <u>ymbe</u> in Middle English with a new spatial adprep, <u>about</u> ("on all sides," "around"). Note that the extended meanings all performed linking functions, which are performed by prepositions today.

In the seventeenth century, Walker (1655) documented the spatially referring adprep meaning as primary. But he listed many additional linking meanings, including "approximately," "concerning," and "ready."

Dictionaries up to the middle of the twentieth century continued to list primary spatiodirectional meanings for <u>about</u> (Webster's, 1957; OED, 1964). These meanings involve adpreps and thus allow particle alternation. In its particle uses, however, <u>about</u> implies an additional sense of continued aimless activity, as in <u>wander about</u>, <u>look about</u>, <u>lie about</u>, and <u>hang about</u>.More abstract meanings are listed secondarily for <u>about</u>: "concerning," "on the verge of," and "approximately." Note that these secondary meanings, like those of <u>ymbe</u>, have once again extended toward specifically linking functions.

All these mid-century meanings are still apparently represented by <u>about</u> prepositions and particles in British English today, according to the 1992 *Oxford English Dictionary*, to word frequency counts (Johansson and Hofland, 1989), and to my own experience as a British English speaker, whose dialect includes such verb-particle constructions as <u>wander about</u>. However, the 1992 OED, unlike the mid-century one, lists the most abstract meanings as primary and spatial ones as secondary:

> about. prep. 1. On the subject of ... 2. At a time near to ... 3. In, round, surrounding ... 4. Here and there ... 5. At a point or points near to ...
>
> adv. 1. approximately ... 2. Here and there ... 3. All round ... 4. On the move ... 5. In partial rotation...

Once again, these extended meanings perform linking functions. Notice that "approximately" is categorized as an adverbial entry; however, this traditional categorization does not refer to particles, but rather to the special, qualifier use of <u>about</u> shown in (18), which actually patterns much more like a linking preposition than an adverbial particle.

(18)   'She said 'they're <u>about</u> ... fifteen years ''behi=nd ,
         in their ''medical 'literatu=re ,   (R:24)

Recent American dictionaries suggest a parallel development for American English. For example, the 1983 *Random House Dictionary* gives the preposition primarily abstract meanings and the particle primarily spatiodirectional and continuative meanings:

> about. prep. 1. in regard to. 2. connected with. 3. near or close to. 4. on every side of. 5. on the verge of.
>
> adv. 6. nearly or approximately. 7. nearby. 8. on every side. 9. in the opposite direction. 10. moving around.

However, this American English dictionary is apparently already out-of-date, according to the conversational corpus for this book, which reveals zero spatially referring tokens of <u>about</u> and zero particle uses. Instead, we find a series of abstract, exclusively linking meanings, among which the all-purpose qualifying function ("approximately") is conspicuous. Francis and Kučera's (1982) much larger sample of 574 tokens supports my own finding: they count <u>about</u> as prepositional 68% of the time; but, since their remaining adverbial 32% contains the qualifying tokens, which also perform abstract linking functions, we can infer that their count reveals a distribution heavily skewed in the same direction as presented here.

The specialized linking functions performed by <u>about</u> in the present corpus are most productive as range markers in verb-preposition constructions (illustrated in example 19) and in qualifying sequences (in example 20).

(19)   *Verb-Preposition Constructions*:

    a. J: Well 'tell me <u>about</u> your ''classes.
       R: I'd thought 'maybe you'd ''forgot <u>about</u> 'that.   (R:14)

    b. She's 'talking <u>about</u> the 'super ''before him.   (U:3)

    c. <''OH> don't 'worry <u>bout</u> it.   (R:24)

    d. Well now 'I don't 'know <u>about</u> on ''pavement but on˜˜   (A:35)

(20)   *Qualifying*:

    a. . .'Usually it 'takes <u>about</u> a ''teaspoon,
       That's <u>about</u> all the 'water they can ''get in their 'lungs,   (C:6)

    b. 'She said 'they're <u>about</u> . . . fifteen years ''behi=nd,
       in their ''medical 'literatu=re,   (R:24)

    c. 'Took you <u>about</u> ''fifteen 'seconds,   (C:27)

About also expresses a series of specific or idiomatic meanings, which can be paraphrased as "concerning" (in 21a and 21b), "more or less" (a specific type of Qualifying) (in 21c), and "on the verge of" (in 21d). All of these meanings license specific types of landmarks; for example, *idea* in (21a) and (21b), *identifying characteristics* in (21c), and *actions* in (21d).

(21)   *Idiomatic*:

    a. 'Now 'how <u>about</u> if I 'put some of ''this in 'here.   (R:18)

    b. it's it's uh it's <u>about</u> ''syntax.   (R:14)

    c. 'He's <u>about</u> the only 'good regular ''out there.   (A:8)

    d. Cause he wasn't ''<u>about</u> to 'sell it.   (A:25)

What is noticeably missing in all of this polysemy is a spatiodirectional sense of <u>about</u>. The closest I could find to such a case is in the qualifying example in (22).

(22)   'Kay 'this is '<u>about</u> where you should ''be.   (C:37)

Since the clausal landmark in this example happens to denote a point in space, we can infer a spatial relation for <u>about</u>. However, the rarity of such examples in comparison with the frequency of those found in (18)–(21) attests to the almost complete reanalysis of <u>about</u> in various abstract linking functions.

It is not too difficult to interpret these abstract meanings as semantic extensions following the universal tendencies outlined in section 9.2.1. First, verb-preposition complexes such as <u>tell about</u> and <u>forget about</u> illustrate tendency 1 in the shift from external to perceptual and cognitive reference. The shift is facilitated by the construction of <u>about</u> with the verb under nuclear scope, so that its trajector is a nonmaterial process rather than a concrete participant. Furthermore, this nuclear scope construction in itself illustrates tendency 2 since the orientation performed by <u>about</u> is now based in the metalinguistic or textual domain, situating a linguistic element rather than a physical entity.

The same is true for the idiomatic constructions, in which <u>about</u> can take almost any linguistic constituent as its landmark, including finite or nonfinite clauses (as in 21a and 21d). The qualifying sequences exemplify a tendency 3 shift toward subjective expression: as a multipurpose hedging qualifier, <u>about</u> expresses the speaker's uncertainty about what is being predicated and disclaims responsibility for its precision.

This variety of extended meanings sets a perfect stage for the historical recycling process described in the previous section. We have a proliferation of specific linking meanings for one lexeme, at least one of which has occasioned reanalysis of <u>about</u> (as a qualifying adverb). These meanings are so different from one other that their common source in the spatial domain is difficult to recover and, at least in American conversational data, seems to have been lost. The next question, naturally, is how the core scope, spatiodirectional meanings of <u>about</u> are formally renewed in American English. The answer is in <u>around</u>, which has emerged as a new adprep.

(23)   a. Basically if 'you're gonna be ''<u>around</u> people who 'know CPR ,   (C:10)

     b. 'Usually . .somebody's ''<u>around</u> or ,
       'help usually ''arrives   (C:20)

We can see in (23) that <u>around</u> allows preposition-particle alternation. As explained in chapter 7, the choice is determined by the speaker's orientational purposes: whether to focus the defining context for a situation, as in (23a), or simply to predicate a state, as in (23b). Both choices are interestingly juxtaposed in the example that follows.

(24)   [It's a lot of fun ,]
     shittin '<u>around</u> <u>around</u> the ''track .   (A:21)

Here, the extensional path property of <u>around</u> is metonymically extended in the verb-particle construction (<u>shittin around</u>) to predicate aimless activity. However, the landmark is still clearly recoverable from the spatiodirectional domain. The same kind of continuative meaning becomes slightly more abstracted from this domain in (25).

(25)   a. Yeah we spent our 'lives looking ''<u>around</u> and ,
       'traveling <u>around</u> and .   (R:23)
     b. You 'guys would all . .'hang <u>around</u> and think 'oh someone ''else will .   (C:8)
     c. When ''I was 'fooling <u>around</u> .   (A:17)

All these verb-particle sequences could be expressed using <u>about</u> in British English and, presumably, in earlier stages of American English. In the current American conversational corpus, however, around takes up these directional and continuative situating functions, leaving about to specialize as a linking element.

Around is a much newer P-form than about: the 1989 OED claims that it was "rare" before 1600 and that its original meaning was circuitive, "in circumference." By the middle of the present century, however, its spatial meanings in British English had generalized to include all those expressed by about, including "on a circuit," "on all sides," and "here and there."

Intriguingly, however, the 1992 OED lists additional, specifically American uses for around: namely, the continuative Aktionsart use and the qualifying use.

What these dictionary notes suggest is a short time lag between British and American English. British speakers are now adopting around as an adprep to carry the original core-scope, spatial meanings of about, as well as the closely related continuative meaning. But in the meantime, American speakers are already extending the use of around into more specialized, abstract meanings—and the direction of extension seems to follow exactly the same linking path as about and ymbe before it.

This dictionary survey is too cursory to justify any solid predictions; but I would speculate that, if around continues to extend in this linking direction, we may once again see a formal renewal of the original spatially referring adprep. About, like ymbe, may become obsolete or persist as a reanalyzed element in its specialized linking functions. But what we can more safely conclude from the survey is that about and around provide a modern English showcase for the cyclical process of adprep emergence, specialization, and formal renewal proposed by Kuryłowicz for earlier Indo-European languages. They also illustrate my hypothesis of semantic and syntactic extension from spatially referring adpreps to progressively more abstract and specialized types of orientation.

9.5. P-Specialization as a "Panchronic" Phenomenon

In light of this typological and historical evidence, we can now represent the synchronic variation and specialization of English P-forms as a diachronic snapshot. In other words, we can interpret their skewed distributions in table 3.1 as a panchronic reflection of both their strategic usage and their evolution over time.

From this perspective, we can position individual P-forms on a continuum of specialization between exclusively situating and exclusively linking elements. The main difference between prepositional Ps (such as in and on) and pure prepositions (such as of, to, and with) is their degree of specialization as linking elements. The latter group have been reanalyzed and grammaticized as case markers and are no longer recoverable as P-forms. About and by also approach reanalysis in some of their specialized linking functions, such as the qualifying adverb or passive agent-marking.

Similarly, the main difference between particle Ps such as up and out and pure situating elements such as too or away is their degree of specialization as situating elements. Up and out are the most specialized situating forms, particularly in constructions such as Aktionsart where their spatiodirectional P-meanings are often unrecoverable. Other P-forms, such as around, through, and over, are less specialized in either direction, and their meanings as adpreps or particles are usually recoverable from the spatiodirectional domain.

Table 9.2: P-Tokens Operating Under Different Scopes, as a Percentage of Total P-Tokens

Scope	Particles	Prepositions	Other[a]	Total %	Raw Totals
Core	30%	24%	3%	57%	710
Peripheral	1%	11%	2%	14%	176
Nuclear	6%	6%	1%	13%	163
NP	2%	5%	1%	8%	94
P	–	3%	–	3%	36
Other[b]	–	3%	2%	5%	66
Totals	39%	52%	9%	100%	1,245

[a]Other includes P-prefixes and P-suffixes, conflated prepositional phrases such as "here" and "there," repeats, uninterpretable repairs, and uninterpretable idioms such as *day in, day out.*

[b]Other refers to scopes not considered relevant to or discussed in this study, namely verb-particle, adjective, and adverb scopes.

9.6.   The Basic Function of P

The preceding diachronic analysis supports my hypothesis that P-forms start out conceptually as spatially referring adpreps (alternating as particles) under core scope. The present corpus also supports this position, by revealing a prevalence for core scope, spatially referring meanings for P-forms in general. The evidence is detailed in Table 9.2, which shows the relative frequencies of prepositions and particles that appear in the database under different scopes.

The table shows that core scope is by far the most frequent locus of operation for both prepositions and particles. Core scope is the scope of adpreps and other constructions with spatiodirectional meanings, such as focal predicator and locative case-marking (which is not grammaticized). Furthermore, all twenty P-forms in this corpus include spatiodirectional adpreps in their meanings, with the exception of about, which was included here precisely because of its intriguing refusal to fulfill the predictions of the dictionary listings in this function.

For prepositions, the next most common scope of operation is peripheral scope. We know from chapter 8 that this scope is the locus for special text-cohesive functions such as subordinator and text-transitional phrases. These meanings exemplify a tendency 2 shift, according to Traugott and König's universal principles, since they refer primarily in the metalinguistic, textual domain.

For particles, the next most common scope of operation is nuclear. We know from chapter 8 that this is the locus for Aktionsart constructions. The domain of reference for these particles, therefore, is also metalinguistic, exemplifying tendency 2 However, it also exemplifies tendency 3 since Aktionsart meanings often imply the speaker's subjective evaluation of the activity involved; it is the speaker's subjective judgment rather than any external reference point that represents an activity as goal-directed or aimless (chapter 8, section 8.4.4). Prepositions under nuclear scope all represent a tendency 2 shift in that they link verbs metalinguistically to range landmarks. In particular, verb-preposition constructions also show an extension toward the domain of cognitive or other internal processes (tendency 1) while qualifying constructions contribute a subjective disclaimer, or hedging quality, in their "approximately" meaning.

NP scope is a less frequent locus of operation for P-forms, representing only 8% of total P-occurrences. These occurrences represent rather unusual extensions, where particles or prepositional phrases perform a function normally associated with adjectives (chapter 8, section 8.6). In a sense, we could say that P-forms under this scope represent metaphorical extension as qualities rather than spatial grams, an extension predicted by Claudi and Heine's grammaticization chain (1986).

Finally, P-scope is exclusively for such compound sequences as <u>out of</u>, <u>up to</u>, <u>on to</u>, and so on (chapter 8, section 8.7). However, this scope is significant as a locus for the emergence of such new compound prepositions as <u>onto</u>, <u>into</u>, and <u>upon</u> — and we could now perhaps add <u>a-b-out</u>, on the basis of our previous etymological analysis. The domain of reference is once again metalinguistic (since the case-marking preposition takes a particle as its trajector) and thus represents a tendency 2 shift.

In conclusion, the synchronic data converge with the historical evidence to support my hypothesis of the core scope, spatially referring adprep as the conceptually basic P-form, and other P-meanings under other scopes representing syntactic-semantic extensions with specialized linking or situating functions.

9.7.   Synchronic Reconstruction

In the present data, there are many conversational contexts where an extended meaning appears close enough (chronologically or semantically) to a spatial one to reveal an obvious possibility for metonymic or metaphoric inference — not necessarily by these speakers, but by these and others before them. By examining these contexts, it is possible to do internal semantic-pragmatic reconstruction of the type proposed by Traugott (1989; also section 9.2.1) as a final line of support for my diachronic P-hypothesis.

This is the purpose of this last section, which will trace a series of pragmatically motivated steps by which speakers may move from one meaning to another along the unidirectional paths elaborated in this chapter. The specific extensions and constructional meanings to be considered here are:

1. From core direction/location to nuclear Aktionsart marker

2. From core direction to peripheral deixis

3. From core location to nuclear range

9.7.1.   *From Core Direction to Nuclear Aktionsart*

The significant extensional properties described in section 9.1.3 for <u>up</u> and <u>out</u> may be the metonymic bridge from core directional predications to telic Aktionsart particles, as we will now see.

To begin, the separation property of <u>out</u>, in some directional contexts, may be expressed as an endstate (as in 26).

(26)   I'm 'afraid if I ''blow on that 'mouth,
      I'm gonna 'blow this 'temporary <LAUGH ''crown <u>out</u>> .   (C:17)

In this core scope meaning, separation is predicated as a resultant state for a core participant: <u>the crown</u> is <u>out</u>. Thus, <u>out</u> implicitly adds telicity to the activity of blowing. Telicity is also added by <u>up</u> to the predication in (27).

(27)   [it's kind of a pleasant place to live],
      and . .''grow '<u>up</u>,
      or . .''drive through 'you know it's ,   (R:34)

<u>Up</u> adds telicity to the directional activity of "grow," not as an endstate, but as an evolving state: the participant is not <u>up</u>, but he is seen as moving in that direction; as Brinton might say, "the situation, if continued, would lead to some end" (1988:183). The positive polarity property of <u>up</u> implies that this end is a desired goal.

In (28), the directional meanings of <u>out</u> and <u>up</u> refer metaphorically to mental activities rather than to physical space.

(28)   a.   'Lemme 'help you ''<u>out</u> 'here .   (C:35)
      b.   But 'that I found ''<u>out</u>.   (U:81)
      c.   I'm 'trying to get things lined ''<u>up</u> for it .   (A:30)

All these predications still occur under core scope. Core participants are viewed as changing their state not in space but in the speaker's estimation of their progress toward an endpoint. For (28a) and (28b), <u>out</u> predicates metaphorical separation — from a sticky situation in (28a), or from a secret source in (28b). For (28c), <u>up</u> predicates incremental progress toward a desired goal — a state of organization. This property, implicit in the directional meaning of (27), becomes explicit in (28c).

The syntactic shift from such core to nuclear scope constructions may be made in contexts such as those in (29).

(29)   a.   I'll 'find <u>out</u> in a ''second .   (U:78)
      b.   'helping ''<u>ou=t</u> with this other 'department that 'needed (help)˜˜   (R:18)
      c.   'Randy I 'better let ''you dish '<u>out</u>.   (R:29)
      d.   an you can . .''open it ,
         . .open '<u>up</u> an make 'sure so you can ''feel ,   (C:13)

The crucial difference between these contexts and those in (28) is that the verbs in (29) have sublexicalized or null complements; thus, there is no semantic patient on which to predicate the evolving state. Compare the (a) and (b) utterances for the same verb-particle combinations, in (30) and (31).

(30)   a.   'Lemme 'help you ''<u>out</u> 'here .   (C:35)
      b.   'helping ''<u>ou=t</u> with this other 'department that 'needed (help)˜˜   (R:18)

(31)   a.   But 'that I found ''<u>out</u>.   (U:81)
      b.   I'll 'find <u>out</u> in a ''second .   (U:78)

Despite their lexical and semantic similarity, these uses of <u>help out</u> and <u>find out</u> are differently construed. The (a) sentences take the semantic patient of the verb as their trajector: you in (30a) and that in (31a). However, in the (b) sentences, the trajector is not expressed, although we could infer it as a null complement. In the absence of a core trajector to be situated, the evolving state is contained within the verb-particle predication itself; there was a "finding-out" or a "helping-out": what or who evolved "outward" is left unspecified.

By the same logic, in (29c) we could infer a null complement (food) as the trajector for out. But since the speaker does not specify this complement, we construe dish out as a self-contained predication. And in (29d), where open up refers to the action of unzipping the jacket on a dummy to expose the chest, we could perhaps recover the jacket as the evolving trajector for up; however, since it is not expressed, the activity of opening itself is construed as evolving toward a desired state without reference to any core argument.

From here, it is a short cognitive step to reanalysis of the particle as a nuclear scope Aktionsart marker. If enough tokens of a particular verb-particle combination are construed in this self-contained way, in a wide enough variety of contexts for a long enough period of time, that combination may come to be interpreted as a phrasal verb, where the telic particle situates that verb. Consequently, we find check out, find out, and help out as separate phrasal verb listings in dictionaries, under the more general entries for the verbs.

If a verb-particle combination becomes reanalyzed in this way, it may then appear with a new complement for the new phrasal verb. This whole extension from directional adverb to Aktionsart construction is nicely illustrated in the following juxtaposed examples for clean up.

(32) a. 'Oh the ''super'll clean it 'up   (U:1)

      b. I'm cleaning ''up , right ?   (U:2)

      c. When we 'clean up the ''table it'll ̃ ̃   (R:34)

The examples in (32) reflect a process of pragmatic inferencing and strengthening for up. The properties of directional extension and goal orientation are first exploited under core scope in (32a), where it refers to glass about to be lifted from the floor. Next, these properties are extended to the metalinguistic domain under nuclear scope in (32b), where the action of cleaning itself evolves in a positive direction. Finally, in (32c), clean up is reanalyzed as a telic unit or phrasal verb with its own complement, the table.

Once the constructional template is established for such telic phrasal verbs, new collocations may be generated in which up and out have a generalized Aktionsart-marking function. For this reason, they are sometimes interpreted as perfective or completive markers for a wide variety of verbs: hook up, end up, banged up, sign up, fix up, burned out, and fade out are a few examples from this corpus.

Within this template, verbs and particles may combine to produce noncompositional, subjective meanings, where the verb is no doubt metaphorically extended from an originally physical domain but now unrecoverable: the corpus includes the lexicalizations mess up, screw up, fuck up, and crack up as examples.

Within the phrasal verb template, particles may even construct with adjectives rather than verbs to denote goal-oriented processes; thus, we have <u>wise up</u> and <u>mellow out</u> in the corpus. But these data offer only a hint of the potential which is undoubtedly being exploited to create new meanings in conversation every day.

So far, we have concentrated on telic Aktionsart-marking, which is by far the most productive type observed in these data. However, the same inferential steps proposed here may also apply to the development of continuative aspect-marking for <u>on</u>.

<u>On</u> does not specialize in these data as a particle P: table 3.1 shows that it occurs 83% of the time as a linking preposition. However, its situating properties are extended enough to produce a sideline meaning of continuative Aktionsart (or, more properly, aspect, according to Brinton, 1988) for inherently nontelic verbs. Since a similar kind of extension has already been noted for <u>around</u>, which is still a relatively nonspecialized P-form, we could speculate that aktionsart marking does not represent a great conceptual leap, in diachronic terms, but occurs relatively soon in the evolution of P-forms. The examples in (33) contrast a series of uses which represent the extension from core scope locational predication to nuclear scope aspect marking for <u>on</u>.

(33) a. Cause you're 'right <u>on</u> the ''edge of the ,
         ''Diagonal .   (R:11)

      b. You're ''right ''<u>o==n</u> there .   (C:27)

      c. ''O=kay , 'pressure's ''<u>o=n</u> .   (C:1)

      d. Did you 'turn it ''<u>o==n</u> ?   (R:2)

      e. 'You all will have to 'carry <u>on</u> ''without us for a minute .   (A:16)

      f. And it 'keeps ''<u>on</u> .   (U:12)

In (33a), <u>on</u> is a preposition that situates the trajector and also links to a location — a road. Through landmark sublexicalization, <u>on</u> becomes a locative particle in (33b), referring to the hearer's physical position as she presses on the sternum of a dummy. Note that the stress and lengthening of <u>on</u> in (33b) reflect its focal status as a situating element — a status which does not obtain in (33a) (see chapter 7, section 7.5.2).

A metaphorical shift from the physical to the mental domain occurs in (33c), which refers to psychological pressure. In all of these utterances, the relational property of coincidence is central to the meaning of <u>on</u>. This relation is pragmatically strengthened from (33c) through (33f) by its persistence beyond the physical domain. Another property, that of a horizontal surface landmark configuration, applies in (33a) and is recoverable in (33b) from the physical domain but it is no longer recoverable for the nonspatial particle in (33c). In its place, a third property, implicitly produced by coincidence with a horizontal surface, becomes explicit here — namely, continuation. To coincide with a horizontal surface means to have continuous, linear contact with it. In (33c), this property is central to the meaning of <u>on</u>, which predicates a state of continued contact or application for <u>pressure</u>.

This metonymically inferred property persists in all three subsequent examples. In (33d), <u>on</u> predicates a quality on <u>it</u> ("it" is a tape recorder); electrical appliances are said to be <u>on</u> when they are properly connected and continuously functioning. The predication in (33d), as with all the previous ones, still operates under core scope, to predicate a state on a participant. In (33e), however, null complementation for the verb motivates the same shift to nuclear scope that I described above for telic particles. The implicit patient of carry (= <u>your business</u>, perhaps) is unexpressed and the properties of <u>on</u> are predicated within the verb complex itself.

Through pragmatic strengthening across several contexts, this reanalysis under nuclear scope may lead to a generalized function of continuative aspect-marking for the verb itself. <u>On</u> may then be construed with a variety of verbs to express continuation in a linear direction, or to reinforce verbs which already express continuation, as in (33f).

9.7.2.   *From Core Location to Nuclear Range*

Unlike the shift to Aktionsart, the shift to range marking in verb-preposition constructions involves extensions of P's linking function. But the same inferential steps are involved here (in a slightly different order) as in the direction-to-Aktionsart shift.

1. In the absence of a core-scope trajector, location is predicated under nuclear scope, on the verb itself.

2. Semantic properties are extended metonymically and metaphorically to non-spatial domains.

3. The verb-preposition sequence is reanalyzed as a verbal unit.

The verb-preposition construction provides a template for defining cognitive, verbal, or otherwise internal processes (chapter 8, section 8.4.2). To get there, we can start by comparing the spatially referring utterances in example (34).

(34)   a. And I'm just 'putting my 'fingers <u>on</u> the ''bo=ny part .   (C:8)

   b. If you 'push <u>on</u> the ''stomach you might get the˜˜ . . . ''acid into the 'lungs .   (C:6)

These examples represent a shift from core to nuclear scope predication similar to that described in the previous reconstructions. In (34a), location is predicated on a core scope trajector <u>my fingers</u>. In (34b), however, the trajector is unexpressed and inferrable only as null complement (= <u>your fingers</u>). Consequently, the location is predicated under nuclear scope, on the activity of pushing. This predication links verb to landmark in a relation which spans both the metalinguistic and spatial domains. The physical landmark defines the spatial dimensions of the verb's activity.

The same situation obtains in (35). In (35a) and (35b), the null complement is a cognate object (= *breath*) while in (35c), it is schematically evoked (as <u>your hands</u>, perhaps) by the act of pressing.

(35)   a. and 'breathe <u>into</u> the ''tu=be ,   (C:7)

   b. and they 'brea=the 'under the ''diaphragm .   (C:8)

   c. . . . and 'press <u>against</u> the ''lu=ngs ,   (C:6)

Once the syntactic shift to nuclear scope is made conceptually, even verbs without null complements may be construed as the trajectors of the following prepositions. Thus, in (36), it is the *looking* which is "on" <u>the recording</u>, the *choking* which is on <u>the apple</u>, and the *shaving* which is <u>off the (shiny) fenders</u>.

(36) a. you 'need to look on the ''recording .   (C:26)

    b. He was 'choking on a piece of ''apple .   (C:37)

    c. [you could] you know 'shave off the˜ ''fenders and .   (A:27)

After this reanalysis of the verb-preposition sequence under nuclear scope, the next cognitive step is a tendency 1 shift, where the whole utterance is predicated in the internal or perceptual domain (example 37).

(37) a. If you're ''spending . .in the ''hundreds of 'dollars a 'month ,   (R:9)

    b. for 'people who're 'spending under ''300 dollars a 'month ,   (R:10)

The Ps linking these verbs to their landmarks have extended their relational properties metonymically. The medium landmark configuration of in implies a range of containment; for under, the proximal relation to an upper boundary implies an upper limit. These properties are made explicit in (37) to denote a numerical range or maximum, so that *spending* may be situated and defined in these hypothetical terms.

The remaining step from such sequences as these to verb-preposition constructions as in (38) involves pragmatic strengthening of the preposition's range properties in the nonmaterial domain:

(38) a. the 'book is 'based on a 'sixth grade ''reading level ,   (C:2)

    b. okay it 'depends on if it's a 'partial or a ''full .   (C:21)

    c. I said 'I'm not ''ta=lking about 'that man ,   (U:2)

    d. . .if 'you believe in that ,   (U:31)

Within the verb-preposition construction template, the preposition may take clauses or larger textual episodes for both its trajector and its landmark, as we see in (38b) and (38d). This construction has become a productive locus for the definition of a wide variety of abstract processes, activities, and situations. In this construction, certain verbs tend to be collocated repeatedly with certain P-forms whose semantic properties are appropriate for the kind of range-marking function required. For example, the verb base, derived from a noun, metaphorically expresses a foundation; so on, with its properties of contiguity and support, provides an appropriate link to the landmark in (38a). Similarly, *talking* is a relatively undirected activity, so a P expressing indeterminate proximity to the landmark (namely, about) is appropriate.

As the same verbs are constructed again and again with the same prepositions, it is natural to reanalyze the verb-preposition construction as a syntactic-semantic unit, an inseparable phrasal verb. As a predictable unit, the preposition is "licensed," in a sense, by the verb in the same way that the dative case marker to is licensed by verbs of giving, telling, and showing. At the same time, since the preposition's function here is fundamentally to link rather than to predicate states, its semantic properties have no focal status. The result is a general weakening of the independent meaning of the preposition in this construction, which is sometimes interpreted as semantic bleaching in the literature or as producing a nonpredicative function such as Julia Jolly describes for case markers (1993:275–276).

This semantically nonconsequential status of the preposition is also revealed diachronically by Visser (1984), who points out that many verb-preposition collocations have replaced their preposition at least once: <u>depend</u> was once constructed with <u>of</u>, then <u>in</u>, then <u>on</u>, and so on (see also chapter 8, section 8.4.2). But the replacements documented by Visser all involve prepositional or primarily linking Ps: we do not find verb-preposition complexes with <u>up</u>, <u>off</u>, or <u>out</u>. Thus, we see that although the semantics of the preposition may be inconsequential, its pragmatic function is crucial: the Verb-Preposition construction is essentially a linking construction.

There is some indication in these data of the way speakers participate in the creation of new verb-preposition sequences. The examples in (39) seem to illustrate a new sequence in the making.

(39) a. And '<u>copped</u> an 'attitude <u>on</u> ''Joe .   (U:10)

   b. And <u>getta</u> ''<u>attitude on</u> me ,
      an I have to ''hit him .   (U:4)

   c. I 'can't talk to 'him because he's liable to ''<u>attitude</u> on me .   (U:15)

In these utterances, all produced by the same speaker, <u>attitude</u> is a core argument in (39a) and (39b). The predication is metaphorical, analogous to the notion of dumping or laying trouble on someone. In (39c), however, <u>attitude</u> has been converted to a verb and, as a consequence, <u>on</u> now refers under nuclear rather than core scope, to situate a verb rather than an argument. The result is an innovative verb-preposition construction.

9.7.3.   *From Core Direction to Peripheral Deixis*

This last reconstruction traces the shift from core to peripheral scope and involves situating P-forms.

As mentioned in section 1.3, deictic particles such as <u>up</u>, <u>down</u>, <u>out</u>, and especially <u>over</u> all share a general property of significant extension for the Path of their trajector. This property extends to operate under different scopes, particularly peripheral scope, where it provides a specific text-orienting function (chapter 8, section 8.5.4). The inferencing steps involved here are (a) metonymic shift of focus from Path to Endpoint and (b) metaphorical shift from physical to textual orientation.

In (40), <u>over</u> predicates direction under core scope, and a core argument (= <u>stuff</u>, or <u>they</u>) is situated on a sublexicalized but recoverable path (= <u>the table</u> or <u>the pasture</u>), which extends from *there* to *here*.

(40) a. You 'wanna hand stuff . . ''<u>over</u> ?   (R:27)

   b. and 'then they'll come <u>over</u> to ''this field over here .   (R:32)

Paths are goal-oriented: they have implicit endpoints (= <u>here</u>, in these examples). The endpoint becomes explicit in (41), where <u>over</u> expresses endstate, rather than direction.

(41) a. I haven't 'even been '<u>over</u> to ''see him lately .   (A:18)

   b. you're ''<u>over</u> there 'visiting ,   (R:3)

These utterances predicate no physical motion, even though they imply the end of some previous motion. They simply predicate endstate (= <u>there</u>) on the core trajector. That state is defined deictically, relative to the viewpoint of the speaker, who is positioned at one end of the intervening path. Once the predication of motion has been lost, we can interpret <u>over</u> as simply predicating deictic state. To this extent, P is a discourse-directional device: it directs the hearer to shift attention from the speaker's viewpoint to another reference point established by the speaker.

Viewed in this way, the P-form becomes reanalyzed as a general discourse pointer that may constructed with any linguistic element that needs to be situated deictically. Thus, <u>over</u> may operate under NP-scope (as in <u>this field over here</u>, in example 40b). But the deictic-marking construction is particularly useful under peripheral scope, where it supports the introduction of new or discontinuous contexts.

(42) a. and they got ''married,
          <u>over</u> ''there.   (R:3)

      b. He got 'barred from running ''go karts,
          <u>over</u> in ''Tiffen.   (A:14)

The predications in (42) involve a metaphorical shift to the textual domain (tendency 2), where <u>over</u> takes the whole clause as its trajector and situates it deictically, directing the hearer's attention, in effect, from the present context to the new one (= <u>there</u> or <u>in Tiffen</u>). Thus, we frequently see deictic particles juxtaposed with prepositional phrases that predicate the new context (chapter 8, section 8.5.4).

As a productive template, this construction facilitates the expression of deictic marking with almost any particle P, depending on its specific semantic properties and the situating requirements involved, as the examples in (43) illustrate.

(43) a. There 'used to be a 'place <u>up</u> in ''Toledo that'd 'make 'em for you.   (A:31)

      b. . . . And then '<u>down</u> at the 'bottom it 'talks more about ''AIDS.   (C:2)

      c. [he could beat his snowmobile]. . . On 'dry ''la=nd.
          '<u>Out</u> on the 'damn ''blacktop.   (A:35)

9.7.4. Summary

In support of my earlier diachronic hypothesis for P (section 9.2.2), the preceding exercise in synchronic reconstruction has traced the extension from spatially referring meanings under core scope to specialized P-constructions with abstract meanings under other scopes. It has analyzed the inferential steps in this extension across a variety of different conversational contexts and shown that they follow the same unidirectional tendencies that Traugott and König (1991) and other scholars have proposed as universals for semantic change and grammaticization. What remains constant through all these extensional steps is the pragmatic function of the P-form as a situating or linking element.

One main purpose of the exercise has been to reveal P's synchronic variations, not only as vestiges of past changes but also as evidence of changes in the offing. In the course of these changes, metonymic and metaphorical inferencing are seen to solve the kinds of semantic-pragmatic problems outlined by Traugott and König: namely, the problem of "representing members of one semantic domain in terms of another" and the problem of how to "regulate communication and negotiate hearer-speaker interaction" (1991:212). These problems are addressed by P's strategic construction under different scopes in progressively more abstract domains.

9.8.   Conclusion: What Do Speakers "Know" about P?

This chapter has traced patterns of semantic extension, specialization, reanalysis, and grammaticization for P-forms both diachronically and synchronically. One big question is provoked by this analysis: that is, what do speakers "know" when they use P-forms in all these extended ways? This question actually comprises three smaller ones:

1. Do the inherent semantic properties of P-forms prequalify them for particular pragmatic purposes, or do they evolve to meet these purposes?
2. Do extensions represent choices at the moment of use or simply the accessing of a set of learned meanings?
3. Does extension proceed chronologically through step-by-step inferencing or in one cognitive leap?

In light of the preceding diachronic and synchronic analysis, I propose that the answer is "yes" to all the alternatives.

In answer to the first question, there is no doubt that P-forms have inherent semantic properties of the type described in Hawkins's (1984) taxonomy. These properties can be traced through all P's extensions and help predict possible paths of change, as the source determination hypothesis claims (Bybee, Perkins, and Pagliuca, 1994). We have seen that not just any preposition will do for any linking job and not just any particle for any situating job.

But we have also seen—for example, in the evolution of to, of, and about— that the meanings highlighted by a given P-form are unstable and susceptible to radical change. Words may develop so many meanings that they no longer fulfill their original pragmatic adprep purpose and become obsolete or formally reanalyzed. Linking prepositions may sometimes be interchanged with little effect on the meaning of the construction (Visser, 1984).

However, this apparent unruliness is constrained and principled. The pragmatic purposes of orientation drive the meanings of P-forms in situating and linking directions which involve the highlighting of certain semantic properties and the suppressing of others.

In answer to the second question, there is again no doubt that speakers draw on a great bank of learned resources and rules when they extend the meanings of P-forms. It is no longer possible to use to as an adprep, for example; and Aktionsart meanings of up and out can be found in any dictionary. However, the diachronic and synchronic analyses of this chapter indicate that speakers build on their encyclopedic knowledge in creative ways. For example, new Aktionsart meanings continue to be invented in such phrasal verbs as wise up and chill out; and new cognitive processes continue to be defined in verb-preposition constructions such as <u>attitude on</u>.

But once again, these creative uses are principled: they follow the rules. Speakers seem to know the constraints imposed by specific constructions and select their situating or linking forms accordingly.

In answer to the third question, I would refer the reader to Traugott (1989), who argues that knowing exactly when new meanings emerge, and the time lag between them, is not always important in reconstructing the pattern of emergence: "What is significant is cumulative evidence from different but related semantic domains and, wherever possible, from other languages, of the same order of attestation among exemplars, whatever the time lag" (1989:34).

Typological, diachronic, and synchronic evidence has been accumulated in this chapter. It traces all the steps of extension attested for P-forms across semantic domains and syntactic scopes to produce the wide variety of constructional meanings mapped out in chapter 8. All this evidence suggests that P's meanings have evolved and still evolve in the direction predicted by universal tendencies (Traugott and König, 1991). The question of whether, say, Aktionsart meanings develop step-by-step from directional meanings at historically different stages or emerge in one cognitive leap is not as important as the fact that every Aktionsart meaning also has a directional meaning that dates back to its oldest attested uses and which performs a similar situating function.

In conclusion, this chapter has traced the semantic-syntactic extensions of P-forms panchronically, finding a unidirectional pattern of synchronic extension that mirrors the diachronic path of specialization and grammaticization. Its analysis has provided substantial support for my hypothesis that P-forms evolve from core scope adpreps to perform progressively specialized situating or linking functions under other scopes. These extensions generate many new meanings for any given P-form, but are always constrained by that form's pragmatic specialization.

Thus, we can answer the questions raised at the beginning of this chapter. We have explained the skewed distributions in table 3.1 as a reflection of P's specialization in either situating or linking functions. We have also explained why English has pure, non-P-prepositions and how pure particles function to take up some of the obsolete situating functions of these prepositions.

We have also explained historically why there should be a stylistic difference between formal simplex verbs such as <u>extinguish</u> and informal particle constructions such as <u>put out</u> (section 9.4.2).

And finally, we have seen some of the motivating factors that explain the lexical creativeness of verb-particle combinations. The polysemy of such sequences as <u>make up</u> and <u>take off</u> emerges through the interaction of several phenomena: the ability of particles to construct under different scopes; their tendency to evolve into psychological, metalinguistic, textual, and attitudinal domains; and the status of the Aktionsart construction as a productive template for constructing a variety of events and processes from the speaker's point of view.

All these questions have found their answers under the present account of prepositions and particles as specialized orienting elements whose meanings reveal not only layers of historical change but also possible ongoing changes, changes in which speakers today are actively involved.

10

The Big Picture

10.1. Summary of the Study

In chapter 1, "the problem of P" was introduced as a list of questions. The larger theoretical question was how to account for the categorial flexibility, semantic versatility, and syntactic constraints of P-forms: in other words, how to explain this "closed class" of words which displays membership in at least two lexical classes, a remarkable range of meanings, and rather idiosyncratic patterns of construction.

That question entailed several smaller ones, often raised by students of English, about the intriguing characteristics of prepositions and particles. This volume has addressed both large and small questions and has resolved several other problematic issues from the previous literature on P, by proposing a new theoretical account of P as an orienting element. This account explains why we have prepositions and particles, why they alternate, why they pattern as they do, and why they have so many meanings. In the process, it has unified syntax and semantics with the pragmatic motivations that drive P's extensions over time and across different conversational contexts.

The interpretation of P as an orienting element helps explain both why P-forms originate in the spatially referring domain and why their meanings can extend so far from this same domain. Orientation, at the most concrete level of real-world reference, involves spatial relations, knowing "where we are" in terms of things around us. But we also need orientation at the more abstract levels of mental perceptions, subjective attitudes, and text organization. For orientation in these domains, we extend the same notions of situation and relationship — containment, separation, evolving states, endstates, and so on — that we use to make sense of the physical world. As John Bowden says, "much of what we talk about in human language is structured in terms of spatial relationships. A great deal of work in linguistics has concentrated on how

172

the semantics of other domains has been structured in terms of the semantics of spatial relationships" (1992:68).

In this report, however, I have tried to go beyond semantic description, to discover how orientational needs cause us to focus things as being either situated or linked, and how this differentiation of focus translates into language use. I have explained what kinds of elements speakers tend to situate, and what kinds of elements they link them to. These discourse-pragmatic tendencies, I argue, drive both semantic structure and syntactic organization for P-forms.

Therefore, as elaborated in chapter 2, it makes little sense to approach the problem of P's categoriality as a purely syntactic one. Syntactic tests for categoriality are bound to produce fragmented results because they do not look at the whole picture. The categoriality of P as a preposition or particle is not strictly binary. P-forms are more or less preposition-like or particle-like, depending on the degree to which they perform purely situating or linking functions. To explain how and why P-forms pattern as they do, it would be more productive to take Dwight Bolinger's (1971) adprep as a starting-point than the more specialized P-constructions traditionally examined in the syntactic literature.

Better results are produced by semantic and cognitive approaches, which abandon the notion of discrete categories for a more coherent account of P's semantic and syntactic structure. Their models have helped greatly to explain the patterns of construction which produce a diverse and intricately connected network of meanings for P-forms; However, as explained in chapter 3, they have not addressed the constraints on these patterns. In particular, they do not explain the strong tendency for P-forms to specialize as either particles or prepositions. Essentially, their models are static, mapping out the meanings of P-forms in a posthoc way that does not reflect how these forms have evolved over time and are evolving now.

Chapter 4 argued for a reconceptualization of the problem of P, that would allow us to look at how P-forms are used in everyday conversation, where language actually lives and grows. From premises already established in the discourse-functional literature, I argued that such an approach would eliminate the risk of faulty intuitive generalizations that obscure actual patterns of speech. We could find out what speakers actually do rather than describing what linguists think they do. I explained how this approach could be implemented for the corpus of five American English conversations, and I introduced the relevant prosodic, semantic, morphological, syntactic, and pragmatic properties that would be coded to produce objective generalizations about the uses of P.

The remainder of the book has elaborated a discourse-functional account of P based on the findings from this corpus. It gradually builds a profile of particles as situating elements that predicate states on different constituents, and prepositions that link those constituents to contexts that define situations for them, according to the speaker's particular discourse purposes. Chapter 5 defined orientation and its strategic subcomponents of situating and linking and illustrated how they work. Chapter 6 explained the special contextual nature of the landmarks that prepositions link to. Chapter 7 interpreted the choice between preposition and particle as a matter of pragmatic focus and provided the pragmatic criteria that motivate and constrain the choice.

The next two chapters examined P's constituency and semantic extensions in detail, in the process answering the language learners' questions from chapter 1. Chapter 8 mapped out a grammatical template for P's meanings, explaining how a wealth of grammatical and semantic functions could be generated by the construction of P-forms with other constituents under different scopes. The patterns of the constructions and the constraints they impose explained the hitherto confusing results of traditional syntactic tests (chapter 2) and synthesized earlier semantic accounts of P's constituency (chapter 3). Finally, chapter 9 placed P's synchronic variation within a universal diachronic frame. It explained a pattern of skewed distribution for certain P-forms in discourse as a reflection of their evolution over time in response to orientational needs. P-forms were unified with other, non-P-prepositions and with purely adverbial particles. Finally, the categorial flexibility of prepositions and particles demonstrated grammar change in progress.

In the course of this text, we have come across several intriguing surprises concerning what speakers actually do with P-forms: their tendency to set off prepositional phrases in separate intonation units; the scarcity of prepositional uses for <u>up</u> and <u>out</u> or particle uses for <u>by</u>; the suppletion of <u>about</u> by <u>around</u> in American English; or the exclusively linking function of <u>about</u> (= "approximately"), despite its traditional classification in this meaning as an adverb.

This text has also clarified many apparent irregularities as principled, logical consequences of their orientational function. Furthermore, it has addressed several issues left unresolved in the previous literature on this topic: the functional differences between prepositional objects and other NPs (chapter 6); the explanatory importance of the adprep as the source of P's meanings (chapters 5 and 9); constraints on landmark sublexicalization (chapter 7); the significance of syntactic scope as a generator of polysemy (chapter 8); the correlations among stress marking, pragmatic focus, and particle movement (chapter 7); specialization tendencies for certain P-forms (chapter 9); and the relation between P-forms and other prepositions or adverbs (chapter 9).

Both the surprises and the solutions have emerged through a line of inquiry that distinguishes this book from the previous P-literature in two ways: (a) in the premise that language needs to be studied empirically, in naturally occurring contexts; and (b), in its eclectic approach, which synthesizes useful insights from many different linguistic theories without being contained by any of them.

10.2.   Questions Answered

We can now recast the language learners' questions from chapter 1 as theoretical questions to highlight the main conclusions from this study and to frame them in the larger context of linguistic theory.

1. What is the categorial status of prepositions and particles?
2. What is the relation between P-forms, which alternate, and other prepositions, particles or adverbs, which don't?
3. How can we account for the idiosyncratic patterning constraints on P-forms?
4. Why are certain P-forms so skewed in their distribution?
5. Why does a supposedly "closed" class produce so many meanings?

The answers to these questions are elaborated in the following sections.

10.2.1.   Categoriality of Prepositions and Particles

The categorial prototype for P-forms is the *adprep*, a spatial gram that allows sublexicalization of its landmark. Essentially, P-particles are adpreps without landmarks, or intransitive prepositions. However, unlike previous analysts, I suggest that neither the categorial status nor the transitivity of adpreps are a priori, stable properties.

I propose that both these properties are imposed by the discourse context in which the adprep is used. In other words, adpreps are not given to us a priori, with transitive properties intact, in our mental lexicon. Rather, they *become* adpreps in certain environments where they serve their prototypical function. This function involves situating a neighboring discourse element contextually; in other words, predicating a state on that element and linking it to a contextual element which defines the state.

In this proposal, I follow the lead of Paul Hopper and Sandra Thompson (1984, 1985), who argue that "categoriality itself is another fundamental property of grammars which may be directly derived from discourse function" (1984:703). Their cross-linguistic analysis of the categories noun and verb brings them to the conclusion that these supposedly basic universal categories are, in fact, "lexicalizations of the prototypical discourse functions of 'discourse-manipulable participant' and 'reported event,' respectively" (1984:703).

In other words, a lexical category is a label that we attach, posthoc, to sets of words that we see doing recognizable jobs in discourse. We label words as nouns to the extent that they seem to refer to participants and as verbs to the extent that they refer to events or activities.

What this analysis implies is that categoriality is continuous rather than discrete. The same word (e.g., stone, kick) may function syntactically as a noun in some contexts, but as a verb in others. A word that functions syntactically as a verb may be less verb-like than another in the same syntactic slot; for example, the English verb be, which does not refer to any event. There are even grammatical forms that code the intermediate status between noun and verb — for example, the English gerund. According to Hopper and Thompson, such categorial indeterminacy is the rule rather than the exception in discourse cross-linguistically. This conclusion leads the authors to posit a principle of iconicity for the lexical categories noun and verb: "the more a form refers to a discrete discourse entity or reports a discrete discourse event, the more distinct will be its linguistic form from neighboring forms, both paradigmatically and syntagmatically" (1985:151).

But categorial indeterminacy is not the trademark of only nouns and verbs; Thompson (1986) finds that adjectives display similar indeterminacy cross-linguistically. In fact, there is no such category in some languages; in others, its status fluctuates somewhere between that of noun and verb. Therefore, the iconicity principle could also be applied to this category.

Hopper and Thompson's categoriality studies deal only with the open-class categories of noun, verb, and adjective. Prepositions and particles are traditionally labeled closed-class, or grammatical, categories. But I would argue that the iconicity principle also applies to them and to draw an arbitrary distinction between open and closed classes in this case would be unproductive (see section 10.2.6). The findings of the present study suggest that adpreps also follow the iconicity principle which Hopper and Thompson apply to nouns and verbs. I would reformulate this principle as follows for adpreps:

(1) *Iconicity Principle for Adpreps*:

> The more clearly a form predicates a state on a neighboring element and defines that state in terms of a definitional context, the more identifiable it will be as an adprep.

The same word may perform this function more or less prototypically in different environments. If the speaker uses a P-form primarily to focus a state without introducing the defining context, it will be realized as a particle. If the P-form functions primarily to focus a context — for example, a new setting or an organizing frame — then it will be realized as a preposition. Adpreps perform both functions.

All adpreps are therefore prepositional because they perform a linking function. But not all prepositions are adpreps. Their status as adpreps depends on the extent to which they predicate states. For example, the verb-preposition construction, illustrated by such sequences as depend on or believe in, uses prepositions that perform primarily linking functions and do not qualify as full adpreps.

Therefore, we could say that P-particles and P-prepositions, as subcategories of the adprep, also have their prototypical subfunctions: to situate and to link, respectively. These prototypical functions are most centrally represented in elements that are grammaticized in one function or the other. The case markers to and of exemplify prototypical linking while too, now reanalyzed as an adverb, exemplifies prototypical situating.

Adpreps are transitive: they come with complements. But transitivity, too, is imposed by the discourse context. Returning to my invented example at the beginning of this study, I suggest that we can label through as transitive in (2a) and intransitive in (2b) only because (2a) happens to include a landmark and (2b) does not.

(2) a. What's 'bad is they could send a 'bullet right through the ''window .   (R:32)

  b. [if you roll an animal onto your hood I'm sure] that it would . .come 'roaring ''
     through .   (R:33)

It was explained in chapter 7 that whether a postverbal P-form is used transitively depends primarily on discourse purposes: on whether the speaker wishes to focus a context or a state. Therefore, it makes little sense to discuss the putative transitivity of P-forms in isolation from their actual use in discourse. Transitivity is not inherent; it happens. It may be observed, but not predicted a priori. The transitivity of a P-form is determined by whether it performs linking in a particular discourse environment. Since adpreps encode the prototypical function of orientation, which includes linking, they will, as a logical consequence, be used transitively.

I would therefore answer this first question by saying that the adprep can be categorially distinguished from other parts of speech by its prototypical discourse function, which is to perform orientation. This function is lexicalized in English in a relatively small class of words known as spatial grams in the literature. Its syntactic position is assigned, in unmarked clauses, between the verb and the following oblique argument. Its position and function in this slot can be identified as far back as Proto-Indo-European, with a tendency for subsequent extension and reanalysis (Kuryłowicz, 1964) similar to the one we find in English. For all these reasons, the adprep, though not recognized in the literature, has clear categorial status in English.

In contrast, the categorial status of prepositions and particles is less clear. First, their constituency does not distinguish them from other elements. Prepositions construct with the NPs following them and particles co-predicate states with verbs. But so do other elements, in different ways. The functions of prepositions and particles overlap with those of other categories — for example, prepositions with subordinating conjunctions (which may be followed by NP clauses or gerunds), and particles with adjectives (which may function as predicate adjectives). Both prepositions and particles have been characterized as elements of two-word verbs or phrasal verbs. Prepositions are sometimes called predicators and sometimes case markers (Jolly, 1993), which occasions further categorial overlap with other elements, such as verbs, or even the possessive case marker in English. Particles are sometimes called adjuncts and sometimes adverbs, which occasions overlap with a huge set of other functions classed as adverbial. Furthermore, the syntax of P-forms is very variable; we have seen that particle movement is commonplace, and so is prepositional phrase fronting, especially for clause-external phrases.

Second, the categorial function of prepositions and paricles is difficult to distinguish semantically, since all prepositions are not spatial grams (for example, since and even, the latter also functioning as an adjective and adverb). Finally, prepositions are diachronically positioned at various stages on the grammaticization chain from adprep to case marker. For all these reasons, even though preposition is traditionally recognized as a part of speech, I would argue that, by the iconicity principle, both prepositions and particles have less clear categorial status in English than do adpreps.

Prepositions and particles can be roughly identified by ad hoc semantic and syntactic definitions, such as those used in the first chapter of this book. But, as we saw in chapter 2, many attempts have been made to identify them as discrete grammatical categories, and they have generally failed. Thus, the most meaningful way to distinguish prepositions and particles from each other (and from other overlapping categories) is in terms of their linking and situating discourse functions.

10.2.2. *Prepositions, Particles, Adverbs, and Other Categories*

The next question to address is how P-forms relate to other, non-P-forms such as pure prepositions on the one hand, and to pure postverbal particles such as back or away, on the other; and, as a related question, how to relate them to other categories that also perform situating or linking functions.

P-Forms were identified in the corpus as forms displaying both particle and prepositional uses. (I also included about precisely because its unexpected nonalternation promised to be instructive.) Twenty P-forms were identified in this way. However, a larger database may have unearthed more alternating forms. The subset identified here should be seen as a focal group whose patterns and functions represent the adprep phenomenon.

In chapter 9, this focal group was positioned on a functional and historical continuum between purely situating adverbs and purely linking case markers. It was argued that this continuum diverged from the central, conceptually basic adprep. It was also argued that those P-forms that perform almost exclusively linking functions are following the same evolutionary path as case-marking prepositions, which also started out historically as adpreps. This path of evolution from spatial gram to case-marker is matched in many related and unrelated languages, according to the diachronic and typological literature.

Thus, we can conclude that pure prepositions are P-forms which have reached the end of the continuum, as it were, and have become reanalyzed in case-marking functions. Some P-forms appear to be following closely behind on this evolutionary path. For example, by, which almost never appears as a particle, performs certain specialized case-marking functions in various constructions: it marks agents in passive clauses; it marks a certain temporal posteriority with time phrases (by then, by the time that); and it marks a sort of instrumental or enabling relation with gerund forms (by doing that, by looking at the lights).

There are other, non-P-prepositions in English that do not mark case or refer in the spatial domain: despite, since, even, and like, to name but a few. They do not derive historically from adpreps but rather from nouns, verbs, and adjectives. They mark different kinds of relations such as concession, cause, and similarity. However, in their use as prepositions, what they share with P-prepositions is a crucially linking function.

Not surprisingly, some of these prepositions, like the more specialized P-forms (e.g., before, after) can also work as conjunctions or subordinators (e.g., since, like). The function of conjunctions is also crucially linking. Prototypically, conjunctions link clauses rather than entities within the clause and refer to nonspatial relations. However, to the extent that some of these subordinate clauses express contexts for other clauses — as a temporal background, for example, or a conditional frame (Matthiessen and Thompson, 1988), we can expect a great deal of functional overlap between prepositions and conjunctions.

Particles operate on the situating end of the continuum proposed in chapter 9, where they predicate a variety of states. They do not display as strong a tendency as prepositions do toward reanalysis and grammaticization. But when reanalysis has happened, as for example with Middle English too, the form has been reanalyzed as an adverb (a problematic traditional label, as I will explain next) which takes up some of the most specialized situating meanings of the original adprep.

Nevertheless, particle Ps lend symmetry to the situating-linking continuum in their tendency to specialize as situating, rather than linking, functions. Their pattern of evolution involves a pragmatic strengthening of their situating properties and a weakening link with their landmarks, in contrast with prepositions, whose situating properties weaken as they evolve toward exclusively linking functions. In the process, specialized particles come to be viewed as adverbs; the 1981 Webster's, for example, lists up and out, the most highly specialized particles, as adverbs first and prepositions second. But they could equally well be viewed as adjectives in some of their functions (you'd be out after that; really high up people). They could even, at their most predicative, be viewed as verbs, for example, in special uses such as to up someone's salary and in the archaic use, the truth will out.

Some other, non-P-particles construct with verbs as focal predicators and are sometimes listed in phrasal verb inventories: <u>back, away</u> and <u>together</u>. As we may expect by now, these forms also tend to be classified as directional adverbs in dictionaries. In fact, these forms should probably not be tagged particle, since they do not derive from original adpreps. Rather, they emerge independently from body part nouns or from conflations of prepositions with nouns, verbs, or adjectives: <u>a-way</u> originally means "on the way," and <u>to-gether</u> originally means "to-gather." In fact, these pure particles represent potential historical sources for adpreps: <u>along</u> emerged in this manner, as did <u>around</u> and <u>before</u>. Crucially, all these particles predicate states.

What unites these forms with particles and motivates their inclusion in phrasal verb inventories is their situating function and the constructional patterns that this function implies. As situators, they co-predicate with verbs, or co-occur with adjectives (*she's back, we're together*, etc.) as independent predicators.

These clarifications bring us to an important theoretical point: the traditional classification of postverbal particles as adverbs is problematic. First, it obscures the functional continuity between postverbal particles and P-forms used nonpostverbally in other situating constructions.

Second, the category adverb is itself problematic, since it has never been clearly defined, to my knowledge. Rather than representing a prototypical function, this category seems to be reserved as a grab-bag for assorted forms which are said to modify anything that is not a noun. Webster's dictionary entry serves as an example of the general vagueness of this category:

> **adverb** ...: a word belonging to one of the major form classes in any of numerous languages, typically serving as a modifier of a verb, an adjective, another adverb, a preposition, a phrase, a clause, or a sentence, and expressing some relation of manner or quality, place, time, degree, number, cause, opposition, affirmation, or denial

To label such an all-encompassing category "adverb" is essentially misleading. Although the dictionary states senses that adverbs typically modify verbs, they are by no means limited to this function. Some of the elements that they modify (e.g., a sentence) may include a verb, but others (e.g., a preposition) may not.

Defining the form of adverbs is equally problematic. Prepositional phrases are traditionally interpreted as having an adverbial function, either as adverbial complements (*I was <u>in the house</u>*) or as adverbial adjuncts (*In a manner of speaking* ...). As noted in chapter 9, the <u>about</u> qualifier (= "approximately") is classed as an adverb in word frequency lists, even though it always constructs with some kind of landmark and does not in any meaningful sense modify verbs. In short, the category adverb, defined as it is, tells us very little about its prototypical function.

We could, however, paraphrase the Webster definition fairly accurately by saying that adverbs predicate states and qualities on a wide variety of other elements. To modify is essentially to predicate some kind of state or quality on an element for purposes of restriction, elaboration, or identification. Adjectives do this for nouns. Adverbs, as defined here, do it for any other element.

In a sense, then, it makes sense to define particles as adverbs. But that does not tell us much. It would be more meaningful to define particles as elements that predicate contextually defined states. Then, rather than asking how particles relate to adverbs, we should first define the category adverb more precisely, explaining what kinds of relations and qualities, other than contextualized states, are predicated by forms within this category.

10.2.3. *Patterning Constraints*

Question number three refers to the syntactic idiosyncracies and irregularities that prompted the syntactic tests in table 2.1. The traditional classification of prepositions and particles into two discrete lexical categories has until now been based on a battery of tests designed to distinguish them in various constructions.

The problem with these tests — that they do not work systematically enough — was fully discussed in chapter 2. The concluding sections of chapter 8 returned to these tests and explained that both their successes and their failures could be accounted for within a template representing the orientational functions of P-constructions at all levels of constituency. We saw that it is the special-purpose construction rather than the categoriality of P that imposes the syntactic constraints observed in table 2.1. The regularities and the idiosyncracies of P's patterning are predictable from my proposed model of prepositions as linking elements and particles as situating elements.

10.2.4. *Specialization Patterns*

The fourth general question raised in chapter 1 dealt with the skewed distribution of certain P-forms across preposition and particle uses, revealed both in my data (table 3.1 in chapter 3) and in larger word frequency counts for British and American English. Although the question has not been examined in the previous literature, it is an important one, since it prompted a line of inquiry for this study that has yielded very fruitful results. In chapter 9, the synchronic skewing was shown to reflect speakers' tendency to select P-forms as either situating or linking elements and to reinforce these functions systematically in a variety of specialized constructions. This tendency is also reflected in the historical evolution of P-forms in English and in other languages. Thus, the analysis of P's distribution opened a diachronic window not only on its patterns of extension but also on the pragmatic motivations for them. In this way, P-forms take their place in the larger picture of universal, unidirectional grammaticization patterns currently being developed by many typological studies.

10.2.5. *Polysemy*

The last question, asking how a closed class of words can produce such a dazzling array of meanings, has been answered gradually throughout this study. A great deal of help was given by previous semantic and cognitive models which map out P's meanings in various ways (Kennedy, 1920; Bolinger, 1971; Brugman, 1981; Lindner, 1981, 1982; Hawkins, 1984; Lakoff, 1987; Svorou, 1994). The models, combining prototype theory with semantic decompositional analysis, generate large numbers of meanings for spatial grams, connected by means of metaphorical networks, radial categories, image schemata, or taxonomic grids of semantic features. As a result, their mental models have impressive generative power, constrained only by the limits of the human imagination.

If we combine the insights of these mental models with the Role and Reference Grammar notion of the layered structure of the clause (see chapter 3, section 3.2.3), we can account for yet more meanings. In chapter 8, I explained how shifts in the scope of operation for a given P-form could produce different constructions with very different meanings. For example, a core scope focal predictor reading would express a very different (and much stranger) meaning for *pick up your room* than would a nuclear scope Aktionsart meaning! And a core scope adprep reading for *I ran in the house* would be very different from a peripheral scope reading that views *the house* as a setting. Furthermore, the constructional patterns themselves offer a productive source of meanings. For example, the Aktionsart verb-particle pattern facilitates an almost unlimited number of creative meanings through the interaction of certain inherently extensional P-forms with the lexical semantics of almost any verb (chapters 8 and 9).

Thus, by combining the semantic possibilities of mental maps with the possibilities of construction with different constituents under different scopes, we can begin to understand P's extraordinary potential for polysemy.

However, mental maps and constructional frameworks may describe P's meanings, but they do not explain them. Nor do they constrain them. They do not clearly define the real-life limits observed in the corpus on P's alternation between preposition and particle.

The purpose of chapter 9 was to motivate and constrain P's polysemy. In the process, it has converted the synchronic map into a panchronic one, which relates semantic extensions in the present to actual historical developments over time. The motivation for P's polysemy is the ongoing need for greater specification of orientation, in progressively more abstract domains. The constraints are produced by channeling this function into situating and linking. Prepositions extend — but also narrow — their meanings to express links with more specific kinds of contexts, as seen in the evolution of <u>about</u>. Conversely, particles extend and also narrow their meanings to predicate very specific kinds of states, as in the development of the modern English <u>over-</u> and <u>out-</u> prefixes or in the development of deictic markers as discourse pointers.

Chapter 9 has also contributed another useful insight into the polysemy of prepositions and particles: they are self-renewing. When the meanings of a P-form proliferate to the point of confusion, or, conversely, become so narrow that the P-form no longer performs its original adprep function, then a new form emerges to take up some of those meanings. Some of these new forms are constructed from combinations of prepositions, such as the P-scope conflations <u>onto</u>, <u>into</u>, and <u>upon</u>. Others, such as <u>around</u> and <u>along</u>, come from combinations of prepositions with adjectives.

10.2.6. *Open or Closed Classes?*

In view of this self-generating potential for P, we may wonder how closed the adprep category is as a lexical class. If we follow a structural definition of an open-class element as one that generates new forms by derivation, then adpreps would qualify as closed-class, since they cannot produce new forms in the way that, say, a noun such as <u>friend</u> can: for example, <u>friendly</u>, <u>friendship</u>, and <u>befriend</u>. But if we adopt a semantic definition of a closed-class element as having a purely grammatical function, then adpreps constitute a considerably more open class than, for example, articles. In terms of the grammaticization chain (Claudi and Heine, 1986), English adpreps such as <u>down</u> and <u>before</u> may be viewed as the products of grammaticization from nouns referring to objects or body parts. But they are not fully grammaticized since, unlike case-marking prepositions, they have independent lexical meanings and, like open class categories, can function in a variety of syntactic slots: <u>down</u> can function as a verb or adjective and <u>before</u> can function as a temporal or spatial conjunction.

The tendency for new adpreps to derive directly from open-class words (<u>along</u>, <u>around</u>, <u>behind</u>, <u>below</u>) highlights the difficulty of labeling them as grammatical elements. Furthermore, dictionaries identify adpreps as adverbs and yet, as Soteria Svorou points out, "adverbs and adjectives . . . have been traditionally classified as lexical classes, and, therefore, not part of the grammar of a language" (1994:50).

I would concur with Svorou, who, citing Joan Bybee (1985) and Ronald Langacker (1991), claims that "lexicon and grammar are not sharply distinct but rather form a continuum. . . . Adjectives and adverbs have elements of open-class items (i.e. contribute some content to the utterance), but they also have some elements of closed class (i.e. express some kind of relation" (1994:50–51).

Adpreps, I would claim, combine the open-class property of predicating states with the closed-class property of marking relations. The more they evolve as specialized prepositions, the more they become closed. But to the extent that they specialize in particle uses, they may be viewed as open.

In conclusion, therefore, I would challenge traditional interpretations of prepositions and particles as closed classes. Rather, they represent specialized uses of the adprep, which displays both open and closed characteristics.

10.2.7.   Summary: Categoriality, Variation, and Specialization

We can now go back to the opening illustration of the "problem of P" (example 4, chapter 1, repeated here as example 3).

(3)   a. She'll cli-'try to 'climb <u>up</u> your ''leg 'man .   (U:83)

    b. An ''I'm gonna clean <u>up</u> the 'me=ss ?   (U:2)

    c. When we 'clean <u>up</u> the ''table it'll˜˜   (R:34)

    d. . . . and I uh-an I . .an I 'messed you ''<u>up</u> .   (U:30)

    e. There 'used to be a 'place <u>up</u> in ''Toledo   (A:31)

    f. laid 'off a . . . bunch of . .'really high <u>up</u> ''people ,   (R:19)

The only "problem" consists in trying to explain these varied meanings of <u>up</u> as either prepositional or particle uses in purely semantic or syntactic terms. For example, (3b) and (3c) seem to involve the same syntactic sequence, yet the sequence predicates a very different effect on <u>the mess</u> than on <u>the table</u>. In (3d) the meaning of the verb-particle sequence is quite unrecoverable from the sum of its parts since there is neither any mess nor any upward movement involved. <u>Up</u> looks more like an adverb in (3e) or an adjective in (3f) than either a preposition or a particle. In conclusion, it was determined in Chapter 1 that it would be extremely difficult to define the function of up coherently in either semantic or syntactic terms since the same meaning was expressed in several grammatical categories and the same category could express many different meanings.

The study reported in this book, I believe, has solved the problem of P by removing the cause of the problem — that is, the assumption that either its categoriality or its meanings are static. In addition, it has proposed a unifying function that accounts for all its varied uses: the function of orientation, which is performed in a variety of specialized ways.

The examples in (3) illustrate some of these specializations for up. The first utterance (3a) involves a prototypical adprep; but all the others present up in its characteristic situating function. The second utterance (3b) involves a verb-particle combination which may be interpreted in two ways. It may operate under core scope as a focal predicator, which situates the mess. In this case, we understand that the mess actually moves or changes its state in some way. Or it may operate under nuclear scope as an Aktionsart sequence that situates the verb clean, with the mess as the complement of the Aktionsart complex. In this case, we understand that the cleaning is carried out to a desired endpoint. The third utterance (3c) requires a similar Aktionsart interpretation.

The fourth utterance)3d) represents a more abstract extension of the Aktionsart construction: mess up expresses a subjectively defined event, where the verb contributes a general sense of negative influence on the complement and up contributes telicity, representing the event as an extended process leading to an outcome. Since neither of its parts makes sense independently of the other, this phrasal verb is a lexicalized unit; however, the particle, as a predicative element, is moved to sentence-final position and stressed, to focus the state of finality.

The fifth example (3e) illustrates the use of up as a deictic marker, providing a discourse pointer from the interlocutors' present frame of reference to a new setting (Toledo). We may interpret its scope of operation either as a broad one, situating the whole clause (There used to be a place) under peripheral scope, or a narrow one, situating a place under NP scope.

The last utterance (3f) uses up to predicate a quality under NP scope in a premodifying construction. In this function, it is distinguishable from an adjective only because the quality is actually a state, which is defined contextually (in terms of the people's position in the company) rather than being an inherent attribute.

Despite its semantic and syntactic versatility in all these uses, up is consistent in its function of orientation (i.e., situating). The versatility comes from extending that function from the spatially referring to the subjective and textual domains, to situate different constituents under different scopes of operation.

10.3.   Questions Unanswered

10.3.1.   *Adverbs*

One large question raised in the preceding commentary but beyond the scope of the study reported here is the categorial status of adverbs. As I pointed out, dictionary definitions tell us little about their prototypical function in English. Furthermore, typological and diachronic studies label spatial grams uncontroversially as adverbs, without explaining what this means. Previous studies of P-forms call particles adverbs when they modify verbs or clauses, as in example (3b) and (3e) of up, but, oddly, they call them adjectives when the same word, with essentially the same function, modifies a noun, as in (3f).

We have seen that certain P-forms (too, about) are reanalyzed as adverbs when they specialize in modifying adjectives and quantitative expressions (_too_ short, _about_ six inches). But unlike other adverbs — adverbs of manner, for example — they do not function independently in this modifying function. They cannot end a sentence and must always be followed by the expression that they modify. For this reason, I defined the qualifying, "approximately" function of about as essentially linking. Even though it predicates a state of approximation, this state must always be linked to a defining range. In utterances such as (4), where that range is a nominal referent or complement clause, we could more concisely define this adverbial use of about as prepositional or even subordinating:

(4)   a.   . .'Usually it 'takes about a ''teaspoon ,   (C:6)

     b.   'Kay 'this is 'about where you should ''be .   (C:37)

I have mentioned that the dictionary definition of adverb could be paraphrased as meaning that adverbs predicate states. A fruitful line of inquiry might therefore be to examine the different functions lumped under this category as situating functions. This might result in more precise, explanatory definitions for a long-underexamined part of speech.

10.3.2. *Emergence of Adpreps*

Related to the previous question is the issue of what determines the emergence of a new adprep. We have seen historically that adpreps tend to derive from lexical classes (down, before, behind, along, around). These words all have inherently configurational properties — in other words, the potential to situate. To the extent that this potential is reinforced within and above the clause, they are likely to be classified as adverbs rather than prepositions.

Other potentially situating forms, however, bypass the adprep route and come into service directly as spatially referring adverbs — for example, back, away, and together. All of these forms function like particles. Why, then, do they not alternate as prepositions? Further examination of this question may produce insights to complement Jerzy Kurlowicz's (1964) Proto-Indo-European model of differentiation and formal renewal. It may also help us identify which spatial forms are likely to participate in the attested universal grammaticization chain (substantive > adprep > case marker), and why.

10.3.3. *Asymmetrical Patterns*

A more comprehensive sample than the one presented in this volume might also explain a certain semantic asymmetry in the emergence of adpreps: Why, for example, does <u>near</u> occur as an adprep but <u>far</u> does not? Why does <u>until</u>, which derives from the spatially referring <u>unto</u> as a temporal preposition, have no particle counterpart?

10.3.4. *Obsolescence and Lexicalization*

It would also be very interesting to identify predictive criteria for the evolution of particular spatial grams. Chapter 9 explained how some words become obsolete and replaced by new adpreps while others simply grammaticize: <u>ymbe</u>, for example, was entirely renewed in all its meanings by the new adprep <u>about</u>. But <u>about</u> is not obsolete. It persists in its abstract linking functions while its earlier situating functions are renewed by <u>around</u>. Other forms simply renew themselves out of their own substance: <u>to/too</u> and <u>of/off</u>.

Some forms have become lexicalized as prefixes that retain their transitivizing or case-marking function: <u>understand</u>, <u>overhang</u>, <u>forego</u> (= originally, "go away from"); other lexicalized prefixes retain their situating function: <u>expel</u>, <u>propel</u>, <u>infuse</u>. Some prefixes have become obsolete (<u>ge-</u>,<u>be-</u>), while yet others are evolving in modern English (<u>outfox</u>, <u>overlearn</u>), parallel to the development of phrasal verbs.

Affixed lexicalizations in other lexical classes are also common for P-forms: <u>outboard</u>, <u>overboard</u>, <u>upbeat</u>, <u>turnoff</u>, and so on. A comprehensive study of lexicalization processes would perhaps trace their development, too.

Many phrasal verbs are also lexicalized as semantic if not structural units: in fact, most of the meanings of <u>make up</u>, <u>make out</u>, <u>take up</u>, and <u>put out</u> are unrecoverable compositionally, although we can certainly detect some telicity in the contribution of the particle. Collocations such as these delight learners of English, partly, no doubt, because of their pure semantic mystery. It would be rewarding to know what determines the evolution of such collocations and what constrains them.

10.3.5. *Adpreps in Other Dialects, Genres, and Languages*

The corpus for the study presented here was limited to 1,245 P-occurrences. Although my findings on distributional patterns were generally representative of English, as shown by their correlations with larger word frequency counts (Francis and Kučera, 1982; Johansson and Hofland, 1989), the specific details are only representative of conversational American English.

It is in the conversation domain that language is seen in action. We have seen throughout this volume that theoretical analyses based on introspection or even on a literary corpus do not capture the creative processes or the constraints that speakers apply to their linguistic resources. Therefore, the genre of spontaneous conversation is a very good place to start.

As well, chapter 9 offers some clues that certain P-forms pattern slightly differently in British English, or in more formal, written genres. <u>About</u> is still productive as a preposition in British English, although it is becoming supplanted, apparently "under US influence" (the 1992 OED) by <u>around</u>. This newer form is also productive as a continuative aspect marker but apparently more so for American than for British English (chapter 9, section 9.4.4). I would speculate that phrasal verbs in general are far more representative of spoken than of written genres. This speculation is supported by Arthur Kennedy's criticism of them as "slang" and "bizarre" (1920:45).

I would also speculate that formal, extended monologues, both written and spoken, make different use of P's constructional potential. We observed that its use as a text-transitional device (chapter 8, section 8.5.3) was rare in the conversational corpus of the current study, despite its rhetorical importance, which is well documented in composition textbooks. Thus, genre seems to have a determining influence on P-usage.

Going beyond English, I would like to know how speakers of other languages exploit the linking and situating potential of spatial grams — for example, with serial verbs and spatially referring affixes. Much work has been done in tracing the semantic extension and grammaticization of these forms (chapter 9, section 9.3), but to my knowledge it has not provided a unifying pragmatic motivation such as the one offered here for P-forms.

10.4. Implications

In general, I hope that the model proposed here for English prepositions and particles will help us understand our language better, document it more accurately, and teach it to learners in a more meaningful way.

10.4.1. *For Language Scholars*

The present work contributes to a growing body of research that encourages language scholars to dissolve the boundaries between lexical categories, across syntax, semantics, and pragmatics, and between synchrony and diachrony.

To the extent that we seek to discover the dynamics of language use and language change, the conclusions reached here should also promote the value of corpus-based analyses (which deal with naturally occurring conversation) over introspective approaches (which deal with invented, decontextualized sentences). The rewards of such naturalistic analyses are in the unexpected findings they produce about the ways that speakers exploit their language in creative but principled ways. The synchronic reconstruction in chapter 9 suggests a practical line of inquiry to reveal how conversational use may extend the meaning of an element step-by-step, via pragmatic strengthening and reanalysis.

In identifying the functions of situating and linking, not only as local concerns below the clause level but also as global discourse concerns, the present work may stimulate scholars to explore the orientational functions of other linguistic elements and constructions.

More generally, I believe that this work encourages an eclectic, cross-theoretical approach to solving linguistic problems. Throughout the book, my own analysis has been informed by the insights of many different and potentially conflicting linguistic theories. None of these theories in isolation could account for the problem of P, since their approaches to the problem are constrained by their theoretical premises and thus yield only fragmentary solutions.

For example, chapter 3 explained that both Sue Lindner's cognitive grammar model and the RRG framework of William Foley and Robert Van Valin overlooked important similarities and differences between prepositions and particles. Chapter 7 argued that Knud Lambrecht's construction grammar approach to prepositions did not explain why these elements should be construed as purely relational. Chapter 9 showed that Bruce Hawkins's semantic analysis of prepositions (also from a cognitive grammar perspective) did not capture the dynamic, evolving nature of their semantic structure.

And yet all these theoretical models yielded crucial clues toward solving the problem of P. Thay also provided indispensable nomenclature for describing the complex functions of P: the trajector-landmark schemata of Lindner (1981); the layered structure of the clause in RRG (Foley and Van Valin, 1984; Van Valin, 1993; Jolly, 1993); the relation between constituency and pragmatic focus (Lambrecht, 1994); and the descriptive inventory for semantic structure (Hawkins, 1984). When synthesized with discourse-pragmatic and diachronic insights in the context of the present corpus-based approach, they facilitated a satisfactory account of P.

Therefore, I feel justified in suggesting that other linguistic problems might be similarly approached and that their analyses might benefit from the cross-fertilization of different theoretical ideas.

10.4.2.   *For Lexicographers*

The previous sections have unveiled certain problems in the traditional dictionary classifications of adpreps and adverbs. Although dictionaries will no doubt continue to list prepositions and adverbs as different parts of speech, it is conceivable that the model proposed here may encourage a more instructive type of listing: one that identifies the adprep, acknowledges its functional links with particles and other prepositions, and defines the function of the category "adverb" with more specificity. More generally, dictionaries may eventually recognize the categorial flexibility of most parts of speech and the continuous nature of open and closed categories.

10.4.3.   *For Language Teachers and Learners*

Finally, the present approach to P-particles and prepositions has practical implications for those who teach English to native or nonnative speakers. Drawing on its insights, grammar textbooks could explain P-constructions in a way that helps learners understand their pragmatic purposes and see how syntax and semantics are manipulated for these purposes.

As Cecilia Ford optimistically points out from the perspective of teaching English as a second or foreign language (TES/FL), the need has already become recognized among professionals "for empirically grounded information on grammar from a discourse perspective and with reference to situated usage" (1993:149). This discourse perspective would reveal functional regularities where only puzzling syntactic irregularities were seen before. P-constructions could be presented as a strategic, purposeful component of communicative competence rather than as a set of arbitrary uses.

In chapter 1, I listed some of the specific questions that language learners ask about P-constructions. I believe these questions are puzzling only in a discrete-point, rule-oriented approach to grammar, which focuses on form rather than function. Language educators have clearly established the value of grammar consciousness-raising activities which allow students to figure out how grammar works by observing and analyzing its use in communicative situations (Fotos and Ellis, 1991; Fotos, 1994). For P-constructions, such activities would focus the prototypical function of the ad-prep and the motivations for sublexicalization. Stress-marking and clause-final word order would be drawn to learners' attention as a clue to the focal importance of particles. Intonation would be pointed out as another clue, revealing speakers' frequent use of clause-external prepositional phrases as discourse settings or transitions.

To explain these functions, teachers could appeal to visual and kinesthetic as well as auditory learning styles. With a little imagination, a variety of aids could be enlisted to represent such concepts as discourse orientation, sublexicalization, particle movement, and setting without the need for a complicated metalanguage. For example, cuisenaire rods (small colored blocks of different lengths) could be juxtaposed in different ways to model the manipulations of clause elements. The discourse stage of the clause could be represented metaphorically, complete with participants, events and landmark props. The need for orientation is one that all learners can instinctively recognize in our attempts to make sense of the world.

Such an awareness-raising approach would discourage the proliferation of obscure grammatical terms. For example, one could abandon the notion of inseparable and separable phrasal verbs (Azar, 1989), contrasting instead the special linking function of (inseparable) verb-preposition constructions and the special situating functions of (separable) postverbal particle constructions. In this way, both types of phrasal verbs could be unified with more transparent, spatially referring P-sequences.

Rather than memorizing lists of phrasal verbs and rules for their word order, nonnative English speakers could learn these collocations as strategies for purposeful communication. M. Swain's output hypothesis (1985) reminds us that syntax is best acquired through the negotiation of meaning with proficient speakers. Given students' natural desire to learn the colloquial forms that characterize social interaction, a little instructional input from their teachers, combined with critical feedback from interlocutors, would soon show them that the choice of a certain particle makes a subtle difference to meaning: for example, that burn down is subtly different from burn up. On the other hand, the choice of preposition in verb-prepositional constructions is often less significant: in or on would both serve fairly well as linking prepositions after think, even if they are not as conventionally accepted as about.

This functionally oriented approach would help teachers to be more selective in their corrections of students' errors, focusing on those errors that impede communicative precision, and defocusing others as part of their students' interlanguage, to be resolved naturally through exposure and experience over time.

A functional approach would also help students relate English P with its counterparts in their own languages. For example, it would reveal the semantic-pragmatic motivations that drive the extension from spatial grams to Aktionsart or case markers as a universal tendency. Semantic and syntactic variation would seem less perplexing in English if students could see that the same kinds of lexical elements follow the same patterns of extension in their own languages.

Furthermore, if learners were allowed to see language structure as a dynamic, flexible organism, they might be encouraged to let go of the inhibiting need for rules (which rarely work systematically anyway) and instead try to exploit syntax and semantics in the creative but principled ways that native speakers do.

Teachers can help students in this enterprise by pointing out the differences that genre and discourse style can make. They could, for example, talk about the relative informality of verb-particle constructions compared with simplex Latinate substitutes, the rhetorical importance of P-forms as text-transitional organizers in written discourse, and their usefulness as deictic markers or pointers in spoken discourse.

10.5.   Conclusion

At the very least, I hope the present volime will highlight an important principle that is still often overlooked in language pedagogy: that grammar is a fascinating functional game whose rules cannot be fully prescribed since they are constantly being developed and modified by speakers in an "interplay between speakers' cognitive plasticity, on the one hand, and linguistic convention, on the other" (Lindner, 1981:52).

The "problem of P" is as intriguing for scholars today as it was for Walker in the seventeenth century and Dryden in the eighteenth. But today we can view P's idiosyncracies less as a problem and more as a tribute to the linguistic ingenuity of speakers. My aim has been to put Bolinger's adprep together with prepositions and particles on the discourse-functional map and to show how the "outpouring of lexical creativeness" so appreciated by Bolinger (1971) is channeled.

Appendix

Methodology: Coding of Features

This Appendix supplements chapter 4 in providing some explanatory details on the coding of significant features for P-units and landmarks.

A.1. Intonation Units: Transcription

P-units were coded following the transcription guidelines of John Du Bois, Susanna Cumming, and Shephan Schuetze-Coburn (1988) (transcription conventions listed in front matter). There are often difficulties in delimiting intonation contours and some subjectivity is involved, especially, for example, in "rush-through" cases with no pause and in idiosyncratic pitch sequences.

It is also difficult sometimes to distinguish an intonation unit (IU) boundary from an IU-internal hesitation. Alan Cruttenden's guidelines are most helpful in this respect. He suggests that the basic criterion for delimitation should be a "minimum internal structure" involving "pitch movement to or from at least one accented syllable." After this, pitch change and increased tempo for initial unstressed syllables, final syllable lengthening, and pausing all help identify the intonation contour as a self-contained unit (1986:35–42).

To help solve the problem of subjectivity, reliability checks were made by a colleague, who coded IUs independently in several different stretches of the database.

Prosodic features regularly marked in the transcription include *juncture, stress, pauses,* and *repairs* since all these features are helpful in interpreting information flow. Other features, such as voice quality and overlap across speakers, were not coded unless specifically relevant (for example, where overlap might cause a speaker not to close the intonation contour for a specific unit).

A.2.   Unit Form

In the present data, the most common syntactic form coinciding with IU form is, not surprisingly, the clause (or multiple clause units). The second most common is the prepositional phrase. Syntactic fragments (i.e., interrupted clauses or phrases) often coincide with truncated intonation contours. The reason for truncation may be speaker repair: repaired cases are noted in the coding, on the principle that repaired utterances are as important as well-formed ones in the staging of information (Fox and Jasperson, 1995).

   Problems of constituency definition sometimes complicate the coding of this feature. In particular, the question of what can be called a clause is now equivocal, in the light of recent syntactic literature. For example, Talmy Givón (1980) counts a gerundial or infinitival complement as a clause, differing from noun clauses only in its degree of dependency on the verb of the main clause. Paul Hopper and Sandra Thompson (1984, 1985) also treat nominalized propositions as clauses.

   This issue is important to the present work because it relates directly to the syntactic function of P. Some P-prepositions may take either nonfinite or fully finite clauses, as well as nominalized verbs, for their objects, as in example (1).

(1)   a.   by [giving two breaths]   (= nonfinite clause)   (C:22)
      b.   after [you call for help]   (= finite clause)   (C:8)
      c.   after [each use].   (= nominalization)   (C:2)

The distinction between preposition and conjunction becomes fuzzy in such examples: the underlined P seems to function in all cases as a proposition-linking device. And yet, (1b) clearly has a different syntactic shape from (1c). The question is how to code the unit form of these P + proposition sequences: as introduced by conjunctions or as prepositional phrases?

   For consistency's sake, my procedure assumed the following guidelines. Ps with nominalized or nonfinite verb complements were coded as prepositional phrases (PP). P-forms introducing fully inflected verbs with all their arguments were coded as prepositions with clausal landmarks (P + Cl). The overlap between prepositions and conjunctions is treated in chapters 8 and 10. Illustrations of coding follow in (2).

(2)   P-unit   IU form

      a.   by giving two breaths   PP
      b.   And after you call for help   P+CL
      c.   after each use   PP
      d.   by the time people determine ,   PP+CL
      e.   It depends on if it's a partial or a full .   CL+(P+CL)

A.3.   P-Form

Coding problems sometimes arise with sequences such as over here/there and on here (examples 3 and 4).

(3)   And then they'll come over to this field over here.   (R:6)

(4)   I don't think it works on here so good .   (R:6)

In (3), I coded both cases of over as a particle, according to the logic explained in chapter 4: that neither of the P-forms is followed by a landmark. Instead, each is followed by what I interpret as a prepositional phrase.

The first case is transparent, involving a preposition with a lexical landmark. The second case is less transparent; however, if we consider the semantic relations of this clause, it is clear that the field is not the trajector of over and here is not the landmark. The sequence could be paraphrased as "this field over in this place" but not as "this field over this place." Thus, here expresses a conflation of location and landmark (= "in this place"), namely, a path-ground conflation in Leonard Talmy's (1985) sense. The word over can be interpreted as a deictic directional particle with a sublexicalized landmark (inferrable, perhaps as "the pasture" or "the intervening fields"). Further discussion appears in chapter 8 about the use of over and other particles as deictic markers.

Example (4) has a different semantic composition. In this example, I code on as a preposition and here as a landmark. The speaker is referring to a toy car that moves better on the floor than on the surface of the table. The sequence could be paraphrased "on this surface" or "on this table." Thus, here acts as a pronominalized landmark rather than as a location–landmark conflation.

A.4.   Stress Marking

Coding for stress marking examines the relative stress marking for verbs, prepositions, particles, and landmarks. However, in practice, the coding of stress placement is not easy: degree of stress is relative, varying across speakers and different stretches of speech; secondary and tertiary levels of stress make the procedure even more complicated (Du Bois et al., 1988). For the purposes of this study, a great deal of the complexity is avoided.

Stress placement was coded in a limited way, to facilitate comparisons only for the relevant elements and to exclude other, less relevant elements. If any of the relevant elements received stress in a P-unit, it was coded. If none of them was stressed, the unit was simply coded "other" for stress placement. If more than one element was stressed, then the relative degree of stress was coded for all elements concerned, as equal (=) or greater (>). This system is illustrated in the sequence in (5).

(5)   Stress Coding

   a.   So it 'ended ''up that~   particle > verb
   b.   'He was ''up on the . . . ''trailer,   particle = landmark
   c.   or 'up on the 'back of his ''pickup truck .   landmark > particle = landmark

The stress coding notation indicates that in (5a), the particle up receives primary stress and the verb secondary stress; in (5b), up receives equal stress to the landmark trailer; and in (5c), the landmark pickup truck receives primary stress, while the landmark back receives secondary stress equal to that on the particle up.

A.5.   Assertion

Assertion is an important pragmatic concept in the analysis of information flow, and is defined as challengeable information that builds on and goes beyond pragmatic presupposition (Givón, 1984b:502–505). Presupposition is defined as the information which is recoverable or predictable in an utterance.

Talmy Givón explains that most utterances are a hybrid of presupposed and asserted information, placing them between the extremes of tautology (with only redundant information) and contradiction (informational incoherence) (1984b:504–505). This balancing act is performed by speakers to facilitate optimal processing of information by the hearer.

Givón provides a taxonomy of properties which (as explained in chapter 7) can be applied to test the assertion status of individual words. Presupposed information constitutes "uncontested knowledge," and the taxonomy lists the following kinds of information that are likely to be uncontested:

1. Deictic obviousness: "held in the immediate perceptual field of both speaker and hearer, or . . . derived from the speaker's direct experience"
2. Shared presupposition: coming from "previously shared information in the discourse"
3. Divine revelation: "information both speaker and hearer subscribe to, due to unimpeachable higher sources" (i.e., socially unquestioned beliefs and assumptions)
4. A priori-synthetic: generic knowledge that comes from "living in the same culture/universe as coded in the same lexicon"
5. Analytic truth: truth that comes from "subscribing to the same mode of thought, logic or rules of various games" (1984b:503)

I would suggest it is possible that, in a prepositional phrase, the preposition itself may be presupposed and the landmark asserted. In example (6), the underlined preposition repeats the preceding particle in and elaborates it by introducing the landmark our own place.

(6)   It 'sure is ''fun , to be ''moved 'in ,
       . .in our ''own 'place ''again   (R:1)

Thus, the coding of this feature, as for stress placement, is localized to the relevant elements in this study. Those elements are prepositions, landmarks and particles. Coding indicates which element is asserted in a specific construction, following a binary yes/no principle: if none of them comes under the scope of assertion, then the whole P-unit is coded negatively. If any of these elements is asserted, then the unit is coded affirmatively, and each element is listed. The principle is illustrated in example (7).

(7)   P-unit   Asserted?
     a.   ''Oh, don't 'worry about it . (R:5)   No
     b.   'Just kinda ''tiptoe because you   Yes: Preposition
           have to go right ''by them . (C:13)
     c.   You'd 'wake them ''up . (R:5)   Yes: Particle
     d.   [Keegan] 'tried to put him 'into   Yes: Preposition/Landmark
           the ''wall . (A:10)
     e.   where they actually ''bring in ,   Yes: Landmark
           an ''MCI line or a US ''Sprint line ,
           ''into your 'office , (R:10)

As a note of clarification to these codings: my decisions concerning assertion/presupposition do not follow the procedures of Lambrecht's (1994) theory of focus. His theory is concerned with how pragmatic relations are structurally encoded, taking phrasal categories rather than individual words as the basic unit for a domain of assertion. Thus, for example, in (7b), the whole prepositional phrase by them would be asserted, plus the verb, in Lambrecht's model. However, my analysis of P-constructions is pre-theoretical and pre-constructional: rather than assuming P-phrases as starting points, it seeks to find out how and why these phrases get constructed in the first place. This argument is elaborated in chapter 7.

Therefore, I coded only the preposition as asserted in (7b), and not the landmark. By is asserted because it contributes unpredictable, potentially contestable information. The landmark

<u>them</u> expresses a "shared presupposition," in Givón's terms, since its antecedent has already been represented and shared in a previous utterance. By contrast, in (8), <u>about</u> is lexically entailed by the verb-preposition construction <u>worry</u> _____ : it is the only preposition that could predictably appear in that syntactic slot.

(8)   ''Oh don't 'worry <u>about it</u> .   (R:24)

In other words, we could imagine the sequence "Oh, don't worry _____ it" in a cloze exercise, where students could make only one correct choice. It therefore represents something similar to Givón's "analytic" information, in the sense of being presupposed by the rules of the game (the game being conventional English grammar). The landmark <u>it</u> is also presupposed (compare with <u>them</u> in 7b). Therefore, for this P-unit, both preposition and landmark are nonasserted and the unit was coded negatively.

For particles, assertion is coded according to the same logic.

(9)   You'd 'wake them ''<u>up</u> .   (R:27)

In (9), <u>up</u> is conventionally associated with the verb <u>wake</u>: presumably, no other particle could be meaningfully slotted in this position. However, I think the particle has a different pragmatic status from the preposition in <u>worry about</u>. For one thing, it does not have to be there; the predication would be logically and grammatically complete without the addition of the particle (*you'd wake them*), whereas <u>about</u> is grammatically required to license the landmark <u>them</u>. Just as *cleaning up* is not the same thing as *cleaning* (see chapter 2, 2.1.2), *wake them* is not the same thing as *wake them up*. The particle <u>up</u> adds telicity, a sense of completion, to the verb and is therefore coded as asserted in example (9).

Coding of assertion as a binary, yes/no category may sometimes be problematic. Some elements seem to represent an intermediate degree of assertion; for example, in (10) (which refers to one racing car driver crashing into another), both the preposition and its landmark are semantically unpredictable and therefore asserted.

(10)   [Keegan] 'tried to put him '<u>into the</u> ''<u>wall</u> .

In (11), however, only the landmark <u>your office</u> was coded "asserted."

(11)   Where they actually bring in ,
         an MCI line or a US ''Sprint line ,
         ''into <u>your office</u> ,

Even though the preposition <u>into</u> is stressed in (11), it does not express any unpredictable information: it simply repeats the directional information already asserted by <u>in</u>. (Lambrecht's explanation for this phenomenon of stressed prepositions is given in chapter 7.) The landmark, however, seems to be added as a kind of afterthought, to clarify the speaker's frame of reference. As the setting for the ongoing topic of conversation, this landmark is to some extent a matter of shared presupposition; however, the fact that the speaker needed to mention it suggests some perceived degree of unpredictability. For indeterminate cases such as this, I decided, for consistency's sake, to code the element as asserted.

A.6.   Scope of Operation

The Role and Reference Grammar model of layered clause structure may be briefly summarized here again (see also chapter 3, section 3.2.3): the verb of a clause is defined as the nucleus for that clause. The nucleus, together with its arguments, form the core while adjunctive prepositional phrases form the periphery. All P-forms are coded according to their scope of operation. Here I explain certain modifications to the RRG model which were required for data-coding in the study reported here.

Within RRG's core scope for prepositions, I have made a distinction between those that involve core arguments in a two-term relationship with the landmark and those that involve only the verb itself. I code the former as core level prepositions, and the latter as nuclear level. The difference is illustrated in example (12).

(12)   a. 'Throw him in the 'goddam ''furnace ,   (= core)   (U:94)

       b. If 'you believe in ''that ,   (= nuclear)   (U:31)

I coded the preposition in (12a) "core" because it takes a core argument of the verb him as its trajector: it is predicated as "in" the furnace as a result of throwing. In contrast, I coded the preposition in (12b) "nuclear" because it does not take you as the trajector but rather the verb believe. The function of this preposition is to relate the verb to a landmark that defines its range — the "believing" is "in" that. The notion of range elements comes from M.A.K. Halliday (1985) and is elaborated in more detail for nuclear scope verb-preposition constructions in chapter 8.

Beyond nuclear, core, and peripheral scopes, the codings also refer to NP-scope.

(13)   you know laid 'off a ... bunch of ... 'really high up ''people ,   (= NP scope)   (R:19)

In (13), up takes people as its trajector and comes under the scope of that NP.

Finally, my codings refer to another scope not mentioned in the RRG model of layered clause structure: P-scope, exemplified in (14).

(14)   I've got ... ''two cousins who are ... out of 'work at the 'moment .   (= P-scope) (R:5)

Sequences such as out of work have not been analyzed, to my knowledge, in RRG; however, I propose in chapter 7 that the prepositional phrase of work operates under the scope of the particle out. The preposition relates the particle to its defining domain, work, just as the nuclear scope preposition relates the verb to its defining domain in (12b); in other words, work functions as a range element and the preposition of functions as a type of case marker for the particle. This interpretation is a logical one if we consider the grammatical relations in this clause. The prepositional phrase may not stand alone without its particle trajector (*two cousins who are of work); it relates to nothing else in the clause. The particle could grammatically stand alone (two cousins who are out) but it is rather unspecified semantically — the hearer would very likely ask Out of what? Structurally, then, this particle-preposition sequence resembles the verb-preposition construction exemplifed in (12b). The explanatory value of this scope for explaining certain P-constructions is elaborated in chapter 8.

A.7.   NP Table: Syntactic Role

The sample in the NP table of the database contains 565 entries. Since all these NPs come from the larger P-unit table (see chapter 4, sections 4.4.2 and 4.4.4), they all occur in an utterance containing a P-form. This fact may have resulted in a rather skewed distribution of syntactic roles. For example, a relatively low total of agents (A) is identified (66), as compared with 180 intransitive subjects (S), 231 landmarks (LM), and 88 transitive objects (O). The relatively low occurrence of A is probably due to the fact that many of these units involve P-prepositions, and clauses with prepositional phrase predications are often intransitive.

It might seem strange that more Os (88) are coded than As (66), since A, as the subject of a transitive verb, presupposes O (the object). This, however, reflects the reality of naturally occurring conversation. Most of these agentless utterances involve zero-realized agents presupposed from the preceding clause, as in (15), or they appear in reduced clauses with implicit agents, as in (16). The Os without corresponding As are underlined in both examples:

(15)   You need to just gently press on the stomach , and
        . .make <u>em</u>- vomit and then turn <u>their head</u> to the side . .and start all over again. (C:6)

(16)   It's really nice just to sit down and stop ,
        lifting <u>boxes</u> and moving <u>things</u> around.   (R:17)

In any case, the small number of As in this sample represents no problem for the present study since the semantic and pragmatic properties of A are relatively uncontroversial. These properties have already been extensively studied in the literature (see especially Du Bois 1987 for a review); my small sample entirely supports previous conclusions in differentiating A from other syntactic roles. The present study is more concerned with identifying the properties of landmarks, and the sample of 565 entries provides sufficient contrastive evidence for this purpose.

A.8.   Semantic Class

The problem with coding this feature is in identifying categories — deciding what labels to attach to semantic classes at what level of generality. My response to the problem was to code in an ad hoc way at first, letting category labels proliferate, and then to synthesize various categories into larger groups with more general labels. NPs were coded for semantic class according to the specific context in which they occurred; for example, the word <u>class</u> was coded as an "activity" when appearing in the collocation <u>take this class</u> but, when referring to a location, as in <u>you're in class</u>, it was coded as a "place."

According to these criteria, the following general categories emerged:

1. Person (including any animals referred to as "he/she")
2. Place and Time
3. Thing (or tangible object)
4. Situation
5. Abstract concept
6. Other

The situation category includes activities, events, states, and experiences (examples are shown in 17).

(17)   a. 'He's being ''ethnocentric by ''<u>doing that</u> .   (E:10)
        b. Okay if you're 'on <u>the ''job</u>,   (C:3)

Note that landmarks such as <u>the job</u> in (17) would be excluded from Thompson's 1993 study of prepositional object NPs because they are predicating elements, which do not function as arguments in many languages. However, I chose to include them because they are syntactic arguments in English, and furthermore quite relevant to the present study in their function as contextual props (see chapter 6).

The abstract concept group includes intangible referents: qualities, ideas, and values, for example. The following utterance comes from a CPR lecture, where the instructor is reviewing topics covered by the training manual.

(18) [Page one talks about ... assessment.] That's your "ABCs. 'That's the 'foundation on
      which you're gonna build "everything else on .   (C:5)

All underlined referents are coded as abstract concepts. The distinction between concept and activity is sometimes tricky; for example, ABCs refers to training instructions in a manual about CPR procedures. As explained previously, the coding decision is made according to the specific context; in this case, the instructions are introduced not as physical activities but as textual details that need to be memorized in abstraction from physical experience. In contrast, accident and CPR in (19) represent physical situations — a hypothetical event and a hypothetical activity in the real world.

(19) You 'come upon an "accident and someone needs "CPR ,   (C:3)

Certain NPs are not easily captured in the larger categories and are therefore labeled Other. They do not occur frequently enough to justify any generalizations, so rather than force them into a larger group I simply coded them under smaller semantic domains:

System: A nonanimate, often technological network, such as AT&T lines or the EMS (emergency medical system).

Organization: A social or professional grouping, such as some companies or the health profession, which may be referred to as an animate referent.

Measure: Often used to predicate distance or quantity, e.g., a stone's throw or millions (of dollars).

Idiom: NPs may occur within idioms where they are semantically too opaque to be included in the larger domains. In such cases, the NPs are coded "idomatic." For example, get on your case clearly represents a situation; but within that idiom, the semantic class of case is unidentifiable.

A.9.   Information Status

For the present study, I adopted Ellen Prince's (1981) hierarchy of assumed familiarity to identify the status of NPs as providing old or new information. This hierarchy differs from Wallace Chafe's (1987) three-way classification (active/semiactive/inactive) because it allows finer distinctions within the broad categories: for example, Prince has the categories Inferrable and Unused. Such distinctions are worth considering since landmarks in this corpus have inferrable and unused status more often than NPs in any other syntactic role (see chapter 6, sections 6.1 to 6.3 and table 6.1).

From Prince's six-point familiarity scale, I have grouped all evoked referents together, as well as all new ones, leaving inferrable and unused as intermediate categories. Thus, for present purposes, Prince's categories can be summarized and explained as follows.

New: first mentions of referents whose identity is not immediately familiar to the hearer. They are often indefinite and introduced in transitive object position (Du Bois, 1980, 1987), as in (20a). These NPs may or may not be anchored by a referent or frame more familiar to the hearer: for example, him in (20b).

(20) New:
 a. and 'then we'll watch <u>a "film</u> , (C:2)
 b. She's 'talking about <u>the 'super</u> ' 'before him. (U:3)

Unused: new information, but retrievable as an element well known to the hearer and therefore needing no anchoring. This category includes well-known names, places, and acronyms (<u>Atlanta</u>, <u>AIDS</u>, etc.).

Inferrable: new, in the sense of first mention, but accessible from the discourse context. This category includes "containing" Inferrables, where the new referent exists in a member-set or part-whole relationship to a more familiar referent within the same NP. Example (21) refers to a racing driver where <u>top</u> is inferrable or "contained" by <u>the car</u>.

(21) Inferrable: and he 'takes his ' 'helmet off an ,
 ' 'CLUNK I it 'goes on '<u>top</u> of the ' 'car . (A:11)

In this category I also include paraphrases of evoked NPs and referents which evoke familiar NPs at a higher or lower level of generality. Thus, in (22), <u>long distance</u> is a first mention, but is Inferrable as a summarizing frame for many already mentioned referents (AT&T cards, international lines, phone bills, and so on).

(22) Does 'your bank ' 'spend a lot , on '<u>long ' 'distance</u> ? (R:11)

Evoked: These NPs are active in the hearer's consciousness. Familiarity may be contributed either by the discourse context, as with most pronoun NPs, or by the real-world context where the referent is physically obvious, as in (23) for both of the underlined NPs (spoken to a child banging a plate on the table).

(23) We're 'just gonna 'take <u>that</u> ' 'away from you, ' 'Okay ? (R:4)

A.10. Definiteness and Referentiality

John Du Bois argues that both definiteness and referentiality are required for a NP to be identifiable in the discourse. Identifiability is only a relevant issue for "referential-specific" NPs (1980:209); therefore, NPs "may fail to receive definite marking, not because they do not refer to an identifiable object, but because they simply do not refer" (1980:272). For example, in the activity represented as "pear-picking," <u>pear</u> is not referential because the speaker is not referring to any specific pears, only to a generic activity. For Du Bois, definiteness is a formal rather than a unitary semantic or pragmatic property:

> The word definite may serve a useful purpose in referring to a formal class of reference items which includes not only noun phrases preceded by the definite article (*the boy, the pears*), but also definite pronouns (*I, you, he, she, it*), proper names (*John, London*), and possessed noun phrases (*his bicycle, the man's pears*). Formally indefinite noun phrases include not only those preceded by the indefinite article (*a boy*), but articleless mass nouns (*water*) and plural count nouns (*pears*), plurals preceded by a numeral (*three boys*), and indefinite pronouns (*someone, something*). Use of the cited formally definite reference items marks a referent as identifiable, as long as the mention is referential-specific. (1980:208)

The definition of "referential-specific" is a little trickier and seems to involve a cluster of semantic-pragmatic features. Du Bois defines a NP as referential "when it is used to speak about an object as an object, with continuous identity over time" (1980:208). I interpret this definition to include objectified concepts and events (e.g., CPR, accident) if their identity is seen as continuous and salient in the discourse. In contrast, predicate nominals and other predicating elements are classed by Du Bois as nonreferential since their function is not to refer to a specific object but to predicate certain attributive or classifying qualities. Examples of nonreferential functions are given in (24) and (25).

(24)   Predicate Nominal:

'"That's the 'foundation on which you're gonna build ''everything else on .   (C:5)

(25)   Predicating Element:

I've got two cousins who are out of work at the moment   (R:5)

The foundation in (24) is nonreferential because it expresses a defining quality rather than a continuous entity. In (25), work is a predicating element which, in conjunction with the preceding verb and preposition, defines a situation: *being out of work* could be paraphrased as *not working*.

Du Bois gives further guidelines for interpreting referentiality. Typically nonreferential mentions include NPs within the scope of negation, attributive nominals (*when I was a kid*), idioms with fixed NP elements (*get on your case*), and predicate conflations such as *pear-picking* (where the NP establishes a narrative frame, within which subsequent mentions of the pears may be referential). In my data, a NP was coded as referential if it conformed with Du Bois's guidelines of continuous identity and did not function as a classifying or predicating element.

Notes

Chapter 1

1. The examples are from the database of authentic linguistic materials used in this study. See section 4.4.1 for coding details, and Abbreviations and Transcription Symbols list, p. 000.

2. Double quote marks before a word indicate primary stress placement for that word (the intonation peak), while single quote marks indicate secondary stress. Transcription follows the guidelines of Du Bois et al. (1988). For a list of the transcription symbols used in the present study, see preliminary pages; see also appendix A for notes on certain transcription decisions.

Chapter 2

1. Poutsma, 1928; Live, 1965; Legum, 1968; Bolinger, 1971; Emonds, 1972; Lipka, 1972; Quirk et al., 1972; Sroka, 1972; Fraser, 1976; Pelli, 1976; Vestergaard, 1977; Dixon, 1982; Lindner, 1981; Visser, 1984; Brinton, 1988; Aarts, 1989; Martin, 1990.

2. The postposition construction in (24b) is not to be confused with a verb-particle construction, as in *I put some money by*. Note that (24b) allows a prepositional alternative with a pronoun object, *Mary passed by him*, which is not allowed with the verb-particle construction **I put by it*.

Chapter 3

1. The abbreviations refer as follows: ARG = NP argument; PRED = predicator.

Chapter 6

1. There is one noteworthy difference between Thompson's findings on LMs and mine. In the present corpus, LMs are definite slightly more often (65% of the time) than Os (60% of the time). I believe that this may be because, unlike Thompson, I have coded all LMs and Os, even predicating ones that "function as part of naming an event, activity or situation" (1997: 11), such as *have a cold* and *on the job*. Thompson excludes predicating NPs because of their questionable status as arguments, since they are, in fact, part of the predicate. However, my own study is less concerned with defining argument status than with identifying the functions of landmarks, including predicating functions. Since many predicative LMs in the present corpus turn out to be definite (e.g., *if you're in the medical profession*; *learn by yourself*), the difference in coding procedure may well explain the lower percentage of definite LMs in her study.

2. This interpretation ties in neatly with Shibatani's (1985) account of the Passive construction as a strategy for representing semantic patients as topical and agents as nontopical.

Chapter 8

1. However, even this syntactic generalization is not a reliable one for naive learners of English grammar, who might be a little puzzled by stranded prepositional examples such as (10d).

References

Aarts, Bas. 1989. "Verb-Preposition Constructions and Small Clauses in English." *Journal of Linguistics* 25:277–290.

Allerton, D.J., and A. Cruttenden. 1974. "English Sentence Adverbials: Their Syntax and Their Intonation in British English." *Lingua* 34:1–30.

Azar, Betty Schrampfer. 1989. *Understanding and Using English Grammar*. 2nd ed. Englewood Cliffs, NJ: Prentice Hall Regents.

Barnhart, Robert K., ed. 1988. *The Barnhart Dictionary of Etymology*. H. W. Wilson.

Bing, Janet. 1984. "A Discourse Domain Defined by Intonation." In *Intonation, Accent and Rhythm*, ed. Dafydd Gibbon and Helmut Richter, 10–19. Berlin: Walter de Gruyter.

Bolinger, Dwight. 1971. *The Phrasal Verb in English*. Cambridge: Harvard University Press.

———. 1986. *Intonation and Its Parts*. Stanford, CA: Stanford University Press.

Boyce, Suzanne, and Lise Menn. 1979. "Peaks Vary, Endpoints Don't: Implications for Intonation Theory." In *Proceedings from the Sixth Annual Meeting of the Berkeley Linguistic Society*, 373–384. Berkeley: Berkeley Linguistic Society.

Brinton, Laurel J. 1988. *The Development of English Aspectual Systems*. Cambridge: Cambridge University Press.

Brugman, Claudia. 1981. The Story of Over. M.A. thesis, University of California, Berkeley.

Brunner, C.J. 1977. *A Syntax of Western Middle Iranian*. New York: Caravan Books.

Bybee, Joan L. 1985. *Morphology: A Study of the Relation Between Meaning and Form*. (= *Typological Studies in Language* 9). Amsterdam: John Benjamins.

Bybee, Joan, William Pagliuca, and Revere Perkins. 1991. "Back to the Future." In *Approaches to Grammaticalization* 2, ed. Elizabeth Close Traugott and Bernd Heine, 17–58. Amsterdam: John Benjamins.

Bybee, Joan, Revere Perkins, and William Pagliuca. 1994. *The Evolution of Grammar*. Chicago: University of Chicago Press.

Carlson, Robert. 1991. "Grammaticalization of Postpositions and Word Order in Senufo Languages." In *Approaches to Grammaticalization* 2, ed. Elizabeth Close Traugott and Bernd Heine, 201–224. Amsterdam: John Benjamins.

Chafe, Wallace L. 1986. "Writing in the Perspective of Speaking." In *Studying Writing: Linguistic Approaches.* (= *Written Communication Annual* 1). Ed. Charles R. Cooper and Sidney Greenbaum, 12–39. London: Sage Publications.

———. 1987. "Cognitive Constraints on Information Flow." In *Coherence and Grounding in Discourse*, ed. Russell Tomlin, 21–51. Amsterdam: John Benjamins.

———. 1988. "Linking Intonation Contours in Spoken English." In *Clause Combining in Grammar and Discourse*, ed. John Haiman and Sandra A. Thompson, 1–27. Amsterdam: John Benjamins.

———. 1993. "Prosodic and Functional Units of Language." In *Talking Data: Transcription and Coding in Discourse Research*, ed. Jane A. Edwards and Martin D. Lampert, 33–43. Hillsdale, NJ: Lawrence Erlbaum Associates.

Chen, Ping. 1986. "Discourse and Particle Movement in English." *Studies in Language* 10.1:79–95.

Clark, Marybeth. 1978. *Coverbs and Case in Vietnamese*. Pacific Linguistics, Series B-48. Canberra: Australian National University.

Claudi, Ulrike and Bernd Heine. 1986. "On the Metaphorical Base of Grammar." *Studies in Language*. 10.2:297–335.

Colman, Fran. 1991. "What Positions Fit In?" In *Historical English Syntax* (= *Topics in English Linguistics* 2). Ed. Dieter Kastovsky, 51–102. New York: Mouton de Gruyter.

Comrie, Bernard. 1981. *Language Universals and Linguistic Typology*. Chicago: University of Chicago Press.

Craig, Colette. 1991. "Ways to Go in Rama: a Case Study in Polygrammaticalization." In *Approaches to Grammaticalization* 2, ed. Elizabeth Close Traugott and Bernd Heine, 455–492. Amsterdam: John Benjamins.

Croft, William. 1990. *Typology and Univerals*. Cambridge: Cambridge University Press.

Cruttenden, Alan. 1997. *Intonation*. Cambridge: Cambridge University Press.

Crystal, David. 1969. *Prosodic Systems and Intonation in English*. Cambridge: Cambridge University Press.

Cutler, Anne. 1984. "Stress and Accent in Language Production and Understanding." In *Intonation, Accent and Rhythm*, ed. Dafydd Gibbon and Helmut Richter, 67–90. Berlin: Walter de Gruyter.

DeLancey, Scott. 1984. "Etymological Notes on Tibeto-Burman Case Particles." *Linguistics of the Tibeto-Burman Area* 8.1:59–77.

Dixon, R.M.W. 1982. "The Grammar of English Phrasal Verbs." *Australian Journal of Linguistics* 2:1–42.

———. 1989. "Subject and Object in Universal Grammar." In *Essays on Grammatical Theory and Universal Grammar*, ed. Doug Arnold et al. Oxford: Clarendon Press.

Du Bois, John. 1980. "Beyond Definiteness: The Trace of Identity in Discourse." In *The Pear Stories*, ed. Wallace Chafe, 203–274. Norwood, NJ: Ablex.

———. 1987. "The Discourse Basis of Ergativity." *Language* 63.4:805–855.

Du Bois, John, Susanna Cumming, and Stephan Schuetze-Coburn. 1988. "Discourse Transcription." In *Discourse and Grammar*. (= *Santa Barbara Papers in Linguistics* 2). Ed. Sandra A. Thompson, 1–71. University of California, Santa Barbara.

Emonds, Joseph. 1972. "Evidence That Indirect Object Movement is a Structure-Preserving Rule." *Foundations of Language* 8:546–561.

Fillmore, Charles. 1986. "Pragmatically Controlled Zero Anaphora." In *Proceedings from the Twelfth Annual Meeting of the Berkeley Linguistics Society*, 95–107. Berkeley: Berkeley Linguistics Society.

Foley, William A., and Robert D. Van Valin, Jr. 1984. *Functional Syntax and Universal Grammar*. Cambridge: Cambridge University Press.

Ford, Cecilia E. 1993. *Grammar in Interaction: Adverbial Clauses in American English Conversations*. Cambridge: Cambridge University Press.

Fotos, Sandra. 1994. "Integrating Grammar Instruction and Communicative Language Use Through Grammar Consciousness-Raising Tasks." *TESOL Quarterly* 28.2:323–351.

Fotos, Sandra, and Rod Ellis. 1991. "Communicating About Grammar: A Task-Based Approach." *TESOL Quarterly* 25.4:605–628.

Foulke, Emerson. 1983. "Spatial Ability and the Limitations of Perceptual Systems." In *Spatial Orientation: Theory, Research, and Application*, ed. Herbert L. Pick, Jr. and Linda P. Acredolo, 125–141. New York: Plenum Press.

Fox, Anthony. 1984. "Subordinating and Co-ordinating Intonation Structures in the Articulation of Discourse." In *Intonation, Accent and Rhythm*, ed. Dafydd Gibbon and Helmut Richter, 120–133. Berlin: Walter de Gruyter.

Fox, Barbara. 1983. "The Discourse Function of the Participle in Ancient Greek." In *Discourse Perspectives in Syntax*, ed. F. Klein-Andreu, 23–40. New York: Academic Press.

Fox, Barbara, and Robert Jasperson. 1995. "A Syntactic Exploration of Repair in English Conversation." In *Theoretical and Descriptive Modes in the Alternative Linguistics*, ed. Philip Davis. Philadelphia: John Benjamins.

Fox, Barbara, and Sandra A. Thompson. 1990. "A Discourse Explanation of the Grammar of Relative Clauses in English Conversation." *Language* 66.2:297–316.

Frajzyngier, Zygmunt. 1991. "The *De Dicto* Domain in Language." *Approaches to Grammaticalization* 1, ed. Elizabeth C. Traugott and Bernd Heine, 219–252. Amsterdam: John Benjamins.

Francis, W. Nelson and Henry Kučera. 1982. *Frequency Analysis of English Usage: Lexicon and Grammar*. Boston: Houghton Mifflin.

Fraser, Bruce. 1976. *The Verb-Particle Combination in English*. New York: Academic Press.

Friedrich, Paul. 1975. *Proto-Indo-European Syntax: The Order of Meaningful Elements*. Butte, Montana: Journal of Indo-European Studies. (Monograph 1.)

Genetti, Carol. 1991. "From Postposition to Subordinator in Newari." In *Approaches to Grammaticalization* 2, ed. Elizabeth C. Traugott and Bernd Heine, 227–256. Amsterdam: John Benjamins.

Givón, Talmy. 1980. "The Binding Hierarchy and the Typology of Complements." *Studies in Language* 4.3:333–377.

———. 1984a. "Direct Object and Dative Shifting: Semantic and Pragmatic Case." In *Objects: Toward a Theory of Grammatical Relations*, ed. Frans Plank, 151–182. London: Academic Press.

———. 1984b. "Prolegomena to Discourse Pragmatics." In *Metapragmatics*, ed. C. Caffi, 489–515. (Special issue of *Journal of Pragmatics* 8.4.)

———. 1991. "Serial Verbs and the Mental Reality of 'Event': Grammatical vs. Cognitive Packaging." In *Approaches to Grammaticalization* 1, ed. Elizabeth C. Traugott and Bernd Heine, 81–128. Amsterdam: John Benjamins.

———, ed. 1983. *Topic Continuity in Discourse: A Quantitative Cross-Language Study*. Amsterdam: John Benjamins.

Goldberg, Adele E. 1995. *Constructions: A Construction Grammar Approach to Argument Structure*. Chicago: University of Chicago Press.

Haiman, John, ed. 1985. *Iconicity in Syntax*. Amsterdam: John Benjamins.

Halliday, M. A. K. 1967. *Intonation and Grammar in British English*. The Hague: Mouton.

———. 1985. *An Introduction to Functional Grammar*. London: Edward Arnold.

Haugen, Einar. 1982. *Scandinavian Language Structures: A Comparative Historical Survey*. Minneapolis: University of Minnesota Press.

Hawkins, Bruce W. 1984. The Semantics of English Spatial Prepositions. Ph.D. dissertation, University of California, San Diego.

Heine, Bernd, and Mechthild Reh. 1984. *Grammaticalization and Reanalysis in African Languages.* Hamburg: Helmut Buske.

Heine, Bernd, Ulrike Claudi, and Friedrike Hünnemeyer. 1991a. *Grammaticalization: A Conceptual Framework.* Chicago: University of Chicago Press.

Heine, Bernd, Ulrike Claudi, and Friedrike Hünnemeyer. 1991b. "From Cognition to Grammar: Evidence from African Languages." In *Approaches to Grammaticalization* 1, ed. Elizabeth C. Traugott and Bernd Heine, 149–188. Amsterdam: John Benjamins.

Hill, Steven P. 1977. *The N Factor and Russian Prepositions: Their Development in 11th–20th Century Texts.* The Hague: Mouton.

Hill, L.A. 1968. *Prepositions and Adverbial Particles: An Interim Classification — Semantic, Structural, and Graded.* London: Oxford University Press.

Hopper, Paul. 1995. "The Category 'Event' in Natural Discourse and Logic." In *Discourse Grammar and Typology: Papers in Honor of John W.M. Verhaar*, ed. Werner Abraham, T. Givón and Sandra A. Thompson, 139–150. Amsterdam: John Benjamins.

Hopper, Paul, and Sandra A. Thompson. 1980. "Transitivity in Grammar and Discourse." *Language* 56:251–299.

———. 1984. "The Discourse Basis for Lexical Categories in Universal Grammar." *Language* 60.4:703–752.

———. 1985. "The Iconicity of the Universal Categories 'Noun' and 'Verb'." In *Iconicity in Syntax*, ed. John Haiman, 151–183. Amsterdam: John Benjamins.

———. 1993. "Language Universals, Discourse Pragmatics, and Semantics." *Language Sciences* 15.4:357–376.

Jacobs, Roderick A. 1993. *English Syntax.* New York: Oxford University Press

Johansson, Stig and Knut Hofland. 1989. *Frequency Analysis of English Vocabulary and Grammar* 1: *Tag Frequencies and Word Frequencies.* Oxford: Clarendon Press.

Jolly, Julia A. 1993. "Preposition Assignment in English." In *Advances in Role and Reference Grammar*, ed. Robert D. Van Valin, Jr., 275–310. Amsterdam: John Benjamins.

Kennedy, Arthur Garfield. 1920. *The Modern English Verb-Adverb Combination.* Stanford: Stanford University Press.

Klein, Wolfgang. 1983. "Deixis and Spatial Orientation in Route Directions." In *Spatial Orientation: Theory, Research, and Application*, ed. Herbert L. Pick, Jr. and Linda P. Acredolo, 283–311. New York: Plenum Press.

Kroch, Anthony S. 1979. "The Verb-Particle Combination in English: Review of Bruce Fraser (1976)." *Language* 55.1:219–223.

Kuryłowicz, Jerzy. 1964. *The Inflectional Categories of Indo-European.* Heidelberg: Carl Winter Universitätsverlag.

Ladd, D. Robert, Jr. 1978. *The Structure of Intonational Meaning: Evidence from English.* Bloomington: Indiana University Press.

———. 1990. "Intonation: Emotion vs. Grammar." *Language* 66.4:806–816.

Lakoff, George. 1987. *Women, Fire, and Dangerous Things: What Categories Reveal about the Mind.* Chicago: University of Chicago Press.

Lakoff, George, and Mark Johnson. 1980. *Metaphors We Live By.* Chicago: University of Chicago Press.

Lambrecht, Knud. 1994. *Information Structure and Sentence Form.* Cambridge: Cambridge University Press.

Langacker, Ronald W. 1986. "An Introduction to Cognitive Grammar." *Cognitive Science* 10:1–40.

————. 1991. *Foundations of Cognitive Grammar* 2: *Descriptive Application*. Stanford: Stanford University Press.

Legum, St. E. 1968. "The Verb-Particle Constructions in English: Basic or Derived?" In *Papers from the Fourth Regional Meeting of the Chicago Linguistic Society, 50–62*. Chicago: Chicago Linguistic Society.

Lehmann, Christian. 1991. "Grammaticalization and Related Changes in Contemporary German." In *Approaches to Grammaticalization* 2, ed. Elizabeth Close Traugott and Bernd Heine, 493–535. Amsterdam: John Benjamins.

Lewis, H., and H. Pedersen. 1961. *Celtic Grammar*. Gottingen: Vandenhoeck and Ruprecht.

Li, Charles, and Sandra Thompson. 1974. "Co-Verbs in Mandarin Chinese: Verbs or Prepositions?" *Journal of Chinese Linguistics* 2:257–278.

Lichtenberk, Frantisek. 1991. "On the Gradualness of Grammaticalization." *Approaches to Grammaticalization* 1, ed. Elizabeth Close Traugott and Bernd Heine, 37–80. Amsterdam: John Benjamins.

Liles, Bruce L. 1987. *A Basic Grammar of Modern English*. Englewood Cliffs, NJ: Prentice-Hall.

Lindner, Sue. 1981. A Lexico-Semantic Analysis of Verb-Particle Constructions with Up and Out. Ph.D. dissertation, University of California, San Diego.

————. 1982. "What Goes Up Doesn't Necessarily Come Down: The Ins and Outs of Opposites." In *Proceedings of the 18th Meeting of the Chicago Linguistic Society*, 305–323. Chicago: Chicago Linguistic Society.

Lindsey, Geoffrey. 1981. "Intonation and Pragmatics." *Journal of the International Phonetic Association* 11.1:2–21.

Lindsay, Wallace Martin. 1963. *The Latin Language*. New York: Hafner. Original edition, Oxford: Clarendon Press, 1894.

Lipka, Leonhard. 1972. *Semantic Structure and Word-Formation: Verb-Particle Constructions in Contemporary English*. Munich: Wilhelm Fink Verlag.

Live, Anna H. 1965. "The Discontinuous Verb in English." *Word* 21:428–451.

Lockwood, W. B. 1968. *Historical German Syntax*. Oxford: Oxford University Press.

Lord, Carol. 1973. "Serial Verbs in Transition." *Studies in African Linguistics* 4:269–296.

Martin, Pamela. 1990. *The Phrasal Verb: Diachronic Development in British and American English*. Ph.D. dissertation, Columbia University.

Matisoff, James A. 1991. "Areal and Universal Dimensions of Grammaticization in Lahu." In *Approaches to Grammaticalization* 1, ed. Elizabeth C. Traugott and Bernd Heine, 383–454. Amsterdam: John Benjamins.

Matthiessen, Christian, and Sandra A. Thompson. 1988. "The Structure of Discourse and 'Subordination'." In *Clause Combining in Grammar and Discourse*, ed. John Haiman and Sandra A. Thompson, 275–329. Amsterdam: John Benjamins.

Merriam Webster's Collegiate Dictionary, 10th ed. 1993. Springfield, MA: G. and C. Merriam Co.

Mitchell, Bruce. 1985. *Old English Syntax* 1. Oxford: Clarendon Press.

Myhill, John. 1985. "Pragmatic and Categorial Correlates of VS Word Order." *Lingua* 66:177–200.

————. 1988. "Categoriality and Clustering." *Studies in Language* 12.2:261–297.

Oxford English Dictionary, Concise edition. 1964. Oxford: Clarendon Press.

Oxford English Dictionary. 1989. Oxford: Clarendon Press.

Oxford Modern English Dictionary. 1992. Oxford: Clarendon Press.

Palmer, F.R. 1974. *The English Verb*. London: Longman.

Pelli, Mario G. 1976. *Verb-Particle Constructions in English: A Study Based on American Plays from the End of the 18th Century to the Present*. Bern: Francke Verlag.

Poutsma, H. 1928. *A Grammar of Late Modern English. Part I, The Sentence: First half, The Elements of the Sentence.* 2nd ed. Groningen: P. Noordhoff.

Prince, Ellen F. 1981. "Toward a Taxonomy of Given-New Information." In *Radical Pragmatics*, ed. Peter Cole, 223–255. New York: Academic Press.

Psathas, George. 1989. *Phenomenology and Sociology: Theory and Research.* (= *Current Continental Research* 215). Washington, D.C.: Center for Advanced Research in Phenomenology and University Press of America.

Quirk, Randolph, Sidney Greenbaum, Geoffrey Leech, and Jan Svartvik. 1972. *A Grammar of Contemporary English.* London: Longman.

Random House Dictionary Concise edition. 1980. New York: Random House.

Rice, Sally. 1987. "Towards a Transitive Prototype: Evidence From Some Atypical English Passives." In *General Session and Parasession on Grammar and Cognition*, 422–434. Berkeley: Berkeley Linguistics Society.

———. 1988. "Unlikely Lexical Entries." *Proceedings from the Fourteenth Annual Meeting of the Berkeley Linguistics Society* 202–212. Berkeley: Berkeley Linguistics Society.

Roget's International Thesaurus, fourth ed. 1977. London: Harper and Row.

Schachter, Paul. 1976. "The Subject in Philippine Languages: Topic, Actor, Actor-Topic, or None of the Above." In *Subject and Topic*, ed. Charles N. Li, 491–518. New York: Academic Press.

Schegloff, Emanuel A. 1972. "Notes on a Conversational Practice: Formulating Place." In *Social Interaction*, ed. David Sudnow, 75–119. New York: The Free Press (Macmillan).

Schmalsteig, William R. 1988. *A Lithuanian Historical Syntax.* Columbus OH, Slavica.

Shibatani, Masayoshi. 1985. "Passives and Related Constructions: A Prototype Analysis." *Language* 61.4:821–848.

Shipley, J. T. 1984. *The Origins of English Words.* Baltimore: Johns Hopkins University Press.

Sroka, Kazimierz A. 1972. *The Syntax of English Phrasal Verbs.* The Hague: Mouton.

Svorou, Soteria. 1994. *The Grammar of Space.* Amsterdam: John Benjamins.

Swain, M. 1985. "Communicative Competence: Some Roles of Comprehensible Input and Comprehensible Output in its Development." In *Input in Second Language Acquisition*, ed. S. Gass and C. Madden, 235–253. Rowley, MA: Newbury House.

Talmy, Leonard. 1975. "Semantics and Syntax of Motion." *Syntax and Semantics* 4, ed. John Kimball, 181–238. New York: Academic Press.

———. 1985. "Lexicalization Patterns: Semantic Structure in Lexical Forms." In *Language Typology and Syntactic Description* 3: *Grammatical Categories and the Lexicon*, ed. Timothy Shopen, 57–149. Cambridge: Cambridge University Press.

Tench, Paul. 1990. *The Roles of Intonation in English Discourse.* New York: Peter Lang.

Thompson, Sandra A. 1988. "A Discourse Approach to the Cross-Linguistic Category 'Adjective'." In *Explaining Language Universals*, ed. John A. Hawkins. New York: Basil Blackwell.

———. 1997. "Discourse Motivations for the Core-Oblique Distinction as a Language Universal." In *Functional Directions in Linguistics*, ed. Akio Kamio. Berlin: Mouton de Gruyter

Traugott, Elizabeth C. 1972. *The History of English Syntax.* New York: Holt, Rinehart and Winston.

———. 1989. "On the Rise of Epistemic Meanings in English: An Example of Subjectification in Semantic Change." *Language* 65.1:31–55.

———. 1990. "From More to Less Situated in Language: The Unidirectionality of Semantic Change." In *Papers from the Fifth International Conference of English Historical Linguistics*, ed. Sylvia Adamson, Vivien Law, Nigel Vincent and Susan Wright, 496–517. Amsterdam: John Benjamins.

Traugott, Elizabeth C. and Ekkehard Konig. 1991. "The Semantics-Pragmatics of Grammaticalization Revisited." In *Approaches to Grammaticalization* 1, ed. Elizabeth C. Traugott and Bernd Heine, 189–218. Amsterdam: John Benjamins.

Van Valin, Robert D., Jr. 1993. "A Synopsis of Role and Reference Grammar." In *Advances in Role and Reference Grammar*, ed. Robert D. Van Valin, Jr., 1–164. Amsterdam: John Benjamins.

Vestergaard, Torben. 1977. *Prepositional Phrases and Prepositional Verbs: A Study in Grammatical Function*. The Hague: Mouton.

Visser, F. Th. 1984. *An Historical Syntax of the English Language* 1: *Syntactical Units with One Verb*. Leiden: E. J. Brill.

Walker, William. 1970. *A Treatise of English Particles*. Menston, England: Scolar Press. Original edition, London: T. Garthwaite, 1655.

Webster's New International Dictionary of the English Language. 1957. Springfield, MA: G. and C. Merriam.

Webster's New Collegiate Dictionary. 1981. Springfield, MA: G. and C. Merriam.

Webster's New International Dictionary of the English Language. 1983. Springfield, MA: G. and C. Merriam.

West, J. 1982. "Preverbs in Gothic and Old Irish—A Typological Parallel?" *Studia Celtica* 16/17:248–256.

INDEX